PRIMAL HEALING

ACCESS THE INCREDIBLE POWER OF FEELINGS TO IMPROVE YOUR HEALTH

Dr. Arthur Janov

New Page Books
A Division of The Career Press, Inc.
Franklin Lakes, NJ

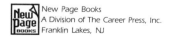

Primal Healing
Typeset by Kate Henches
Cover design by Lu Rossman/Digi Dog
Printed in the U.S.A. by Book-mart Press

To order this title, please call toll-free 1-800-CAREER-1 (NJ and Canada: 201-848-0310) to order using VISA or MasterCard, or for further information on books from Career Press.

CAREER PRESS New Page Books

The Career Press, Inc., 3 Tice Road, PO Box 687,
Franklin Lakes, NJ 07417
www.careerpress.com
www.newpagebooks.com

Primal Therapy is dangerous in untrained hands. If you have any questions about those who claim to be Primal therapists please contact the Primal Center at primalctr@earthlink.net.

For information about proper Primal Therapy please see our Website: *www.primaltherapy.com*.

Library of Congress Cataloging-in-Publication Data

Janov, Arthur.
Primal healing : access to the incredible power of feelings to improve your health : a revolutionary new therapy from the creator of Primal Scream / by Arthur Janov.
p. cm.
Includes bibliographical references (p.).
ISBN-13: 978-1-56414-916-9
ISBN-10: 1-56414-916-1
1. Primal therapy. 2. Emotions—Health aspects. I. Title.

RC489.P67J356 2006
615.5--dc22

2006012349

Dedication

Adieu,

Michael, Matt, Mimi, Nanou, Michel, Larry, Helmut, Eddie, Bernie, Jack, Marion.

ACKNOWLEDGMENTS

I want to thank Dr. Paul Thompson of the UCLA Neuroimaging Center for his help in my effort. Thank you, too, to Dr. David Goodman of the Newport Neuroscience Center for his contribution to my statements in neurology; also a word of thanks to Dr. Jonty Christie. My gratitude to Dr. Mike Makepeace, who was very helpful in improving the language in this book, as well as to my research assistant David Lassoff, who spent many hours verifying sometimes obscure references. Thank you to editor, Kathy Wyer, for her many hours of editorial help and also to Randy Malat, my editor for many years. Thanks go, as well, to Drs. Geoffrey Carr and Peter Prontzos for their valuable input. My thanks, finally, to editor Elizabeth Lyon, who really brought this book together, spending long hours refining it.

My deepest appreciation to my wife, Dr. France Janov, who read and reread these chapters offering invaluable insight along the way. As director of clinical training at our center she has helped develop the theory and techniques of the Primal approach. Her additions and corrections to what I write are everywhere throughout this book.

Finally, I want to thank my recently departed long-time colleague, neurologist Dr. Michael Holden, who nurtured my interest in neurology and taught me so much.

Design of three levels of consciousness image on page 59 by Dr. France Janov.

For more it is than I can well express
And that deep torture may be called a hell
When more is felt than one hath power to tell.
The Rape of Lucrece
—Shakespeare

We must pursue the duty of memory to its conclusion.
—Jacques Chirac, President of France

Memory is a duty.
And memory is medicine.
—Dr. Arthur Janov

Contents

Introduction

As a clinical psychologist with more than 50 years in the field, I've come to appreciate that if we are to effectively treat mental health problems, we must combine the best of both worlds and integrate the discipline of neuroscience with that of psychology. A deepening exchange is needed, a cross-pollination of knowledge and practice between these two fields.

In this book I shall try to fuse neurology, psychology, and biology into one organic whole so that we humans will no longer be dissected into separate parts for convenience of study. This will allow us to explain human beings in a truly holistic way, seeing how psychology interacts with neurology to determine our behavior and our symptoms. Thus, when we make a psychologic diagnosis it will also encompass other sciences, at the same time making a diagnosis of how our physical system works along with the emotional one. For example, we shall not only discuss obsessiveness but also where it occurs in the brain and what the factors were in history that gave it its start. And sexual impotence—how neurologic factors affect it, and where in the sufferer's history experiences occurred that might have given rise to it later on. In this way, we shall cut across several disciplines to help us understand who we are, and how emotional factors affect the brain and body, and vice versa. We are of one piece. We can abstract different aspects of us for convenience of study, but the fact remains that we are one organic whole. At some point we have to put all of the pieces back together to provide holistic, organic answers for the human condition.

Those of us who have been trained extensively and practice Primal Therapy at the center believe that for the first time we are establishing the first science of psychotherapy. We videotape all sessions and we go over them. When a mistake is made we know it immediately because the therapy is precise and ordered. This was never the case when I practiced psychoanalytic psychotherapy. What this means is that we now have a systematic therapy that can truly make people better. I hesitate to use the word "cure" because it has an opprobrious connotation, but the fact is that in many cases that is exactly what happens. This is because we are able to probe into the depths of the brain and into the antipodes of the unconscious to ferret out traumatic elements that have lain there for decades, hidden and deep, doing all kinds of damage, affecting our behavior and what kind of ailments we shall suffer. I believe that this book is an avatar for our field equivalent to Sigmund Freud's 1902 *Interpretation of Dreams*, which laid out for the first time the nature of the unconscious and how it might affect us. We have a more detailed understanding of that unconscious now because we see it in therapy every day. We peer down into the past of our patients and see how ancient history evolved. We observe someone in therapy and begin to understand the history of mankind. We see patients reliving their pasts and observe our ancient past at the same time. We see the reptilian/salamander brain in action by observing the birth trauma and comprehending what it has done to us throughout our lives, from attention deficit disorder to migraines and high blood pressure. Without that understanding we shall never understand ourselves, much less treat those conditions effectively. That is saying a lot, but I hope that this book will clarify what I mean.

Because behavior and cognitive/insight therapies have focused solely on behavior for diagnosis and treatment, current research involving the brain has largely gone unnoticed. So although psychological theories abound, they lack an anchor in neuroscience, and neuroscience offers a wealth of information that can inform clinical practice. I propose creating a bridge between the two.

My attempt is one of the first steps toward this goal and not a final, definitive answer. Having had the privilege of many decades of clinical work, I've observed how personality evolves, where neurosis begins, and learned where a cure lies. Thanks to neuroscience, we now have a vast body of knowledge to mine, a deeper more certain understanding of how the brain relates to behavior. Unlike years past, today we know a great deal more about the nature of feelings and the limbic system. Most importantly, we know how to rid the system of engraved, enduring pain.

Although there are scientific references and citations throughout this work, we should not lose track of the overarching truth—feelings are their own validation. We can quote and cite all day long, but the truth ultimately lies in the experience of human beings. Their feelings explain so much that statistical evidence is irrelevant. Cognitive therapy seeks statistical truths to corroborate their hypotheses and theories; these theories are too often intellectual constructs that do need statistical validation. We are after biological truths beyond mathematical facts. The studies I cite do not prove anything. What they do is indicate a kind of universality, a continuum, to all kinds of organic life. These studies are corollaries, not separate, inviolate realities; a kind of intellectual genuflection to the left brain. But without contact to the right brain those realities are confined to the intellectual. Anything can be true with statistics because they ignore biologic realities. They can be manipulated in all ways. All this may escape those who have no entry into the right-brain unconscious, where history and feelings lie. Animal research is interesting, but we are not trying to understand the psyche of rats; we need to understand our own psyche by analogy or corollary. Those who suffer, who have faulty gates, have a sort of inchoate entry into the unconscious. We have an experimental laboratory in our work where we see the unconscious every day with patients. We do not need statistical truths. We have biologic ones.

Those in cognitive therapy are able to "feel better," but confuse that with getting better because they can use language and words to suffocate pain. They use thoughts to anesthetize feelings and imagine and think that all is well.

There is a world of the deep unconscious that needs to be explored; an unconscious from our animal legacy. That unconscious can never be understood in verbal language. We can't talk to a salamander and we cannot talk to the salamander brain residing in each of us. If there is no place in a theory for that unconscious, there is no way that one can be cured of all sorts of emotional problems; problems that may have their origin in the residue of reptilian life. To observe patients writhing in reptilian fashion when they are in the grips of an ancient, unevolved brain makes all of that clear. It can never be clear as long as we remain on the cognitive level.

Let us not forget that in the world of cosmology there is the discovery of dark matter that makes up the majority of what we used to call empty space. We are part of that universe; our dark matter is called the unconscious. Heretofore, psychotherapy has dealt with only the tip of the iceberg, leaving an unexplored universe untouched. Although cosmology usually deals with the external universe, we are also part of that universe, and the laws that apply to external cosmology must also apply to us humans. After all, most of our biologic bodies are made up of stardust—carbon, hydrogen, oxygen, iron, and other elements. Carbon combined with hydrogen and oxygen form organic compounds. The laws that apply uniquely to the universe above must also apply to the universe below. There is no simple dividing line between the two. The history of the universe abides in each of us. Nothing is lost in our evolution; we simply add on. We still have part of that ancient brain encased in our skulls. We are the history of the universe incarnate—walking histories—a fact that is largely ignored in the field of insight psychotherapy. The more we discover about the laws of the universe, the more we shall learn about ourselves. The key here is that the more we travel back in personal time, the more present we can be; for it is fact that the past is imprinted in our systems, and until we relive and connect it to consciousness, we will be enslaved to our histories. The deeper we travel into the antipodes of our unconscious the clearer we see our ancient history. Chronic high body temperature speaks about our history. It shouts its meaning, but too often it remains incomprehensible to the sophisticated intellectual.

We need to consider Primal psychology a branch of cosmology—a study of the inner universe. How can we learn about the laws of human intercourse if we never delve into the dark mass of the unconscious? Otherwise, we are pushed by forces over which we have no control. We develop symptoms for unknown reasons, and fall ill for reasons quite mysterious. It does not have to be this way. The unconscious speaks to us all of the time in its own language, but too often we don't know what it is, nor can we speak it, for it has nothing to do with words. Proper therapy must use nonverbal language.

Eventually, there must be a connection between the deep unconscious and the upper level prefrontal neocortex. Without that connection, there will be no control of the unconscious. It will continually exert its force creating, inter alia, addictions, high blood pressure, and seizures. With connection those can often be normalized. To treat behavior—addiction—

as a thing in itself is never to solve the mystery of neurosis. Stopping drinking alcohol is not a cure; it is simply stopping drinking. Drinking is usually not a disease in itself (Alcoholics Anonymous notwithstanding), it is a symptom of one. We will learn how basic built-in need, when unfulfilled, becomes transformed into the "need for" drugs, food, or alcohol. We need to address basic need, not the various and sundry "need for."

In cosmology we ask the questions, "How did it all begin? What made it begin? What is the universe like? How did the Big Bang happen?" We need only ask those same questions of ourselves. In Primal Therapy we revisit the years with our parents, race back to our grandparents' times, and from there (over months or years) move down to our primate ancestors. From there we travel to lower animal forms—again, the salamander. And then back to the elements of which we are made: the atoms and molecules of stardust. Of course, we do not go back to that point, but patients do arrive at the salamander brain, where they slither and make sinusoidal movements, where there are no cries, no tears, and certainly no words to blanket feelings. We can do that. We have learned that primitive language, and through it we open up the unconscious for our patients, deepen their identity and broaden their frame of reference to understand themselves, their inner universe, and their current behavior.

The further we go out into the outside universe, the closer we become to our origins, reaching back to the beginning of time. The deeper we go into the dark matter of the unconscious, the more we understand our origins and our present. Dialectically, the further we regress, the more we can predict future problems, whether of anxiety, drug addiction, or sexual impotence. There exists a relationship, for example, of anoxia at birth and later suicidal tendencies. The more we explore the birth trauma, the more we understand about uncontrolled addictions. We can foretell sexual frigidity decades later. We will learn about all of this in the following chapters.

The Big Bang that began our universe some 14 billion years ago has a corollary in the internal universe. We see our ancient past in the far-flung stars racing toward infinity, and we see our personal past in the "far-flung" symptoms of our biology. We see evidence of our early traumas in the measurement of the muscle tension in the space between the eyes, and we see the pre-birth trauma in the levels of cortisol and serotonin, some 30 years later. These are the far-flung sequelae of early imprints, of our personal "Big Bang," if you will. We can trace back to those early events from the high levels of neurochemistry we see today. Those levels are attached to and evolve from specific traumas that happened to us even before our birth. They are reminders of what happened to us and keep those early events alive. We must not simply beat back those fragments of memory with medication, whether of palpitations or high blood pressure; we must connect them to those things that occurred early on that caused the dislocation in our biology.

The purpose of science is to make predictions; however, prediction is not possible until we know origins. To focus only on the present is equal to astrology. To focus on dark matter, the history and the origins, is the domain of astronomy. The latter is strict science. The value of a science is only as good as its criteria of proof. If the proof in psychotherapy ignores history, if it is phenotypic and couched in ahistoric terms (for example, stopping alcohol for six months), it cannot succeed. It can only produce current temporary changes that cannot last because dark unconscious forces remain at work. We remain captives of history, not just the history of early childhood but well before when life-and-death traumas dislocate and deviate normal functioning.

If we are ever to discover a fuller universe that explains human pathology, we need to explore the inner cosmos, the mysterious unconscious that yields up its truths hesitantly but surely and ends the mystery that was the unconscious. We will never truly understand depression without a voyage to the zone of the interior. How do we know? The tendency toward depression, and often suicidal thoughts, continues until we explore the deep, remote past and relive it. It is that reliving that normalizes both chemistry and behavior. Reliving means hurtling through time to a timeless state where the present and past merge into one. One *is* the past, then current behavior becomes clear: "I have migraines because there was so little oxygen at birth." Or, "I drink because there was no mother for weeks right after I was born." No insights necessary. The unconscious explains it all. Let us consider our field that of Primal Cosmology, where we are no longer content to look only at the present; we must revisit the past and be submerged in it. Only that will liberate us. There are no Gestalt exercises, no insights that can accomplish that. There is no present without that past.

Primal Therapy is the first psychotherapy to effectively gain access to the deepest layers of the brain and consciousness. To help people, to get rid of terrible symptoms and suffering and to put an end to their depressions and anxieties, we must move beyond the Freudian and behaviorist legacies that have done so much to help, but which are now so limiting. We must move the art of psychotherapy more toward a science.

The notion that thought is first and the brain second, which distinguishes intellectual from feeling therapy, goes back to the old dispute between the logical positivists of the 19th century who saw the mind as primary, and the empiricists, who put experience first. It clearly goes back to the notions of Socrates. Matter, the brain, obviously preceded mind. There was the existence of billions of years of organic life before there was a thinking brain that could conceive ideas.

Psychology can no longer be merely a "behavioral science," but rather something that takes into account our physiological selves, the forces that drive behavior—*a science of feeling*. Psychology must become the science of the human condition; all of it, not just the mental aspect. In order to establish the first science of psychotherapy, those of us at the Primal Center formulate hypotheses and put them to the test. We have completed four significant brainwave experiments as well as several double blind studies, and have examined patients' neurochemistry and immune functions. We monitor our patients for years after therapy to verify that their progress is sustained. We measure each patient's vital signs before and after every session. We recognize that when there are specific vital sign configurations, certain kinds of pathologies will reveal themselves. Changes in those signs give us a measure of progress. Our techniques, refined through years of practice, are precise and quantifiable.

I have remained true to the research I have investigated, and I have reported it faithfully, stating when something is speculation or supposition as opposed to established fact. Our clinical work is well recognized after 33 years of treating 5,000 patients from more than 20 countries.

I dedicate this work to my patients who through their commitment to treatment have helped me formulate ideas, and who have had the courage to go where no psychiatric patient has ever gone before.

1

It's All in Your Head

I have set for myself a rather daunting task: to demonstrate that no therapy that uses words as the predominant mode of treatment can succeed at creating any profound change in the patient. This includes all insight therapies, cognitive therapy, rational emotive therapy, hypnotherapy, psychoanalysis, biofeedback, eye movement desensitization and reprocesssing (EMDR), and guided imagery/directive daydreaming. All of these can help, but none can make a profound change in personality or provide profound, lasting relief.

I would have disagreed with this proposition when I originally practiced psychoanalytic, insight therapy many decades ago. My patients agreed that they felt differently after treatment, and believed that they had made major changes in their lives. Now I am more than skeptical. I have now seen what more is possible. Profound personality change is impossible on the level of words, or even on the level of emotions; there is no venting or "getting it out," such as crying and screaming, that will bring about any true or lasting change.

For true and lasting change to occur, deep levels of the brain must change physiologically, enabling key structures within the brain to recalibrate to optimal, healthy levels. Furthermore, such change will only come about when those parts of the brain that hold deeply imprinted memories can connect neurochemically with the parts of the brain that underlie the more rational, thinking aspects of our minds, such as the frontal neocortex. No amount of talk-based therapy will ever bring about such a connection because there is little activation of the subcortical structures that mediate the deeply imprinted memories, yet this connection is vital if more substantial progress in psychotherapy is to occur. In these pages, I will show how our mental health, as well as much of our physical health, is determined by the physiological function of that gray matter we call the brain.

Conventional psychotherapy has been imbued with the belief that good mental health is a product of your mind—a result of your thinking, logical, rational, prefrontal cortex; in brief, that you can think your way to health. The logical corollary is that you get sick in your mind; in effect, you think your way to sickness. Conventional psychotherapy believes that if you change your state of mind, you change your state of health. Yet neurosis, a physical and mental deviation of a normal system, is not laid down in the brain as an idea but as an experience, one that leaves a physiological trail. Because of this, any psychotherapy that relies on words and ideas cannot change neurosis. There is an article in the September 2005 *Science News* that found that positive thinking can have a long-range effect.[1] Even the expectation of pain can be processed by the same brain nerve circuits as in actual pain; and the converse is also true: thinking about relief brings relief. This, unfortunately, has led many professionals to believe that one can think one's way to health. We can only think our way to a deceptive state of health, while roaring pain seethes below.[2] So the belief in relief has a sound neurologic basis and is not solely a whim of the "mind." The problem is that it remains a belief and not an actual full physiologic state. This is one way there is a disconnect between body and mind: the mind becomes disengaged and alienated from our true physical state.

Neurosis is a significant level of pain imprinted neurochemically into our systems early in our lives, which causes major dislocations of function, both mental, emotional, and physical. In psychotherapy we must not ignore the full physiological effect of experience by attending solely to the cortical, thinking mind. It is obvious, yet most current therapies separate mind from brain, and brain from body, so that therapy has become a fragmented enterprise. If we see mind as a reflection of the sum total of the entire system, we begin to understand that we can only get well if we recognize it as an integrated system.

If "wellness" were simply a matter of what we think about ourselves (or what a therapist thinks of us), then all the religious conversions and resultant epiphanies would be just as valid a cure for neurosis as any psychotherapy. After all, if we subscribe to conventional psychotherapy, and believe that we get well only in our minds—in what we think about ourselves—then what is in our minds is paramount, whether it's an idea of being saved by a deity, or saved through an insight we may have about what our mother did to us while we were growing up.

However, because the cortical—thinking—mind has a capacity for self-deception, we cannot rely on what patients conclude; nor can we rely on psychological tests to give us accurate information about a patient, because such tests deal only in ideas and exclude the body, the physiological. A case in point: A study by a group of British neurologists found that the name of a scent overrode the actual sensory experience. So they mislabeled various scents and found that the study group reacted to the labels rather than to the experience. This was verified by magnetic resonance measurements. In brief, cognition dominated feelings and instincts. If the subject reacted to the wrongly labeled scent, the parts of the brain that should have lit up to cheese, for example, did not because it had a more pleasant label. In brief, we can twist perceptions and cognitions any which way, and it can override experience. We will see how important this is later on when we discuss cognitive therapy.

> *For true and lasting change, deep levels of the brain must change physiologically, enabling key structures within the brain to recalibrate to optimal, healthy levels.*

For true and lasting change, deep levels of the brain must change physiologically, enabling key structures within the brain to recalibrate to optimal, healthy levels. For true and lasting change, deep levels of the brain must change physiologically, enabling key structures within the brain to recalibrate to optimal, healthy levels.

We must be precise in our diagnosis at all times. We wouldn't give antibiotics for a viral disease simply because the patient thinks she has a bacterial infection. In general medicine, we do not accept the patient's own diagnosis—we run tests to determine the truth. We must do the same in psychotherapy. We must test not only the psyche, but the physiologic system, as well. The physiologic effects and the ideas we hold about ourselves come from two different brain systems. Often, there is poor communication between those brain systems so that what we think and what we feel are quite different.

Most therapists only test the patient in terms of psychologic states. Their questionnaires focus on mental health. If a patient says, "I cry often, but I feel fine," is this something that we should believe? If we test the patient's stress hormone level (cortisol) and see that it is high, we must be suspicious if the patient claims that she feels fine.

I saw one woman with what is known as a masked depression; something she was not aware of, but she acted "dead and down" nearly all of the time. Her entering vital signs were low, and her cortisol level (a stress hormone that we measure by taking swabs of the mouth—saliva) was quite high. Though she said she was not aware of any deep suffering, she claimed to have a slight malaise. Her physiology was screaming volumes, and later so was she; that is, when she developed access to her unconscious. Our job, in one respect, is to merge the unconscious with the conscious, to put us in touch with what our bodies are saying. For that we need to learn the language of the deep brain, something that speaks to us constantly, if only we paid attention, yet only rarely can we speak to it. We need to learn its language, which is not much easier than learning French. What is worse, we cannot learn it through words; never through intellectual exercises, only through feelings. If we don't learn to speak the language of the unconscious, which has its own syntax and lexicon, we simply cannot make profound change.

The painful aspect of a memory occurs when feelings butt up against repression. When a person feels, and there is no longer a reason for repression, there is that much less hurt. As feelings rise in a session, so does the pain. It becomes real suffering as it approaches conscious-awareness. And then suddenly—relief. The feeling is addressed and felt. The only other choice someone who is in conventional therapy has is to push down the pain with medication. Or drown it in a flood of words and ideas. It is clear to me that as one opens up to oneself, one is much freerer, open, and loving.

Thirty-three-year-old Amy reported to her therapist at the Primal Therapy Center that her week was rather dull. "Although I cry once in a while, I seem to be doing okay." Yet her body betrayed her. Even with a

> *Modern-day psychotherapy often reinforces the split, or disconnection, between the deep primal universe and our thinking frontal cortex.*

"dull, calm" environment, her stress hormone (cortisol) level was high. She was clearly under stress and didn't know it, which is the case with many individuals who suddenly come down with a bleeding ulcer and have no idea as to why. Her body, her unconscious, knew the truth even if "she" didn't. That is one key reason we must have access to the unconscious, aside from the fact that it would no longer drive us. It would stop sudden inexplicable illnesses from befalling us. People in pain don't always suffer. Their repressive, inhibitory systems are functioning well. Suffering is the aware part of pain, not the conscious part. By that I mean that we can be aware of a certain discomfort, of feeling lousy, but not know why. Whereas when we are consciously aware, we feel pain and know why and where it comes from. That is knowledge as a result of access to our unconscious.

The suffering in depression should not be a mystery. There are specific events that caused it, and it can be accessed in an orderly, sequential fashion. Amy found later, after recounting how her mother always yelled at her that anyone that angry all of the time cannot love. Though her mother sporadically confessed love, it was never really evident in her behavior. And behavior is what counts, not just words. Amy's needs were sequestered as was their deprivation. They were evident in her act-outs, where she clung onto female friends, needing their "love" and approval all of the time. She was so desperately clingy that she drove some of her friends away.

A whole universe of experience lies so deep in the brain that most of us have no idea it exists. That universe drives our behavior and gives rise to mental and physical symptoms. We must ask ourselves some important questions: How do we know about that universe? How do we gain access to it? And, most important, how do we integrate it into our consciousness so that we are not driven by unconscious forces?

Regrettably, much of modern-day psychotherapy reinforces the split, or disconnection, between the deep primal universe and our thinking frontal cortex. The feelings leaking up from the primal universe are treated by most therapists as aberrations requiring suppression by our thinking minds, the cortex. We now know differently. That universe not only exists and is quantifiable (feelings can be measured along with the level of repression) but is also crucial to our health. The body has a voice, and it tells us that if the level of cortisol, our stress hormone, is high, and if serotonin, a brain chemical that suppresses other brain activity, is low, the body can override anything the cortex would have us believe. If there is a discrepancy between what we believe and what physiological tests indicate, we should be suspicious.

One patient began therapy saying that he was coming for intellectual reasons because he believed in our philosophy. Little by little we found that he could not sleep, was agitated constantly, and could not relax. He organized his day so that he always had something to do and some place to go. His vital signs were high—a heart rate of a constant 95 beats per minute and blood pressure of 160 over 100. He wasn't seeing us for philosophical reasons. He was ashamed to be "neurotic" like everyone else and could not stand being a "nut case." This man had what I call leaky gates. His inhibitory, repressive system was defective. There are many reasons for that, as we shall see later. One important reason is the birth trauma, heavy anesthetic, which inhibits the frontal inhibitory cortex from proper development. He had trouble controlling his impulses, which surged forward during sleep, waking him up, causing him to ruminate and think about any number of trivial things. His gating system was inadequate for proper sleep.

We (together with Open University, Milton Keynes, England) have done imipramine binding studies (blind) of blood platelets. Blood platelets have a high degree of biochemical resemblance to nerve cells, including neurotransmitter uptake and binding sites. We reasoned that we could measure through the blood, by surrogate, the serotonin production in the brain. Imipramine has a role as an antidepressant. It blocks the uptake of serotonin so that more of it remains to help repression. That is why it is important that levels normalized after one year of Primal Therapy.[3] Our informal analysis of a number of patients in Europe found that manic patients were low on binding. It is something we expected, as their frontal control mechanisms were faulty. We assumed that early trauma compromised the development of prefrontal brain tissue.

Within our brain system resides the left frontal cortex, which has a tremendous capacity for self-deception. Once we understand its role in evolution, we should be wary of relying on it for accuracy and truth about internal experience. We can rely on the left frontal cortex for external perception because that is its role, but not for internal understanding. If we want to know about our primal universe of feeling, we must appeal to the right brain and right prefrontal cortex. We can trust the right side; it is the repository of truth. Unfortunately, it forces the left side to lie and deceive; above all, to lie and deceive the self.

We shall see how receiving love early in life, even in the womb, sets the systems and structures of the brain and determines lifelong mental and physical health.

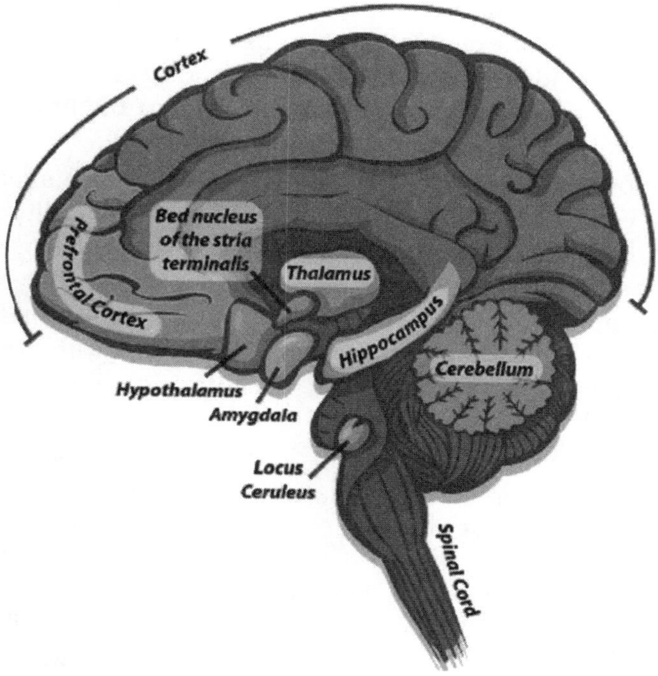

Recent brain research (cited later) has found that if we suffer a lack of love early in life, there are fewer key cells to help us think, concentrate, focus, and connect our thoughts with our feelings. Once we understand that hidden feelings drive much of our behavior, we will then understand how important it is to connect our thoughts with our feelings. Without connection, we cannot control the behavior or the physical symptoms that grow from such feelings.

In conventional psychotherapy, we manage through various insights and drugs to achieve temporarily what should have occurred had we had loving parents very early on. Both drugs and therapy allow us to achieve at least a temporary state of ease through enhancing the effectiveness of the defense system. I submit that cognitive/insight therapy is, in effect, a tranquilizer and increases left hemisphere repression to the detriment of feeling.

Drugs kill the pain from not being loved early in our lives, making us believe for a time that we were loved, or at least allowing us to think we are doing just fine. Because early love optimizes the amount of repressive chemicals we secrete, when there is an absence of love, we have a loss of those chemicals and are rarely comfortable in our skin thereafter. When someone has a traumatic birth, the entire biochemical system is altered, and the body may, for example, produce less alerting, vigilant chemicals, rendering an individual sluggish, passive, and non-aggressive. Such early life experiences are imprinted neurochemically into the brain and influence our lives in adulthood.

The notion of the imprint is key to our work and to an understanding of neurosis. Once an experience is imprinted neurochemically, our neural connections are permanently affected, meaning that it remains within our brain's system for a lifetime. However, it appears that it is possible to change the imprint through reliving the experience in Primal Therapy. The distress caused by the imprint may be diminished with drugs or alleviated to a degree with conventional psychotherapy, but the imprint is indelible, and ultimately wins out.

As we shall see, the imprint is laid down in every cell of our bodies. It distorts organ function and reregulates key set-points of hormone and neurochemicals, such as serotonin. For it to be changed or eradicated, we need to go back to the moments when it was set down, relive the experience, and normalize the system. There is no act of will, no trying, that will normalize; only reliving the time of deviation will do it, and it will happen all on its own. That is why a depressive can come into a session with a 96-degree (F) body temperature, relive a deep early hopelessness, and leave with a more normal reading. Why? Because the imprinted sensation/feeling no longer holds the deviation in place. That is, deviated readings are a product of the imprint. The body must react to deleterious early events; it doesn't develop low body temperature capriciously. It is part of an ensemble of reactions throughout the system that keep depression intact. It is all part of the memory. We can fix this reaction (blood pressure and heart rate) with vitamins or New Age techniques, but to change the whole cascade of reactions, we must address the time of the primal event.

When we address whole man or woman, we get a different set of reactions from when we address a symptom here or there. We don't want to make the *symptom* well, we want to make the *person* well, and the symptom will often take care of itself. That is why, in our hypertensives (high blood pressure patients), there is a significant permanent drop in their readings after one year of therapy. We don't work on symptoms directly, we often know little about the minutiae of a symptom. We know about the human condition that gives rise to symptoms. Specialists often know more and more about less and less—more about one specific reaction (which is very valuable) but that often will not explain its origin and how to get rid of it. Instead they have learned through medication how to control and manage it.

One depressed patient came into sessions chronically fatigued and lacking energy. She relived a birth where the mother was heavily anesthetized—she could not get out no matter how hard she tried. She finally was brought out with forceps. But the fatigue was imprinted, as was the lack of energy. Prior to therapy she was diagnosed with chronic fatigue syndrome and was treated with various drugs. But the fatigue *was a memory*, which could only be treated with memory—going back to where it all started and feeling the fatigue in context. Then her vital signs came back to normal, as did the energy levels. This didn't happen after one session, but after many.

Just as conventional psychotherapy ignores the organic disposition of the brain, there is a converse problem in some circles of medicine where health problems are reduced purely to brain function, disallowing any psychologic factors. Thus, in the current zeitgeist, an eating disorder such as bulimia exists because of low serotonin levels, a hormone produced by the brain, with many concluding that it is a function of genetics.

The belief that only physical factors matter is demonstrated in an arena of medicine known as biofeedback, which maintains that we can change a mental health problem such as anxiety by temporarily redirecting brainwaves, for example, by having a patient imagine relaxation and then directing her brainwaves to the alpha range, which some therapists equate with a calm state. But is this sufficient criteria toward determining whether a treatment has been successful?

In biofeedback, a notion of normality is applied to the patient rather than allowing the system to normalize through a natural evolutionary process of therapy. It is the *therapist's* idea of normality. It is taking a piece or fragment of our psyche and treating it as if that were the be-all and end-all of the matter. Imagine that you are hooked up to an EEG machine and that you try through visualization, such as that in biofeedback, to change your brain waves to so-called normal. It is pure mysticism to believe that this will overturn the effects of a lifetime with an alcoholic mother and a violent father. Such a therapeutic process is dependent on imagining a normal state, which means thinking your way to health. What one achieves is an illusory state; in short, something that isn't real or lasting.

To treat a patient successfully it is imperative that we take into account his psychological history, a history that might contain incest, abandonment, and neglect. Most importantly, we must consider an individual's early physical and psychological development, and examine that critical period from gestation through the first three years of life, which science is just now beginning to recognize has so much to do with problems later in life. It is necessary to look at the person as a whole and consider the patient's early history, taking into account physiological as well as psychological factors.

I call the gap between feelings/sensations and their psychologic counterpart the *Janovian Gap*. We shall see how important this gap is in determining how long we live and how early in life we may fall ill with any number of diseases, both physical and psychological.

The only progress in psychotherapy is to become whole again, to retrieve a self that was lost long ago and to recapture feelings that we disconnected from at the start of our lives. Only a therapy based on the experiential, on the development of the individual's brain, can succeed. The patient's whole system must be considered in such therapies so that the whole system can get well, not just a part of it.

Symptoms are the expression of an imprinted memory—memories of experiences we had in our earliest moments that have been laid down neurochemically within our brain and nervous system. That is what lies in the primal universe—monumental emotions of imprinted memories that have been sequestered in the far reaches of the brain. For a patient to get well, it is necessary to access those memories in a safe way, bring them to conscious-awareness and finally to integrate them. When that happens, the individual's entire system is harmonized, key hormones are normalized, and the system is finally righted. After a connection is made between feeling-sensations and the thinking mind, perceptions are more accurate and a sense of calm and relaxation never before known is finally experienced.

We feel better all over after we've made a connection between our thinking minds and our imprinted pain because the traces of trauma can be found in every part of our systems. When a real connection is made to the imprint and its attendant feeling-sensation, we see changes in system

After a connection is made between feeling-sensations and the thinking mind, perceptions are more accurate and a sense of calm and relaxation never before known is finally experienced.

levels in the patient's brain, biochemistry, hormones, and blood. Such measurement of progress in psychotherapy is possible, and must encompass those various systems. However, doctors often prescribe drugs as a way of correcting these systems. Doctors will offer Zoloft, Prozac, Wellbutrin, Paxil—the list keeps growing—to help the patient feel better, and sometimes they do. They may stop drinking or bingeing or then may finally be able to relax. Is that better? Of course, but the patient pays a big price: the drugs perpetuate a deep repression by widening the gap between the imprinted experience and the thinking mind, keeping the patient unconscious of his feelings. This may possibly give rise to serious disease later in life.

The major point of all of the previously mentioned drugs is to help repression, to block feelings. The real killer today is repression; many diseases lie above that bedrock. When there is a force holding down pain, the system does what it can to fight back. (Way back in the 1970s, psychiatrist John Diamond wrote about how the body doesn't lie.) The energy of the pain has to go somewhere, and it travels to various organs—the kidneys, liver, heart, or blood circulating system. One way we know this is that after a patient has relived major early traumas, including the lack of love, symptoms disappear, and blood pressure and heart rate normalize. Most of our entering patients have high levels of stress hormones, and we know that long-term elevated stress hormone levels can lead to a number of diseases, not the least of which may be Alzheimer's. Let's be clear: if the actual pain traveled upward and forward and made a connection, the energy would not travel to various organs, those most vulnerable. But when there is a disconnection, only the energy portion of the feeling is liberated to meander here and there in the system. The pain has an energy source that has to be dealt with somehow. It drives us; very much like a motor that constantly accelerates. As I discuss elsewhere, long-term high stress levels actually diminish the size of the hippocampus—the seat of memory—thus adversely affecting memory.

Drugs deepen the disconnection between deep pain and the conscious mind. That is not a way to dissolve neurosis; on the contrary, they enhance it, and the so-called improvement is artificial. We think we feel better, but the body knows the truth. And problems continue.

If we neglect an understanding of the brain and its systems, then we may draw conclusions about our patients that have no basis in physical reality. When we adopt palliative, intellectual approaches, therapies that address only the top level of the brain (the left prefrontal cortex), we may be unaware of a boiling and roiling cauldron of pain circulating down below. And that pain is likely to continue to cause mental and physical problems until the thinking mind connects to it neurochemically.

> *Drugs perpetuate a deep repression by widening the gap between the imprinted experience and the thinking mind, keeping the patient unconscious of his feelings, potentially giving rise to serious disease later in life.*

I am proposing a radical paradigm shift for the field of psychology, one based on new theoretical frameworks that employ specific techniques to access the deepest levels of the brain so that we can free the brain's systems and allow it to function at normal levels. To do this, however, we must understand how the structure of the brain and its organic function affects our overall health. We do know, for example, that the right brain—where feeling rules—develops and is impacted before the left—where thinking reigns. Obviously, effective psychotherapy will connect the two sides and integrate them. That is the meaning of integration, of getting it "all together." It means being whole; thinking what we feel, and feeling what we think. It means the end of hypocrisy.

We will discover the importance of connection between the right and left brains in any effective psychotherapy. We will learn about the front part of the prefrontal cortex and its role in connecting thought to feeling, and we will see how memory is imprinted and lodged in our systems.

For example, we are limited if we try to understand from only a purely intellectual point of view how birth trauma has impacted a patient's health. Yet, if we understand the language of the brainstem, which is the deepest channel of the central nervous system, we can actually learn what happened during gestation and birth. If we can guide the patient as he follows the trail that leads from his conscious mind down through the deepest levels of his brain to connect with an imprinted memory and "relive" his experience in the womb, we can provide effective treatment that will alleviate a litany of health problems.

One patient came in with chronically high blood pressure. She relived the birth trauma over and over again; fighting to get out, using all of her energy in the battle. The prototype for high blood pressure had been set down at that time. Her blood pressure did not lessen when she relived many later childhood feelings of neglect. After six months of sessions, her blood pressure finally dropped from 180 over 110 to 135 over 90. For her, Primal Therapy was lifesaving.

For more than three decades of practicing Primal Therapy, we have seen that a cure for being neurotic or even seriously mentally ill may be achieved through a carefully designed therapy based on neuroscience research and years of experience. The systematic process enables a patient to consciously relive history by connecting neurophysiologically to past traumas. It means that the patient has the undivided attention of the therapist, and is seen daily for three weeks. It means a soundproof room with low light and calm surroundings. It means no interruptions by telephones or secretaries. The patient is the total focus. Thereafter, there are groups and continued individual sessions, although not every day. All patients are presented to staff and the treatment plan is discussed so that all therapists in group therapy know how to approach the person.

Trauma is not necessarily engraved in a person in one grand, dramatic moment. It can be caused by simple neglect inflicted day after day over many years early in life. The baby who is not picked up when he needs it suffers. When that suffering goes on for a long time, it becomes trauma and is imprinted neurochemically into the brain.

When trauma happens early in life, the nervous system is not fully developed, and it can only process a limited amount of stress before there is an overload of pain. That overload is not ignored by the body's system; instead, it is put in storage in the brain neurochemically and is held as imprinted memory. Later, that imprinted memory may give rise to behavior that reflects a self-image of, "They don't care about me. What's wrong with me?" It becomes, in the current psychological vernacular, a lack of self-esteem. At its worst, imprinted memory may give rise to depression, anxiety, or high blood pressure, as well as any number of various mental and physical maladies.

It is important for psychotherapists to address a patient's history in an orderly fashion, to gradually uncover pain that is held in storage as imprinted memory. In Primal Therapy we begin with the most recent, less painful memories and continue on to the more remote and extreme early traumas, tracing our way back to the deepest levels of the brain slowly and methodically, over time.

There is nothing so simple as feeling our feeling, nothing so clarifying as that experience, and nothing so relieving as having a unified system—brain and body—at last.

There is nothing so simple as feeling our feeling, nothing so clarifying as that experience, and nothing so relieving as having a unified system—brain and body—at last.

A common myth states that it is dangerous to open up the psyche. This belief has been ingrained in us since the admonitions of Freud. I have found, by contrast, that opening up the psyche in a gentle, systematic way—one that accesses all levels of brain function—is the only way to eliminate ingrained patterns and enduring inexplicable symptoms.

2

How Love Sculpts the Healthy Brain

How we develop is best understood as the transformation of the external into the internal. We internalize our outer world experiences even from the start, and our neurophysiology is re-formed in the process—our experiences literally become a part of us. Receiving love, or experiencing an absence of it, early in life changes the brain permanently. If external life is harsh and unloving, even in the womb, that will be internalized, and that environment will shape the brain.

Early love, or a lack of it, has profound effects on our physiological development. When we receive love early in our development, our brain and body will run at optimal levels. The degree of love we receive in infancy can determine how well we get along with others, whether we are able to give and receive love, how stable our relationships will be, how intuitive and empathic we are, how well we learn, and how healthy we will be. Indeed, oxytocin and vasopressin are often referred to as the hormones of love, and low measurements of these chemicals may well indicate a lack of love and attention early in life. Changes in these two hormones in adulthood may tell us a good deal about early abandonment. They may also indicate how able we are to sustain a loving relationship later on. The imprint of alienation and anomie may dictate how close we can be with others. (There will be a full discussion of these hormones in Chapter 4.)

Personality develops differently in an absence of love, as does one's physiology and way of living. A lack of love conditions how we think of the world and ourselves, and how well we feel or don't feel. It determines how much impairment the feeling structures of the brain may have sustained. Those who experience impairment are not going to have their full powers of concentration, intellectual tenacity, and sustained interest. They are not going to learn as well as others, and that will have a great impact throughout their lives. A lack of love will also alter production of most of the key hormones and will leave the afflicted with a higher level of stress for life. It may affect what diseases people suffer from later in life, and, above all, how long they may live.

According to Allan Schore, professor of neuropsychology at UCLA, during pregnancy and for the first critical months of a baby's life, the mother is downloading her limbic system onto the baby's. Feelings by the mother sculpt the feeling centers of the baby's brain, creating a kind of symphony, or synchrony. The mother's patterns and rhythms of mood, any hormonal imbalances she might have, as well as over-excitement or depression are being experienced and integrated into the limbic area of the fetus/infant. The download forms the matrix for the child's physiology and brain development.

If we want to achieve a healthy, integrated brain, where do we start? We start with love—love in the most encompassing, broadest sense of the term. *Love is the single most important ingredient in determining how the brain develops.* It establishes how successful connections are made between key brain centers, and it influences the degree of access we will have to our feelings throughout life.

Loving a child means fulfilling his needs. A baby has needs in the womb, at birth, and after. This means nurturing the child and not inflicting trauma on the baby, from conception on, and particularly not during pregnancy and the child's first three years.

A baby's development in the womb is critical, because the baby is going through critical phases of development. Set-points for many physiological functions are established in the first months of gestation. Love between mother and child expresses itself in many ways, including fulfilling the physiological needs of the baby, such as its need for oxygen and proper nutrients during gestation. A loving mother will not go on a drastic diet just to keep her figure while she's pregnant, nor would she drink alcohol or smoke, knowing that these are damaging to the fetus. She will not rev up her system—and her baby's—by ingesting caffeine in soft drinks or coffee, not to mention taking diet pills or cocaine.

Giving birth with love means the mother will avoid taking an anesthetic to ease her own pain because she knows it will deprive the baby of oxygen and shut down many of her baby's systems. Because birth is often a life-and-death matter, a trauma inflicted here becomes imprinted and can endure for a lifetime. After birth, for a mother to love her baby, she must hold it close and breast-feed so that she and her child can develop a strong bond.

Much more than that, real love means the baby will experience a closeness to both parents and receive lots of warm physical contact such as holding, hugging, and kissing. In addition to holding an infant and caressing her, "loving" means looking at the infant with warm eyes, paying attention to her moods, listening to her, and caring for and soothing her. It means being empathic, sensing what she needs when she requires attention, and even when she doesn't, although some children are hugged, kissed, and coddled far too much—out of the parent's needs, not the child's. Love means encouragement, praise, and allowing the expression of feelings. It means guidance and protection, helping the child feel safe at all times.

As the brain matures, we develop other needs—such as the need for intellectual stimulation, praise, and discussion—from our mothers and fathers. In sum, we have physical, emotional, and intellectual needs, and we suffer when they are not met.

The more these needs are met, the more healthy brain development will be, thus producing a healthier and happier the baby. But when these needs are not met, when love is absent, there are immediate and enduring consequences. When a mother is not loving, not emotionally soft and warm, if she does not caress her baby often, she shapes a different kind of feeling structure in the baby's brain. This is particularly true of the baby's right brain, where the earliest imprinted memories take hold (this topic will be discussed in a later chapter). Part of not loving is not matching the baby's moods. Perhaps a young child is exuberant and playful, and the irritated mother is shushing and castigating her. Or the child is sad, and the father tells him to stop looking despondent and act cheerful.

The Outside Dictates the Inside

From the moment of conception, the driving force in human behavior is to minimize pain and maximize comfort. To that end we have an elaborate painkilling system mediated by neurotransmitters that enter into the synapses between neurons to block the transmission of the message of suffering to higher centers. Our ability to feel comfortable depends on optimum levels of the inhibitory neurotransmitter *serotonin,* and of the *endorphins*, an internally produced morphine of the brain and body. Early love normalizes these levels. A sense of calm in the mother while she is carrying the baby, and intimate, loving contact between mother and child in the first months of life give the baby a stronger brain.

The mother's state of being during pregnancy, whether she's calm or anxious, happy or depressed, whether she wants the baby or not, influences hormone output that will affect the baby's brain development.

Love regulates the opiate receptor system in such a way that optimum levels of endorphins in the mother's system make her comfortable and allow her to manage pain more easily at all times. One might call this a higher pain threshold, which only means that repression in the healthy person is more effective. This proliferation of endorphins will give the child an enhanced ability for contentment and joy. This also means a better handling of stress and adversity as she goes through life. As an adult, she has a calmness that is translated to her own baby, and responsiveness to the baby's experience. She is able to make her own children comfortable, enabling them to handle stress without being overwhelmed.

One mother we saw reared a "Primal baby," a child totally loved. The child was never afraid of new experiences, not afraid to change schools or make new friends, and not afraid to tackle new learning. She was operating with her whole self, and that means access to her feelings. Because she was not overwhelmed all of the time by internal pressure, she could handle a good deal of stimulation. The person in pain is already overwhelmed by internal input so that the slightest addition of pressure becomes too much. She seems to crumble from the overall load.

The mother's state of being during pregnancy, whether she's calm or anxious, happy or depressed, whether she wants the baby or not, influences hormone output that will affect the baby's brain development. More and more scientific research is confirming that children of mothers who underwent stressful conditions during pregnancy "show greater susceptibility to a wide array of health problems, including diabetes, obesity, high blood pressure, and heart disease."[1] A report in the October 2004 *Science News* noted, "A childhood filled with psychological or physical hardships contributes to a person's risk of developing heart disease."[2] Researchers from Atlanta and San Diego looked at the records of more than 17,000 adults to identify risk factors for heart disease. The more problems in childhood, the more likely there would be heart disease later on. What the investigators did not look at was how *early* those risk factors might occur. A high level of anxiety in the mother will contribute to stress for the fetus. An anxious, pregnant mother—responding to her outer world—is stirring up the metabolism of her fetus, who is also responding to his environment. If the mother's anxiety goes on long enough, it will become a permanent state in the fetus, and will change her child for life. The mother's anxiety will overstimulate the fetus and impair its nervous system, creating a child with an imprint of a high level of stimulation, which could leave her feeling overwhelmed by every little thing that happens throughout life. As an adult, she might respond to her husband's request to bring the salt to the table with an angry, "Do you really expect me to do everything? Get it yourself."

The outside dictates the inside. For a fetus, the mother's womb is the external world. A womb environment that keeps the fetus in an alert state eventually becomes part of the baby who will be a more aggressive, hyperactive child who cannot sit still or concentrate. He will grow up hypervigilant. This may be useful if he becomes a Hollywood agent or an undercover cop, but is bad for his longevity. Conversely, if the carrying mother is depressed for a lengthy period of time, her baby goes into "down" mode.

A common myth states that it is dangerous to open up the psyche. This belief has been ingrained in us since the admonitions of Sigmund Freud. I have found, by contrast, that opening up the psyche in a gentle, systematic way, one that accesses all levels of brain function, is the only way to eliminate ingrained patterns and enduring inexplicable symptoms. It is strange indeed that modern psychotherapy still subscribes to the ancient religious notion that we are inhabited by demons that must not be approached. It is pure mysticism to think that the unconscious is full of phantasmagorical entities, dark sinister forces that must be avoided at all costs. None of that is true; we have taken our patients to the very depths of the unconscious and have found no mystical demons. All we find are memories, memories of our lives. Painful, gut-wrenching memories, but memories with which we can live.

I call the process of connecting to imprinted memories "reliving" and/or a "Primal." Without reliving, the part of the memory that could not be integrated at the time the trauma occurred is doing continual damage to our system. But we can only do this when we are older, stronger, and more mature. As adults, we are strong enough to face our pain.

Despite a plethora of different therapeutic approaches, I have found no way out of neurosis except through connection, from the lower levels of consciousness to the higher, and from the right prefrontal brain to the left, all of which means reliving pain. There is nothing as simple as feeling our feelings; nothing so clarifying as that specific experience, and nothing so relieving as having a unified system—brain and body—at last. By feeling unloved, for instance, we allow ourselves to feel love again. It means we can feel, really feel, at last.

Depression may spell low dopamine levels in the fetus; this in turn may later direct a personality that is phlegmatic, passive, and nonaggressive. If the mother drinks a cocktail, the baby will get dizzy and drunk. If she smokes, the baby will choke. All this may endure, as various set-points are being imprinted into the baby's nervous system. Remember that low dopamine can lead to an addiction for the kind of drugs that boost it; for example, cocaine. In short, a person's emotional capacity and physiological system may already be compromised by the time he comes into life, even before he can fully process emotions.

When there is a lack of mother's love at the very start of life, the baby's brain will produce fewer inhibitory chemicals, which are responsible for holding back pain. If an infant does not get fed when he needs it, but when it is convenient for his mother, he suffers. If a toddler does not get the closeness, hugs, and kisses he needs from his mother and father, he suffers. Producing suffering in another is not an expression of love. Denial of the child's need is often done unconsciously, such as saying, "You know I love you, but I'm just not demonstrative." A parent may want the child to understand why he or she can't love him, but all his unconscious system knows is that he is suffering from his unfulfilled needs. I have not found experimental evidence to indicate exactly what happens in early pain in regard to serotonin production, but it seems logical that great pain first causes a leap in serotonin output followed by a quick depletion. It is as though the level of pain is such that production cannot be sustained, and then there is a depletion. It has been found, for example, that in chronic depression, serotonin levels are low. In some respects it parallels what happens in the blood system when early imprints cause constriction first followed by vasodilation, which is a widening of the blood vessels.

Receiving love early in life promotes the development of a comprehensive network of dendrites, which are the parts of brain cells that receive information from other cells. Neurons "speak" to each other via this vast network of branch-like connections of dendrites. The more dendrites we possess, the better our cells can communicate. This can mean increased access to our feelings because we literally have more lines of communication available.

Just as positive experiences early in life can stimulate neurons to develop new synapses and dendrites that enable more diverse connections to other neurons, in circumstances where there is an early lack of love, we are deprived of many of the synapses we need for integrating feeling with conscious awareness. We are, quite simply, not playing with all of our marbles. We may think that one sibling is stronger mentally than another in childhood due to genetics, but it may well be due to womb-life, which gave the brain of one child better and stronger neural connections than the other. The mother may have been calmer during one pregnancy than the other.

A study discussed in an October 2004 *Science News* article compared two sets of mice. One set was normal; the other had a gene for serotonin secretion knocked out. They were then treated with the equivalent of Prozac (serotonin enhancers) at the ages of 4 days to 21 days (corresponding to ages from the third trimester of gestation to 8 years). When the mice matured, they were put under stress (foot shock). The mice that received "Prozac" early in life displayed anxiety and depression, showed less interest in exploring their environments, and took longer to avoid the foot shock. What the study explained was that serotonin plays a pivotal role in normal brain development, and if we interfere with the serotonin output early in life while the brain is still developing, there could be permanent effects on mood and its control later on.[3] I am suggesting that trauma, even in utero, can do exactly that—make someone susceptible to anxiety and/or depression later on.

Love is especially important for the development of the prefrontal cortex (the section of the brain that lies behind the forehead and eye sockets), where we connect to, control, and integrate our feelings. With love, we grow a greater number of neurons, key nerve cells that translate and transmit information. The growth of the synapses, which provide the interconnectivity between neurons, flourishes, rendering a stronger brain, especially in the prefrontal cortex/control center. Trauma during womb-life can blunt healthy development of this area so that the baby is born with fewer neurons. It can weaken the development of the prefrontal cortex, resulting in a susceptibility to problems with impulse control later in life. We may see this in an individual who cannot wait or control impulses. The result can be bed-wetting in a child or premature ejaculation in an adult. It may lead to a person having difficulty focusing or concentrating.

Once the cortex is diminished, with fewer dendrites to receive other neuronal messages and synapses to carry the message to other neurons, it is not going to flower in adulthood. And brain scans bear this out. For instance, there is less activity in the prefrontal area in certain impulse states. Criminals dominated by their impulses have a greater tendency for impulsive behavior. Daniel Amen, a specialist of the brain, has done SPECT scans (brain scans) on individuals with a variety of psychological states. He found that in attention deficit disorders, where the subject is given a task that requires concentration, brain energy shifts backward instead of moving to the frontal cortex, where it should be. The brain is frontally deficient, I believe, due to early trauma or toxic insults so that it doesn't have the equipment for proper focus: neither the connecting gaps between neurons, nor the actual brain cells to process abstract thought. It doesn't have all its marbles and cannot do what other brains can do. We cannot afford to overlook all of this in treating patients in psychotherapy. We may be trying to get a brain to do what it cannot do neurologically.

Critical Periods: Is It Ever Too Late to Be Loved?

Critical periods are the times when needs for love are at their maximum and must be fulfilled. The pain impressed into the system when needs are unmet during a critical period remains for a lifetime. There are no substitutes that repair the damage—not love or caring later in life, not success, not "awareness" gained through therapy, not drugs or alcohol, nor belief in God.

The only way to undo the damage is to access the neural connections that were laid down at the time of the original pain and trauma so that they can be modified. Because these neural connections include primitive regions of the brain, including those underlying basic emotions and survival functions, a cerebral talk about what happened in the past will have little effect. Instead, we must allow ourselves to fully experience, or rather reexperience, those early painful, traumatic experiences as an adult who can tolerate the feelings. This is what Primal Therapy offers.

Although it is pointless to give a six-month-old extra oxygen because she lacked it in the womb, there indeed might be a solution. Any serious trauma during gestation or birth becomes imprinted and may endure for a lifetime. But we now have the techniques to go back in history and undo the effects. For example, we can go back to when a patient, as a newborn, lacked oxygen during birth. The patient will turn red because at that moment he is lacking oxygen, a sensation that his brain has stored as a memory. (Our research, discussed on page 63, at the UCLA Pulmonary Laboratory confirms this.) Because the lack of oxygen skewed the system, the reliving can now resolve the trauma and reverse the deviations caused by the original experience (often causing breathing problems or shortness of breath). We have all seen children who, under stress, will hold their breaths for an inordinate amount of time, which is often an indication of oxygen deprivation at birth.

Healthy development of neurons during the last trimester of pregnancy is especially critical, for if trauma occurs during this time, the developing brain can be changed for life. If the newborn is not touched in the first hours or days after birth, a terror and loneliness can be imprinted that stays with her for life.

Several studies have found an association between a mother's nurturing and the future mental health of her children. Recent animal experiments led by Michael Meaney, a professor of medicine at McGill University in Montreal, Canada, reported by Emma Ross revealed that the way a mother cares for her baby can determine how stressed out the child will be as an adult; her nurturing can permanently change the way the infant's genes operate.[4]

Meaney set out to test whether baby rats who are licked more turn out differently from those who are licked and groomed less, and, if so, why. These studies on the origins of adult disease rigorously tested whether it really is the mother's behavior that makes the difference and showed what happens in the brain of the offspring to produce the adult characteristics. Meaney and his research team found that baby rats that were licked by their mothers a lot turned out to be less anxious and fearful as adults, and produced lower levels of stress hormones than those who were groomed less. "All the mothers nurture their pups, provide ample milk, and the pups grow perfectly well," says Meaney, "But there is one behavior, called licking and grooming, that some mothers do much more than others—four or five times as much. The pups who are licked more are less fearful, they produce fewer stress hormones when provoked, and their heart rate doesn't go up as much, so they have a more modest stress response than the pups who are licked much less."

The scientists even took the mothers out of the picture altogether and stroked the baby rats with paintbrushes. Meaney maintains, "It does the same thing that maternal licking does." The change in the production of the brain receptors was apparent by the second week of life.

"This is a very important study," said Peter Blackman, a professor of pediatric and prenatal biology at the University of Auckland in New Zealand, who was not involved in the research. He pointed out that the expression of genes in mammals can be permanently changed by how mothers and infants interact and how that can have long-term effects on behavior and psychiatric health. If those baby rats were licked just as much weeks later, the critical period would have passed and the lifelong effects would not be evident.

The following remarks are from *Monkeyluv* by Stanford University biologist and neuroscientist Robert M. Sapolsky. We see in his reported research on mice how early the critical period can be. As we shall see, not only are early childhood events important for later life, but even more important is fetal life. Sapolsky comments on how genetic influences are not the be-all-and-end-all that we sometimes believe. Life circumstances are important, but pre-birth influences can be critical.

> Relaxed-strain [from the genes] mice that were raised from birth by timid-strain moms grew up to be just as relaxed as any other member of their strain. With the same kind of technology used by clinics performing in vitro fertilization, the investigators cross-fostered mice as embryos. [Letting one strain of mice raise a genetically different strain of mice.] They implanted relaxed-strain eggs into timid-strain females who carried them to term. Some relaxed-strain pups were raised by timid-strain moms, and others by relaxed-strain ones. The result? When the supposedly genetically hard-wired relaxed mice went through both fetal development and early puphood with timid-strain moms, they grew up to be just as timid as any other timid-strain (inherited) mice. Same genes, different environment, different outcome.[5]

Sapolsky then goes on to comment: "Environmental influences don't begin at birth. Some factors in the environment of a timid-strain mouse mother during her pregnancy—her level of stress...are affecting the anxiety levels and learning abilities of her offspring, even as adults." He emphasizes that "relaxed-strain mice aren't relaxed only because of their genes; their fetal and neonatal [around birth] environments are crucial factors."[6]

I am going to discuss these early influences, so we should be aware that there is a body of research in animals that seems to corroborate my point: birth and pre-birth events can help determine our behavior as adults; and, if we neglect these influences, we shall not fully understand who and why we are what we are. Moreover, we shall not know how to treat and reverse all manner of problems we have as adults. From conception on we are building a superstructure. We need a solid foundation for that superstructure so that we can be integrated adults who can withstand the impact of the elements. Conclusion: genetics is important, but life experience, even in the womb, can be equally, if not more, important. Whether we manifest high blood pressure, asthma, or migraine headaches not only depends on genetics, but our early experiences. If we ignore experiences in the womb, we are leaving out critical moments that can affect us for a lifetime.

You may wonder, "Can we really go back and reexperience fetal events?" In evolution, each new level of brain development incorporates lower, earlier levels. The thinking neocortex is a sort of an add-on from previous animal brain forms. So, at birth, there are already sensations from pre-birth that play a part in how the newborn reacts to that birth trauma. When a patient relives a birth trauma (if there were one), she is in fact also experiencing sensations (the base of feelings) that occurred previously. As we shall see later, this is how we can relive pre-birth events without being aware that they come from experience in perhaps the fifth or sixth month of gestation.

As a general rule, the earlier in life a need goes unmet, the more devastating the later effects of deprivation will be. The closer to the "critical period" a trauma occurs, the more harmful it is. One way we can define *critical period* is the irreversible quality of its effects. The more time that has elapsed after a critical period has passed, the greater the force required to create an imprint. It takes a tremendous trauma after the critical period to have a profound and lifelong effect. Why do needs go unmet? For a passel of reasons, but it is often true that parents are so immersed in their own unmet needs (with the resulting narcissism) and pain that they simply cannot attend to their child.

We have learned from our patients' feelings, supported by vital signs taken before and after each session, that not being touched at age 7 years can never match that same trauma at age 6 months.

A divorced father, who left his family when the daughter was 6 years old and the son 8 years old, came back into the family's life when the children were in their late teens. He was hoping to make up for lost time. It was not to be. Their rapport was seriously ruptured, their pain of the loss deeply ingrained. In order to overcome the blockage of the earlier pain, the children have to go back to the time of abandonment, feel its hurt, beg Daddy not to leave, and then at the point maybe they can accept their father a little better into the family.

In fact, any deep pain and repression can close up the system so that love can hardly get in. Pain is the enemy, but repression is both a friend (needed originally to keep a steady course) and an enemy (when we want to love later on). It comes into being as a handmaiden of pain. Once pain has been resolved, there is less need for repression.

We have learned from our patients' feelings, supported by vital signs taken before and after each session, that not being touched at age 7 years can never match that same trauma at age 6 months. For example, lack of close physical contact in the first months of life after birth can mean less nerve fibers connecting the brain's right and left hemispheres, and, as a result, a lack of access to feeling. (See Chapter 3 for more information.) Lack of close contact after the age of 5 would not have the same effect.

If we don't caress a child at age 7, disastrous consequences will not happen, and critical changes to brain structures will not occur. The child will hurt, but his whole brain system will not be changed. It will be a painful memory, but it will not be an imprint in the same way as if it happened during the critical period. Traumas in adolescence, such as not being hugged, understood, or listened to, are still painful, but not as painful as earlier deprivation. Indeed, the later pain is usually a result of it triggering feelings related to the earlier pain, even though we may be completely unaware of it.

In contrast, *imprints*, a special category of memory, have enduring and widespread effects. They change our whole physiology, determine set-points for key structures within the brain, and shape personality accordingly. Thus, a lack of touch can have immense consequences for a baby when it first comes into the world and its emotional brain is still developing. Not being touched will trigger the production of the stress hormone cortisol, which can rise to catastrophic levels and adversely affect brain structures. Because they occur during critical periods, imprints, by definition, are largely irreversible—unless they are relived neurophysiologically.

A number of animal experiments demonstrate that the newborns that had their eyes bandaged during the critical period for developing vision became blind. Two Harvard scientists, Torsten Wiesel and David Hubel, in a now classic experiment, bandaged the eyes of kittens right after birth. When the bandages were later removed, the kittens were blind. Although their eyes worked, their brains had lost the ability to process visual information because they lacked this input during the critical period. Similarly, people who have been blind from infancy but whose vision is later restored through new medical techniques find it too difficult to "learn" to see.

The same is true for how love impacts the brain's development. Love means meeting a need at the time when it is crucial. You can't make up for it years later, such as a mother whose husband left her when the children were young. She was depressed during her children's infancy. When the children were older, the mother wanted to make up for time lost to her depression, but alas, it could not be done. The children gave up trying to receive love from this single, depressed woman who could barely get out of bed each day. The child can forgive the mother, but the unmet need for her when the child is young is merciless and unforgiving. These children came to the Primal Healing Center as adults, and were able to go back and feel, crying like young children with the original child's brain. As noted earlier, it is a cry that cannot be duplicated later, after a session. An odd dialectic: *feeling* the pain made it go away. Why? Because it was never fully felt before. It is held in storage until the person is strong enough to face it. Trust the system; it knows what to do.

When a patient is told what to do or how to behave by therapists, generally, this implies that they do not trust the patient's system. We do not develop symptoms or behavior for no reason. The system is eminently logical. We have only to find out what the logic is behind a specific behavior or symptom. Our therapy is not about screaming at the behest of a therapist, nor about pounding the walls after being told we are angry at our fathers. It is about allowing ourselves to feel what is already there, often locked deep inside, and giving those feelings their full expression. It is about a systematic journey to the antipodes of the mind, where the brain of the patient leads the way.

The Fulfillment of Love

The need for love is every bit as important and biologic as the need to see. Once deprived, we lose part of the ability to give and receive love. So let us not say, "Look, why are you depressed? You've got a girlfriend who loves you." She can never fill the hole, and that contributes to an endless search for what was missed, which often manifests in infidelity. Having a wife or husband who loves us can never make us feel loved once we feel unloved. It is like trying to undo the imprint. Let me be more specific: one can feel comfortable with a spouse but below the comfort and "love" one feels in the present is the ubiquitous sense of lacking. Still, the feelings we have for and from others counts a good deal; it does help quiet the anguish. Once deprivation is installed, we may try to fulfill it with many other partners, and it never works and is never totally satisfying. The infidelity goes on and on. Remember, in infancy the brain is still developing. A lack of love early on can interfere with that development. We see evidence of this in the desperation and paranoia one feels with a partner. The minute the other person talks to someone else, jealousy sets in—then anger, recriminations, and suspicion. The greater the earlier deprivation, the less it takes in the present to set off the pain. One musician I saw demanded that his girlfriend keep her eyes on the floor when at parties. He never wanted her to look up at a man.

If we don't praise or at least look carefully at the young child and what she creates throughout her infancy and childhood, we can cause an imprint and change the child's neurophysiology. Thereafter, all encouragement and praise will fall on deaf ears, or at least on a deaf limbic system—brain areas that mediate our feelings and emotions. The critical period will have come and gone. The need for praise at 6 months of age may not be essential, but it is crucial at age 5. It is no wonder then that a movie star who grew up in an orphanage will never feel fulfilled no matter how much adulation and love she gets later in life. Current love helps; it may attenuate the hurt she feels, but it never changes it. If it did, then perhaps Marilyn Monroe would not have gone in and out of relationships looking for that elusive thing called love.

It is also true that the deeper the lack of fulfillment experienced during early development, the greater the struggle will be to fulfill that need throughout life. One may get the applause of thousands, yet it still doesn't satisfy. If love could be made up later in life, then the rock stars I see in therapy would be comfortable. They rarely are. Mothers who were left by their husbands during pregnancy may have children with a greater tendency to become homosexual. It has been established that sex hormones can be changed by the carrying mother's stress situation.[7]

For example, researchers found that female characteristics were permanently altered when the fetus was exposed to high levels of testosterone in the womb. Certain adverse characteristics during womb-life will masculinize female offspring. Female rats, for example, will play like males and demonstrate mounting behavior.

Is homosexuality a choice? Not likely. If the father left after the third year of the child's life, the impact would not be so catastrophic, as in the critical period when sex hormones are being set during gestation. But with a stressed mother during pregnancy and later deprivation of a father who has left the household, we have the possible makings of frank homosexuality in a young male child. The loss of paternal love merely compounds the early changes in sex hormones and may create latent homosexuality. This is not necessarily true in every case, but it is something to be aware of. Different circumstances would apply to a female child.

The critical period for intellectual development is much later than that for physical love. A 5-month-old baby is not going to feel dumb no matter how he is treated. But when there is adequate intellectual development later in childhood, the child is then susceptible to emotional influence and can be made to feel dumb. If we feel dumb because that is the way we were treated from ages 6 to 15, chances are we will believe we are dumb thereafter. No matter what accomplishments we might achieve, we will still think we are dumb.

Intimate contact between mother and child in the first weeks and months of life regulates the opiate receptor (pain-killing) system in such a way that there are optimum levels to make us comfortable. When we mature into adulthood, therefore, we are then able to make our own children comfortable, as well, enabling them to handle stress without being overwhelmed. A parent who was loved as a child has a calmness that then translates to her own baby. A tense mother who handles her child roughly is not imparting a sense of calm to him. A mother who desperately needs love may use her baby to fulfill her own needs, demanding too much from him so that he cannot be himself.

We recently saw a young male homosexual whose father did not leave home but was emotionally gone. He was a boxer and a tough guy, wanting his son to follow in his footsteps. Hugging and kissing his son was out of the question. His machismo would not allow it. He would box and wrestle with his son, but never offer a tender touch. This is what our patient would seek out later in life—a little tenderness. He was never aware of it growing up, but his body stored the need until it could express itself in a love relationship with another man. The time distance between a lack of cuddling from his father and his later need for male love was such that putting the two together seem out of the question. When he came to us, he cried and screamed for that love from his father.

Pain and Repression

Earlier I noted that mother's love during the critical periods early in life is like a drug. But in the absence of that mother's love, we hurt. A lack of love is *pain*. A baby cannot survive feeling that mother will never come or that everything is deeply, utterly hopeless. Luckily, the baby doesn't have to tolerate such pain. The baby's brain will adapt to the lack of love and will find a way to cope with it, through *repression*.

As a survival mechanism, repression allows feelings to be blocked and rerouted, and then dislocated, so the baby no longer needs to feel a dire sentiment such as, "I'll die if my mother doesn't love me." Of course, such feelings are never articulated, they are merely sensed. Yet they are imprinted into the brain as a feeling of "I'll die if she doesn't love me." Years later, when the baby has grown into a man and his girlfriend leaves him, he may tumble into a deep depression, which is what we see currently in one of our young patients. He was actively suicidal—he felt he could not go on and did not want to go on. We found that it was the same feeling he had when his mother ran off with another man and left him to be reared by his father. The imprint triggered the feeling of abandonment ("I'll die if she doesn't love me"). The connection between the thought and the feeling is literally a series of related nerve networks, each nerve cell or circuit setting off the adjoining one; they then jointly call a meeting, an assembly, and the generating source is revealed. We have to be present at that assembly. D.O. Hebb discussed the assembly of neurons some 50 years ago.

Although repressed, the overwhelming pain from the early lack of love is constantly knocking on the door of awareness. The system does everything it can to block that awareness because it means feeling hurt. But when early trauma depletes some of our body's own internally produced painkillers—neurotransmitters such as serotonin—the brain's ability to keep pain at bay is weakened. The person may feel compelled to turn to drugs or alcohol to do the trick. Many tranquilizers, for example, do what our own body would do on its own had its capacity to produce its own painkillers not been damaged by trauma and lack of early love. Or the person may become addicted to something that can make him feel good, such as cocaine, which raises dopamine levels (the "feel good" hormone) and takes the place of his mother. It makes him feel strong and warm, and gives him a sense of "can do," all of the things that his mother should have done early on. He is seemingly addicted to cocaine, but it is really a substitute mother who is addicting. His mother could have given him lifelong optimum dopamine levels. Now it is too late. So he settles for a substitute.

Many tranquilizers, for example, do what our own body would do on its own had its capacity to produce its own painkillers not been damaged by trauma and lack of early love.

Similarly, a therapist's concern and kindness is worth a temporary 20 milligrams of Prozac, a substitute for serotonin. This is why many people become addicted to therapy. We go back for it over and over again, often not knowing why, yet having someone to listen to us exclusively is very comforting. What most of our drugs do is replace the chemicals lost or diminished during the imprint. Early love provides the optimum amount of serotonin in our systems. But lack of love creates deficits. Prozac steps in to do what mother should have done. The need for heroin and any other painkiller is that very same need early on for mother. It was and is a matter of life and death. Taking drugs is, in short, trying to make up for a lack.

Is addiction a bad habit? I contend that mostly it is survival. It should not be cast as a moral judgment. Is being off drugs something to brag about? The Alcoholics Anonymous people think so, and obviously, it is important, but there has to be knowledge of what to do after withdrawing. Otherwise, the system feeds on itself, destroying organs, which will eventually foreshorten our lives. The need does not go away. It remains pristine and pure all of our lives. It is untouched by experience because it is inured to any experience that doesn't fill the need, even symbolically. We are stuck in a time warp.

Later we will see how the words of a therapist, no matter whether right or wrong, can be soothing to our agonies. We can be fooled into thinking that the "insights" *we* have in therapy are what make us feel better, but in reality it is the caring, reassuring tone of the therapist, all along. It dampens pain, the pain of a mother who was unaffectionate and inattentive; the pain of a father who never cared, was never soft, and whose tone was unrelentingly harsh. The therapist's presence says, "I'm here now. It's going to be all right." Just being in his office can make us feel better.

Feeling better is fine. But we must keep in mind that the caring we get now cannot make up for the lack of it when it was critical. The critical period has passed. If it hadn't, then the doctor's caring would heal us. Because it is after the critical period, it is only palliative. It may help stabilize a shaky defense system, but it never eradicates need. I will repeat ad nauseam: *we cannot love neurosis away.* Even if we could resurrect Momma and have her kiss and hug her grown-up child, no amount of love in the present can reverse the damage. That is why a kindly therapist, who is concerned and interested, cannot reestablish equilibrium in his patient. No amount of his caring and insights will induce any profound change. No psychotherapy can alter those needs, nor can the drug-taking or other act-outs they drive, once they are sealed in.

More broadly, we must keep in mind the futility of using *ideas* to treat the effects of deeply ingrained traumas. As we shall see, it is not possible to use ideas and thinking processes, which literally came along millions of years later in the evolution of brain development, to affect what is lower in the brain and evolved millions of years earlier.

Case Study: Stash

I was born weak and exhausted. The drugs given to my mother had passed through her system into mine and were trying to kill me; that is how I felt it, that something's trying to kill me. I was slapped repeatedly and dunked in alternately hot and cold water to revive me after the caesarian to save me from death from medically induced drugs.

I never had a break; I never had the opportunity to heal and recover. I was expected to be a normal baby; in fact, an excellent baby, the perfect baby one could be proud of. I needed rest and a lot of nurturing, not to be living up to expectations; and why would anyone have expectations of someone so new to the world anyhow?

I've always retreated to the past. The past always seems like it's better to me than the present. I remembered being probably about 1 [year] or less and being in what I believe is my parent's apartment. All I remember is being alone, in a crib, the room being muted, but it was sunny and warm outside, curtains blowing lightly from a large open window or French doors. The important part is that I was alone, and felt very, very alone. I had this melancholic feeling, which is the underpinning of all my feelings all my life, a yearning for the past. Imagine yearning for the past at the age of less than 1! To me, it's a feeling of wanting to go home; to go back to a place of where I feel okay and there's no more melancholy.

This was the beginning of my depression, and it only got stronger from there. I believe that what I was pining for was to be back in the womb, where all was whole and taken care of, and, most importantly, I was never alone. I know that it still wasn't ideal there because my mother was an alcoholic and smoker, but compared to the stark loneliness I was feeling at the time, it was a far better place.

All I ever wanted was to be what my parents wanted me to be, especially my father. I wanted to be everything they wanted me to be, and more. The truth is all I ever wanted was to please my parents, in spite of how I acted as I got older and grew rebellious and angry.

The most prevalent theme in my life, repeated over and over in a myriad of ways, is that I have to always deny feeling weak and act strong. Weakness is incredibly threatening to me, is what I'm always terrified people will see in me and will reject me for. I can never give into it; I've expended untold energy constantly keeping it at bay. I couldn't help but indulge it occasionally, but could never let it take over because that's a hole I would never be able to crawl out of; it's death to me.

I always felt that something was wrong with me. This was twofold in that there's truth to it, as well as simply not being able to live up to the anticipations of my family. I believe humans (and animals, for that matter) have hardwired expectations in our genes. One of which is to be born via the birth canal and to experience it, both mother and child. When that doesn't happen as it's supposed to, something doesn't feel right, and will never feel right until resolved and being nurtured. So I've always felt something was wrong with me because there was; I wasn't born the way I was supposed to and didn't feel the way I was supposed to. As a matter of fact, it went very wrong, and I've even felt that I wasn't supposed to have been born, that I should've died.

Doing anything has always been twice as difficult for me than others who didn't have such trauma. I not only had to perform as well or better than others, but I also had to repress this overpowering feeling of tiredness and weakness at the same time. I was expected to excel at everything. Neither my parents nor anyone else had the understanding that I had started life with a huge deficit and therefore needed help, nurturing, a break, lower expectations, etc. So I was expected to excel, and there's no reason why I shouldn't. After all, I had no handicap in their eyes. And so when I didn't excel, it meant there was something wrong with me, a double whammy. And when I did, well, it was simply expected. No one had any idea for me it required twice as much energy, heartache, and effort as most people.

So I've lived my whole life fighting this incredibly threatening feeling, feeling/thinking that there's something wrong with me, that I'm inferior, etc. Even the slightest failure was huge in that it would open up this can of worms. Yet my system was always trying to reach normalcy by going back to this experience, to feel this feeling, and resolve it. And here I've been thinking I'm a loser, a failure, not worth knowing or being around, not having talents, skills, just being generally unworthy and someone to be ashamed of, wondering why anyone would like me or want to be my friend. Always just wanting to have the opportunity to just take a break, catch my breath, rest for a little while...and always wanting to have the chance to start over and do it right this time.

I'd binge on drugs and alcohol. Cocaine was a favorite for the energy, omnipotence, and numbness it would give me. I'd then "crash" from the partying, have reality match the hung-over feeling inside, then recuperate before I'd begin the cycle again. This is exactly how my birth went, drugs and all. Somehow I managed to work/run my own business during this time, as well as work out at the gym most every day, play in a band, and date a lot of women.

So I'm exhausted. This is the essence of depression. It's the feeling of the original high-valence trauma creeping into consciousness combined with the huge amount of repression constantly required to keep this catastrophic feeling unconscious. You have to severely deaden yourself to keep the feeling of the trauma from taking over. There's a price for this, though, which is a deadening of all experience, and a profound melancholy, which is a yearning for how things should be. We're all created hardwired with this expectation. In a funny way, we know what we're supposed to feel and be like, and when it doesn't happen, there's melancholy; for life isn't all that we know it should be.

3

Where Ideas Spring From: The Different Languages of the Brain

If we want to understand why we behave the way we do and why we suffer from various afflictions, we need to have a basic understanding of the brain and how it works. We need to know where emotional pain is rooted and how it got there before we can begin to understand how to reach it and resolve it. This is especially important in psychotherapy because, as someone once said, "When you get on the wrong train, every stop you make will be the wrong one."

Trauma and lack of love put us on the wrong track right from the start. This is literally true when it comes to the brain, for there are nerve tracks that become deviated and rerouted due to early pain; it's like a house that isn't wired correctly, so all of its electrical circuitry will lead to the wrong outlets. If we don't know about a deviation, then we won't know where the normal route should be. And worse, because we tend to think that the deviation is purely "psychological," we end up overlooking the physiological in its entirety; we think that ideas seem to "go off" or happen by themselves, while the rest of us remains steady and fixed.

We have seen many patients who are pure intellectuals who have no idea about the universe of feelings. Our therapists need to have knowledge of what brain system the patient is using. For example, we may see what I call "first-line intrusion": the patient begins to feel about neglect in his childhood only to begin coughing, experiencing excess oral fluid, choking, placing his arms in the fetal position, and so on. We know what the signs of intrusion are; meaning that we understand that deep brain imprints are surging forward and obfuscating the feeling currently being dealt with. We then have a choice: either deal with the intrusion or use medication to subdue it for a time so that the patient can feel her feelings. We need a gestalt/neurological understanding to make our choice. In any case, we see by this intrusion that the inhibitory repressive system is faulty.

We have a French patient, who tries to feel events from childhood, but as soon as he has access, the birth signs come up and block any ability to feel. He turns red, lacks oxygen, chokes, and simply cannot continue with his childhood memories. Here the childhood memory—"I am all alone, I don't exist to them" (which can later lead to "I don't exist," otherwise known as low self-esteem)—dredged up the Primal aloneness right after birth when he was left alone for three days, with perfunctory care. There is no separation between levels of consciousness, so the patient feels overwhelmed all of the time. There are certain pathognomonic (sure) signs of birth intrusion that cannot be faked any more than a patient can fake a body temperature drop of two degrees.

Chances are that by the time a patient comes for psychotherapy, he or she carries a neurotic behavior that is so deeply ingrained that the origins of it are virtually inaccessible. Conventional therapies, such as behavioral, cognitive, and insight, don't have the tools to find the early imprints that are the origins of the patient's neurosis. If a patient is to heal, then the psychotherapist must have the tools to find the pathways to the roots of the patient's emotional and physical turmoil. Understanding the brain—of how its pathways and circuitry are laid out—is essential if we are to find our way to the root of any problem. The aim of therapy must be to establish fluid lines of communication among the levels of consciousness. That is what constitutes *full consciousness*.

The brain actually has three levels of consciousness, not two, which most think of simply as the conscious and subconscious mind. But when we understand the three levels, we come to see how certain experiences are imprinted into specific levels of the brain depending on when they occurred and how much force was behind them. When someone takes drugs or tranquilizers, for example, they are calming different levels of consciousness and the imprinted memory of the experience that's giving rise to the pain.

Research shows that there must be great emotional force driving a trauma for it to imprint the brain. There is a good deal of work on the retrieval of memory and which brain systems are charged with doing it.

We shall discover the route that feeling takes in the brain, how it gets blocked, and what happens to us once it is blocked. We shall also find out why feelings must be the sine qua non of any proper psychotherapy.

The Three Levels of Consciousness

We basically have three brains in one: the brainstem, the limbic system, and the neocortex; each of these constitutes a level of consciousness, and each has its own memory system. We remember smells, sensations, even conversations, all on different levels of the brain, yet they are all connected.

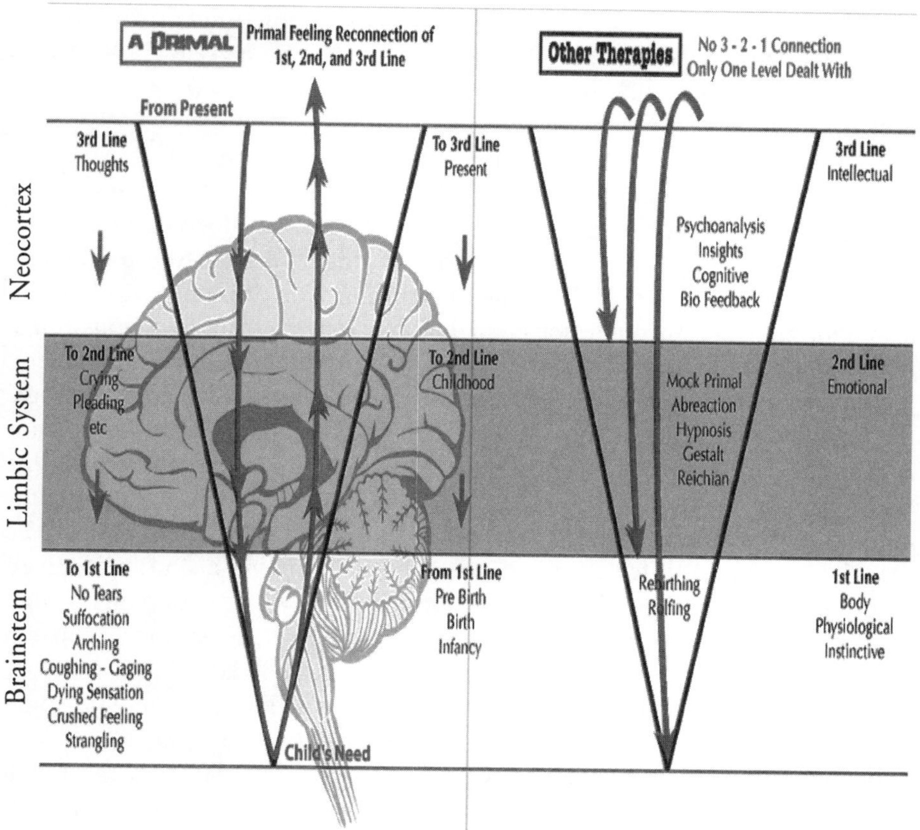

First Line: The Brainstem

The first level, the brainstem, is a primitive or reptilian brain (I sometimes refer to it as the *salamander brain* because the limbic system and brainstem constitute a good part of the whole brain of the animal), which is our oldest brain system. The brainstem was the first to evolve, and the first part of the central nervous system to develop in human evolution. Salamanders, incidentally, have pretty much the limbic system we have, in primitive form. The eminent neuroanatomist E.J. Herrick identified them as a walking, swimming, living brainstem. It seems that we never lost that part. We just added new brain tissue on top of it. When patients are down on that level, there are never any words nor adult-like screams—mostly grunts.

The brainstem leads out of the bottom, rear of the brain down through the spinal cord. It deals with instincts, basic needs, survival functions, sleep, and basic processes that keep us alive, such as body temperature, blood pressure, and heart rate. I call this the "first line," or survival, brain.

The brainstem takes form around the 33rd day of gestation. After the first month in the womb, we have a fairly complete brainstem, and with it comes the ability to code and store trauma. Besides very deep breathing, the brainstem is also involved with taste and hearing. We can store a mother's depression, anxiety, stress, drug-taking, smoking, or drinking. Mother can also communicate, through her changing hormones, her unconscious rejection of her coming baby, which then becomes stored in the baby's brainstem. Such experience is not stored as ideas, obviously, because we don't yet have a neocortex, which is our thinking, intellectual mind. But what is important is that the imprints in this storehouse will later motivate certain thoughts and aberrations of thinking. They will follow the nerve tracts to higher centers of the brain that then will elaborate upon the experience of the original trauma in different ways and sway our thinking accordingly. Even without the top-level, thinking frontal cortex, which will express pain through words, animals and humans can still scream and cry. First-line brainstem imprints are so powerful that they can interfere with all later brain development. Emotional evolution can be so fragile that a person, even with some love in childhood, can never manage to feel strong, to hold a job, to be steady and solid as a human being. The deep imprints, despite later love, can still effect bedwetting, nightmares, high blood pressure, and premature ejaculation. Often what Freud thought was hysteria was simply first-liners who lacked structure and who seemed to be all over the place. Those early imprints often run our lives—make us impulsive and unable to concentrate, cause us to suffer from deep mid-line symptoms (such as intestinal and breathing problems), and they set the stage for later migraines.

There is a common myth that emotional pain is different from physical pain. There is a study out by a UCLA team of psychologists who investigated the two kinds of pain. Using MRIs (magnetic resonance imaging) to monitor brain activity of a group of students, a game was rigged so that the subjects would feel rejected—an emotional pain. The brain scan indicated that the locus of this kind of pain was in the center of the brain in a structure known as the *cingulate*, together with parts of the right prefrontal cortex.[1] (We will see later in the chapter on the left and right brains how the right prefrontal area is the higher processing locus for feelings.) The cingulate is also key in processing physical pain. In other words, the brain doesn't differentiate among various kinds of hurt—a hurt is a hurt no matter the origin. An emotional illness is something that really does hurt, and the system shuts down when the pain of either variety becomes too intense. An emotional hurt early on becomes embedded in the physical system, and there it remains. Being abandoned, which is perceived by children as extreme rejection, is a *physical* agony, often too fierce to feel. Some say, "Ah, it's just in your head. You'll get over it!" No so fast. In psychotherapy we need to be reminded that to address emotional pain means experiencing all of its *physiological* accoutrements. Shedding a few tears or sobs won't get the job done; not if we want to undo the damage of emotional deprivation in infancy and childhood.

And why do emotions hurt so? Because we need strong emotional interaction with our parents if we are to survive (see Chapter 2). Animals with damaged cingulates no longer attempt to keep their offspring nearby, and the babies (who have damaged cingulates) no longer express a cry when separated. The cingulate is important because that cry is necessary to keep mother running to child.

As the brain develops, the memory accompanies its development to higher places and takes form within the new higher nervous system. Any trauma we undergo will be absorbed first into the limbic system (feeling) and then into the cortical apparatus (thought, logic, reason), which will distort it accordingly.

By the seventh month of gestation, most of the brainstem structures are ready to fire and their fiber connections are all in order. Even if the frontal cortex were destroyed at this point through some trauma, primitive brainstem reflexes, such as sucking, grasping, and withdrawing, would continue to function. However, the fetus can only communicate in the language that its brain has the capacity for at this given time: writhing, grunting, turning, twisting, butting against an obstacle, spitting up, and turning red. Along with these are the vital signs triggered at the time, a fast heart rate and high body temperature, for example.

In a Primal session, patients may regress to relive an experience that happened during their gestation or birth. In such an instance, as the frontal cortex quiets and recedes and lower brain centers assume control, the patient will experience coughing and gagging as they tap into brainstem imprints. During a primal reliving, the late-developing frontal cortex is relatively inoperative while the lower levels are activated. Thus, there are less and less thoughts, less articulation of words as the patient slides down into feelings and sensations, and then later, into pre-birth memories. There are never any scenes to go with these events, just the physiologic reactions. Of course, there are never any words; it is one way we know what brain level with which we are dealing. They are distinct. It is difficult to believe that reliving a churning stomach and difficulty in breathing is a real memory, but it is a primitive memory, lived in the only way the brain is capable.

In some respects, a session is very much like dream sleep. During dream-life, the prefrontal thinking cortex remains relatively inactive while the feeling centers are working away. To put it differently, if the prefrontal cortex is quite active, there will be neither dream sleep nor a primal. After a session, the patient usually has no idea how much time he spent in feeling, just as in a dream, because the time-keeper is the top level neocortex, which took a brief vacation during that time. Indeed, if the patient has a precise notion of the time spent in the session, it may be because he was not wholly into a feeling. Some patients report that it is almost dreamlike when they are submerged into areas of consciousness below the cognitive level. Descending down the brain to feeling levels leaves the patient with little awareness of the therapy room; she is engulfed on a lower level of consciousness. She is inwardly directed rather than outwardly, which I believe is an essential for cure in psychotherapy; not the inward direction governed by the frontal cortex which *discusses* feelings, but the part of the brain that controls internal awareness (again, more on this in detail later). In summary, dropping into a feeling during a session is much the same as dropping into a dream state; the difference is that in dreams the feelings are symbolized so as to protect the manufacturer of the dream (this is to keep the pain sequestered so as to protect sleep). In therapy, one is plunged into the feelings *below* the symbols; in this way, patients who have felt for some time as therapy proceeds report less symbolic dreams.

We must remember that a brainstem memory means a brainstem *reaction*. This means that high vital signs that accompanied the original trauma must be in evidence again during a session if we are to resolve primitive memories. When patients relive pre-birth and birth imprints, all of the sensations mentioned can be involved, and should be if the memory is complete. Without complete reactions to a memory, the improvement is only partial, as partial as the reactions permit.

It is a reminder of an experience that was undergone and blocked out of the conscious-awareness. That is how some afflictions such as colitis or bleeding ulcers happen; the imprint is churning away on the deeper levels of the brain, yet we have no conscious awareness of it. Some forms of apnea, which is a loss of breath, can be attributed to first-line intrusion.

We did research at the UCLA Pulmonary Laboratory with a young man in his 30s. After reliving a birth sequence, he suddenly went into apnea and stopped breathing for a full minute. This was not a voluntary act. He replicated what happened to him at birth. It was a wordless reliving that achieved some kind of awareness that was not totally verbal. In fact, it was a connected sensation that heretofore played out in his sleep, in which he suffered from periodic apnea. If we relive an early terror before we have words to wrap around it, it still can be a connected event. It has entered awareness. Afterward, it is no longer a vague, inexplicable anxiety. It is what it was: terror.

I have pointed out that the brainstem speaks the language of high blood pressure, palpitations, and shortness of breath—the silent killers. It houses many of our instincts; our terror and furor; and our basic, primitive needs. It contains the secrets of our birth and of our lives before birth in the womb. If we want to know what kind of birth we had, it will tell us in its own way. It will be precise and unmistakable. Its wonderful quality is that it cannot and will not lie. If we claim not to be afraid, but down deep there is unabated terror, there is no argument. A chronic symptom of palpitations is testimony to the possibility of an old imprint lying deep in the nervous system. A memory imprinted in the brainstem may have serious consequences for many survival functions.

> *Chronic high blood pressure is a good example of how memory lives within our brain system—it is an expression of a memory, a neurological imprint, which manifests physiologically.*

Because the brainstem continues to develop for several months after birth, what happens to us emotionally during the few months of life on earth can affect our heart function, most of our survival mechanisms, and our brain development. When we discuss breathing difficulties and heart problems later in the book, we must think about the brainstem and the memories it holds. These ailments speak of preverbal trauma and therefore may dictate where we eventually will have to go in psychotherapy. Any deep symptoms such as a constant low-grade fever or chronically elevated body temperature all point to the brainstem. To reiterate, early traumatic imprints have direct connection to heart function. The problem may not become visible for decades, and therefore we cannot imagine how early someone's heart problem began.

The brainstem imprints the deepest levels of pain because it is developed during gestation and handles life-and-death matters before we see the light of day. Almost every trauma experienced during womb-life is a life-and-death matter. The brainstem doesn't speak English or any other language. Imagine trying to communicate with words about the brainstem's pain when there aren't any. People develop problems such as high blood pressure or colitis when the brainstem is carrying an imprinted memory of a trauma and it tries to tell the frontal cortex about its near-death experience. The high blood pressure or colitis is a warning about stored terror. The brainstem is screaming at the neocortex, the thinking mind, "Listen to me! I need to tell you about something, you've got to hear this. I've got a connection to make. Let me through." It is screaming by way of high levels of biochemicals, such as noradrenaline, glutamate, and cortisol, the language of its biology. And the cortex is saying, "Sorry, you've got information I don't want to know about. Try later!"

"Yes, but if you don't let me out, my blood pressure is going to rise dramatically."

"Sorry."

A good example of how we see the vestiges of an imprint to the brainstem is expressed through sleep disorders. Actually, we could use the word "footprint" here because a brainstem imprint is widespread and covers many brain functions, affecting everything from eating to sex to sleeping. We could say that the reason someone cannot fall asleep is because he has so many thoughts going on—a racing mind. The true reason is that his thoughts are being driven by brainstem imprints that are completely "mindless," in the sense that words have no relevance at the brainstem level, yet brainstem imprints drive a continuous flow of ruminating ideas. This is because it contains long-reaching nerve tracks that go directly to certain areas within the thinking, cortical mind, and consequently drive incessant thoughts, even when we're asleep. But these are not "thought disorders," they are the result of nonverbal imprints affecting our global life.

Early in gestation, the fetal brainstem will respond to external noises, even the sound of the mother's voice, with head turning, reflective body movements, and heart rate changes. If there is a serious accident to the mother while she is carrying, it will undoubtedly affect the brainstem of the fetus, with possible effects on its heart function as well. The baby may be born fragile and delicate, plagued by a constant underlying fear and will be easy to startle.

One patient I saw, Edith, relived a scene when she was in her eighth month of gestation. Her mother was driving a car and not wearing a seat belt when she missed a curve, rolled over several times, and was pinned against the steering wheel. There she was, eight months pregnant, crushed inside the car for more than two hours. The mother thereafter was in a state of shock with constant anxiety attacks right up until she gave birth to Edith. Her baby, my patient Edith, was born a fearful child who would overreact to the slightest noise. She was filled with tension, had trouble getting and keeping a job, and was unstable in relationships. Although she had a fairly loving early home life, as she got older she became afraid of almost everything, especially death. As a child, she carried with her a feeling that was deeply impressed into her system, yet she could not make sense out of it. She went to many doctors, none of whom could even guess the origins of her problem. She got into all sorts of belief systems and cults as an adult to ward off the feeling of impending death and, above all, to explain the unexplainable. She was, by any standard, a frail human being. She was imprinted by deep terror and the constant activation of brainstem mechanisms.

What does a fetus do when faced with trauma? It reacts viscerally. If a person has had this kind of trauma, he will have a predisposition to go on acting viscerally for the rest of his life. He then develops stomach problems, colitis, ulcers, cramping, and breathing problems, and doesn't know why. It is why, during Primal Therapy, we often know the origin of a problem when a patient presents us with colitis, for example. If a problem is solely and seriously visceral, chances are its origins date back to birth, or before. Look to the brainstem, and you'll find the source. For

Edith, who has spent her life in a constant state of agitation, tranquilizers are obligatory to enable her to function on a daily basis. She has suffered for her entire life, in spite of a loving childhood.

Second Line: The Limbic/Feeling System

The second level of consciousness is the limbic system of the brain, which is responsible for feelings and their memory. It provides images and artistic output, processes certain aspects of sexuality, and is partly responsible for anger and fear.

The limbic system possesses some key structures that affect brain function, including the *hippocampus,* which is the guardian of emotional memory; the *amygdala*, which I believe may provide the "feeling" (sensation) of feeling, the visceral components of feeling; and the *hypothalamus* and *thalamus.*

The thalamus is the relay station, or central switchboard, of the brain, sending feeling messages upward and forward for understanding and connection. It can decide a feeling is too powerful to be felt and orders that the message not be relayed. The hypothalamus works with the lower structure, the pituitary, to govern the release of key hormones, not the least of which are the stress hormones. When a person has strong emotions, it is the hypothalamus that organizes her response.

Within the hypothalamus lie two different kinds of nervous systems (both work automatically): the sympathetic and the parasympathetic. The latter governs repair, healing, and repose. The sympathetic is the one that controls aggression and assertiveness. When there is a strong trauma in utero or just after birth, one of these two systems comes to dominate our lives and dictates whether we shall be passive or aggressive in the face of problems. It helps shape our personality.

The limbic/feeling system is a repository of emotional truth. It lies at roughly the temple area and winds back on the sides of the brain like a ram's horn. This feeling system goes on developing for at least two to three years after birth, although one of its components, the hypothalamus, is fully functional when we are born. This is why we can have physical ailments from birth; colic may be one example of the effects of stress to the hypothalamus from birth trauma or even before.

The Amygdala: The Feeling of Feeling

The amygdala is one of the most ancient structures of the brain and the oldest structure of the limbic system. It is formed long before the new (neo) cortex both in personal time and in the long history of mankind. It can be damaged, along with the brainstem, by pre-birth trauma such as stress from an anxious, or drug-taking mother, from birth events, as well as by infancy deprivations. The amygdala is the hub of the emotional system; the gateway to feelings. It gives us the sensation behind feeling, while the later-developing hippocampus registers those feelings as facts. The imprints here will help determine the growth of the physical system—our bones, blood, and muscles—and the personality.

It is possible to access memories of feelings without eliciting the feeling of feeling. The sentiment "I remember when my mother gave away my dog" can be remembered by the hippocampus without the full participation of the amygdala. When that happens, there can be no lasting change in therapy because a good part of the memory is not retrieved in the reliving. Our job is to help the retrieval of all of the event, including the exact emotional response as it happened originally. Only then can it be integrated and cease directing our lives. Because the original trauma pervaded every part of our systems, the reliving must do the same. Otherwise, it is only a partial reliving and is not curative.

The amygdala warns of a menace and tells us to get ready for danger. It helps activate us, calling for even more stress hormones. Early traumatic memory is consolidated by the amygdala. It processes the guts, literally the visceral aspects, of feeling. The amygdala is dominant in processing emotional information up to six months of age. The critical period of the amygdale, when it is most susceptible to imprinting from trauma, is the last trimester before birth and the first few months after birth when the development of the synapses and the dendrites of the brain are maturing. Imprints at this time are determinantal. The amygdala has a more direct effect on the neocortex, dictating which memories get stored and how, and how powerfully those memories will affect thought processes.

Words in therapy later on can never alter the memories of trauma that the amygdala has sustained. Luckily, when the going gets rough, it can help manufacture its own opium to hold back pain. In this way, it helps us remain unconscious. It is truly a wonder that this small brain structure "knows" when to stop pain and can release a poppy derivative to help. In addition, it tells other brain structures about how much to release and when to stop. It is not about a conversation so much as communication. Many plants do the same. When there is too much sunlight and therefore a danger, decreasing photosynthesis, there is a tendency to shut down. This indicates that the process of overload and shutdown can be traced back to plant life. In the case of overwhelming sun energy, two researchers point out that the leaf damage is the same as a sunburn. Plants seem to have a warning system that puts other parts of the plant not yet exposed on alert.

What we often see in therapy is that after a primal reliving, the system automatically shuts down for the moment. As if to say, "I've had enough for the day." It is a time for the patient to rest, not to be pushed further into an overload.

The Hippocampus: The Seat of Memory

The hippocampus contains the archives of early experience, particularly trauma, and also puts a damper on amygdala activation so that our reactions themselves do not become a danger; after all, continually high blood pressure and heart rate threatens existence. The hippocampus has a high density of stress hormone receptors and is therefore quite sensitive to stress. The context of a feeling is organized by the hippocampus. It gives us an anchor for our feelings—a time and place—and allows us to connect to our feelings.

The hippocampus is not as old as its confrere, the amygdala, which is why a massive early trauma may be processed by the amygdala without a specific time and place, and without any concepts or words to understand it. It needs the later-developing hippocampus for that. Connecting with preverbal traumas is a matter of awareness of specific sensations in context—such as feeling a drowning sensation during birth and knowing its origin. We can undergo pre-birth, birth, and infancy traumas but cannot remember them because one responsible system (the hippocampus) is not yet up to speed. So while we cannot consciously recall these very early events, the "memory," or imprint, is still registered by the amygdala, and we are affected by memories we can't remember. As the neurophysiologist Joseph LeDoux states, "For this reason the trauma may affect mental and behavioral functions in later life through processes that remain inaccessible to consciousness." He believes that "memories are indelibly burnt into the brain and are with us for life," which, given all the late information, has become a rather established fact.[2]

What is crucial about the hippocampus is that early trauma and lack of love can cause a shriveling of its dendrites, eventually leading to memory loss. Long-term imprints affect the hippocampus so that it would not be surprising if deficiencies in memory occur in later life.

The Hypothalamus: The Translator of Feelings

The hypothalamus, also part of the limbic system, helps organize stress hormone release, specifically cortisol. Cortisol increases the rate and strength of heart contractions and affects many of our metabolic processes that respond to stress. The hypothalamus looks today pretty much like it did a million years ago. It manages the secretion of hormones, controls eating and drinking, and drives rage. It provides a physiologic force to feelings. It deals primarily with our internal world and is partly controlled by other limbic structures such as the amygdala. The hypothalamus has connections to the brainstem and translates feelings into biochemical processes. It is very much a translator, taking feelings and organizing physiologic reactions for them.

The Thalamus: The Messenger of Feelings

The relay center of the limbic system is the thalamus, which sends feelings higher to the frontal cortex for comprehension and integration. When the pain is too intense, it will not relay feelings; rather, it acts like a mail carrier and will return them to sender, marked "address unknown." One of the highest concentrations of repressive agents, inhibitory neurotransmitters, is found here. The thalamus needs help to stop too much pain, and it gets it. Actually, the thalamus does double duty because it is related to two different pathways: it sends information to higher centers (prefrontal cortex) and at the same time to the amygdala. The amygdala gets the message and sends it to the brainstem, which then provokes an alarm, putting the body in an emergency state. If the amygdala is out of commission, there is no alarm state.

The thalamus is the switchboard of the brain, relaying certain aspects of feeling to the frontal cortex, which is involved with thought, ambition, planning, seeing the consequences of actions, and, above all, repressing—holding back feelings from full awareness. It is the final checkpoint before messages of feelings converge, surging toward the prefrontal-awareness area. The thalamus talks straight neurochemical talk, a language that expresses itself wordlessly. Yet it can translate painful messages into something understandable by the frontal cortex. If the pain is too much, the message that arrives is garbled. If it is acceptable, the gates open and the message is clearly understood. We know what we feel.

Its job description is outlined by pain. Certain neurotransmitters "know" when to intercede. Later on in therapy, the thalamus will transmit messages to the cortex and then we will at last put words to this process. "Love me, Mommy. Tell me you like me just a little!" It has its own kind of awareness because it can decide that emotional pain is too much and not relay it up to higher levels. The thalamus looks out for the prefrontal cortex and takes care not to overwhelm it. It is not that we were once conscious and then suppressed the feeling. It is that key emotional messages never made it to the prefrontal area.

Let me say again that the emotional centers can be active before awareness sets in. It means, among other things, that they drive us unconsciously. It is one reason why we do not realize we are in danger from hidden feelings; we are only aware of great discomfort. Here is a good example of being aware and being unconscious at the same time. One new patient used to leave her child with babysitters whom she really did not know well to go to seminars on awareness. While she was gaining awareness, she was acting unconsciously. We can say something that seems to pop out of us before we have a chance to think about it. Our feelings are active before inhibition takes over. We can shout at someone with rage before we even have a chance to see what effect it might have.

The Third Line: The Neocortex

The third line is the neocortex, the part of our brain that was the last to evolve and the one responsible for intellectual functioning, generating ideas, and thinking. The *left prefrontal area* deals with the external world, helps us repress and, when able, to integrate feelings. It comes online at about the third year of life. The *right prefrontal area* is internally oriented, deals with our feelings, and is responsible for bringing feelings over to the left prefrontal area for comprehension. Although it develops rapidly in the first three years of life, there is another burst of growth just before adolescence. Ostensibly, as the hormones begin raging, there is at the same time a greater amount of frontal cortex to control the impulses. In short, here is where repression really begins its life. By the end of adolescence, repression seems to be in full force, but it is too late: the adolescent has already acted wildly and out of control. Too many hormones and too little prefrontal cortex.

> *The neocortex is the first door we walk through toward retracing our history and understanding our pain.*

The frontal cortex is part of the feeling system to the degree that it gives meaning and understanding to our physiologic-emotional reactions. The neocortex serves as a portal for entry into the suffering component of memory, a portal that cannot operate by itself. It's the first door we walk through toward retracing our history and understanding our pain. When the prefrontal cortex is impaired or damaged due to early trauma, it is difficult to block feelings that arise from lower brain levels. When it operates less efficiently, imprinted memory seeps up to the surface. There will be panic, malaise, and anxiety, all driven by an imprint, which may also show itself in compulsive worrying.

In psychotherapy it is very important to treat the problem, and not simply the symptom, which, unfortunately, is what happens all too often. For instance, *worrying* is not a problem, it is the symptom of something that is occurring physiologically within the brain—what causes the worrying is the problem. Worry is what happens when early fear shoulders itself against the frontal cortex. Fear is the province of the limbic area; amorphous terror belongs deeper, by and large, to the brainstem. Unyielding symptoms such as phobias usually derive from the brainstem. Worrying is something that plagues many of us, and is usually expressed as, "What if this or that happens?!" The constant worry is anticipating catastrophe, but what we don't realize is that the catastrophe already has happened; we simply have no access to it. The prefrontal cortices (right and left) are the assembly area where aspects of our history join to become whole, where we gather in disparate aspects of our history. If one goal of psychotherapy is to make a person whole, then memory must be complete and connected.

Essentially, neurosis is driven by lower brain centers that are trying to communicate to the left neocortex but can't because a disconnection has occurred, a disconnection caused by the imprint of an early lack of love that spells hopelessness and helplessness. For instance, the limbic system, the brain's second level, is able to react all on its own before the neocortex is even engaged, so we react systemically before the frontal cortex is even aware of what's happening. It is not ideas coming from the prefrontal neocortex that drive a reaction within our bodies and nervous system, but emotional processes that are unfolding neurochemically from the limbic area.

One patient of mine, Eva, when blocked from getting her passport from the passport office flew into a rage because this frustration—being stopped from progressing and from getting ahead—was resonant with first, being blocked from any desire by her parents, and then being blocked from getting out during her birth when her mother could not seem to open up. This rage and drive was life-saving originally because it signaled "give it one last try." She demonstrates what I call "struggle-fail" syndrome, where she tries so hard, is blocked, and then meets insuperable odds, and finally has to give up. She has a drive to succeed as an adult, but she is easily discouraged. She started so many projects full of determination and enthusiasm only to give up at the slightest obstacle. Then she would fall into a depression, a feeling of "What's the use of struggling?"

In what might be called her "manic" phase, she was duplicating her own birth sequence. She was stopped cold when her mother received a massive dose of anesthetia that also shut down many of the baby's systems, not the least of which was respiration. At this point she was plunged into failure, despair, and resignation; these were the prototypes for many later reactions. She was diagnosed as "depressed," but now we know what it really is. The injected anesthesia immersed the baby into what I call "the trough," which is the parasympathetic system taking over. The trough is the point at which the struggle to be born is blocked either by a cord around the neck, massive anesthesia, or other obstacles. It sets up a "struggle-fail" syndrome, and shifts brain gears into a repressed mode (parasympathetic). This is the meaning of resonance: something in the present triggers off the second-line–related feeling and then down to the first line, but only when the patients is ready.

Eva was driven to keep from slipping into the trough where death lurked. Death loomed, and "getting out"—her escape—was impossible. The need to "get out" later in life had a life-and-death urgency to it, which is reflected in her initial drive to start new projects. Let me reiterate here that this is not a theoretical construct, but an actual observation of patients over time as they are taken very deep into the remote past.

Depression is life in the trough, not an attitude or a series of negative ideas. It is being immersed in one's history and not being able to get out of it. Worse, it is not knowing one has sunk into that history.

Ideas arrived millions of years after instincts and feelings. Ideas are not the problem; they signal the problem, providing the words for it all. The suffering system is one of the most ancient in the brain. Monkeys suffer but can't describe it in words. Humans can. But primates and humans suffer in the same way with pretty much the same brain structures. The top level of our brain—the neocortex—only indicates what feelings are on the rise. It doesn't suffer by itself; it is aware of suffering and talks about it. It remembers and thinks about life and childhood, but the suffering part lies sequestered in its lair, waiting for the opportune moment and the opportune therapy.

When all else failed, Eva tried suicide. Death was a memory, a memory of the end of agony. When she was triggered during the day by someone who stopped her from doing what she wanted to, she sometimes went into a funk—back into the original situation of birth where she was blocked and helpless. We need to keep in mind that there are connected nerve tracks that form a vertical nerve network (I will discuss the horizontal networks in a moment). Something in the present triggers a feeling, which then descends down to the prototypic nerve network. There is the original sensation-feeling, which is elaborated upon as we, and consequently our brains, mature. Thus, a session is de-evolution, going back in time. When Eva was triggered, the feeling could end up in a nightmare. In that nightmare, she felt helpless, scared, unable to move or scream, and she felt death approaching. In her sleep she fabriacted a story to make her feelings rational—the essence of neurosis. Feelings as a dream or nightmare are not capricious. They are not invented out of thin air. They are based on history.

Again we see that feelings drive ideas and not vice versa. Even the ideas and images in a dream are driven by the deep unconscious. The ideas follow evolution—sensations first, feelings second, and finally, ideas. When Eva couldn't struggle to make something happen in life, she got severely depressed. It took her back to where her struggle at birth did not work; where death threatened. She was back where she couldn't move to live, and she was helpless again. Any kind of helplessness meant death to her early on; hence, depression. She avoided any kind of helpless situation, of being in anyone else's power, of having a boss, for example. The prototype involved helplessness and almost dying at birth.

She had to deny the hurt from the start of her life: "There is no one there to help me. I have to do it all myself." As a child she never asked for help because of her imprint; and, in fact, never got any help from her parents because she never looked like she needed it. She was determined in everything she did. All this reinforced her unconscious feeling, "See, there is no one to help. Better to do it all on my own." That need got waylaid and never made it to the top level, never allowed her to feel and know that she needed anyone in life. She left every boy she dated as soon as he gave her any orders or tried to control her. The slightest demand by someone became a fascist dictum, something to rebel against.

By the time we observe her adult behavior, its origins are overlaid and unrecognizable, so it is understandable that therapists focus on the here-and-now. The basic feeling is ramified and convoluted by later childhood events. The original big feeling is now found in minute behaviors, such as hesitating to ask a waiter for water. She could not have a sustained relationship because she didn't want to be dependent on anyone for love. Her parents, who did have that power, abused it and gave her very little love. Her present relationships with boys resonated with that abuse, and made her afraid.

How Repression Works

There is a gating system in the brain that inhibits or slows the message of feeling when it is too much to bear. When the amygdala's gating mechanism against rising feeling fails, there is a more direct impact on the frontal cortex, causing it to be activated; to race; to manufacture ideas and beliefs; and, in general, to do what it can to attenuate the onrush. If the hippocampus is overtaxed with many painful memories, then it may be helpless to inform the hypothalamus to soften the amygdala's output of feelings. The amygdala has direct connections to the frontal cortex so that feelings can also directly affect our thought processes; and, of course, it has direct connections to deeper levels of brain function. When gating mechanisms fail, feelings that are rooted in lower levels of the brain, such as terror, can escape control and rise to the prefrontal cortex to signal danger. The prefrontal cortex may label this an anxiety attack, and the individual is then aware of great discomfort.

A cognitive psychologist might try to deal with that anxiety as if it were a cortex-only phenomenon, and attempt to control it through ideas, thoughts, logic, and so on: "Look here, you are overreacting. There is no reason to be so excited." Yet reactions are nearly always correct; they tell us what's really happening on lower levels of the brain, even though the original context of how they were imprinted may be unrecognizable. We shouldn't deny or change reactions, but rather find their origins so that the reactions make sense. Without access to our feelings, we would be forced to conclude that some current behavior is irrational because we are unaware of its antecedents; for example, phobias.

Driving our behavior, our own feelings, can be a danger to us because they are too much for the higher levels of the brain to accept and integrate. The brain has a warning system that alerts us against potential overload—more feelings than can be experienced and integrated. It says "gear up" for the onslaught of pain, and the system obeys. But if the inhibitory gating system is "leaky," it allows too much pain to get through. As this overload of pain/hopelessness begins its march to the cortex, alarm bells are set off. Cortisol is one of these alarm chemicals. The alarm is general, however, and many systems are affected. The brain's own hippocampus can be damaged by too much cortisol secretion over too long a time, resulting in a weakened memory. It is not surprising that those of us who were anxious throughout childhood barely remember anything. Eva hardly remembered anything of her childhood; it was all a "black hole." She did tell us in the intake interview that, vague though it was, she believed she had a "fairly happy childhood." This wasn't exactly the case, as she found out in therapy.

A good example of overload is a recent case where a 40-year-old patient who at the age of 9 was taking a bath with an electrical heater sitting beside the tub. She reached over to move the heater and received a massive shock. She became immediately unconscious, but the violence of her flopping/seizures tore the heater plug out of the wall and saved her life. She went downstairs to tell her mother, who was ironing. Her mother said, "Oh, that's too bad. But you seem okay now." She went on with her ironing. The meaning to her daughter at the moment, which summed up many moments before, was, "She doesn't care. There's no help for me. She really doesn't love me."

Over several months she has been reliving that shock—flopping, seizing as violently as when it happened. (This has been filmed.) She had no idea that shock was still in there. It was pure electrical energy with no content, yet it shut her down totally. She had a rigid, immobile facial set that did not ease nor loosen until months of reliving the shock. Her whole body froze at the time of the shock, and, even today, making easy, fluid movements is difficult for her. Her whole system seems to have contracted permanently; a total overload. Her "Primals," as we call them, are both of the seizures and then "She doesn't care. There is no help. There's no place to turn." That realization was tremendous pain because it was an augury of her coming life. She almost died. Her mother hardly reacted. The most important thing she gets out of these Primals is that she was never able to express herself. Everything was locked inside; she seemed dead. Now, finally, as she expresses the shock, she can also express herself emotionally. Her face has expression, whereas before it was expressionless and immobile. She has had constant fears of dying, and it hasn't just been an idea. It was a real experience. Her nightmares were filled with danger where she was on the verge of dying. I have seen many patients who had those fears and it was not like something in the future—it was immediate: "I am going to die now!"

If she never relived the shock, we would never have known of her actual near-death experience. In cognitive therapy, her fears may have been treated as irrational ideas. The electrical shock in the bathtub is no different from an overload by a feeling: "It is all hopeless. No one will ever love me." That too, is electrical. But it has content. The shock did not. That is what made it so devilish to discover. There was no specific scene to rely on. It was a "neutral" experience; pure electricity, which allowed us to see the overload clearly and how it operates. This overload, although having nothing to do with sex, can and did stunt sexual expression, as well. And any early trauma can accomplish the same thing.

Traumas can be laid down in the viscera during womb-life and at birth, when the highest level of neurologic function is the brainstem/limbic structures. When patients complain of visceral symptoms such as Crohn's disease, we have evidence of how early the trauma was set down. The signs of an early imprint are sensations—stomach churning, tightness in the chest, difficulty breathing, sensations of being squeezed or crushed, and a general sense of agitation.

Thus, the amygdala and the hippocampus can control the release of stress hormones. As the system is flooded with cortisol, the hippocampus, for example, can send the hypothalamus a message to ease up. In some respects the amygdala is pleading, "release!" while the hippocampus is begging, "hold back!" We want to be just stressed enough to handle emergencies but not so much as to be overwhelmed. We want to be sure that the signal of danger does not become a danger itself. We do not get panicked out of some irrational force. There is a good reason for it; something in lower levels of the brain are driving it. The panic (and panic attacks) is a response to an alarm, a danger. In brief, panic attacks may be quite rational, responding to real imprinted events. Too often we try to remove the danger signal while leaving the danger intact. This often happens when the danger is situated down in the brainstem and out of sight. As long as we deal in words and explanations, we can never arrive at the original danger, by definition.

Panic is a terror from early in the gestation period. It, by itself, has weakened the repressive, gating system so that any current lessening of vigilance can set it off. It predates by a long time the affliction of depression because it occurs before the full development of the inhibitory, gating system. It is purely physical and seems such a mystery—until the person gains deep access. Then it is no longer a mystery. It is the most primitive of reactions; words will not touch it. It represents the highest level of brain function at the time. Look at its manifestations: shortness of breath, chest pain and pressure, rapid heartbeat, choking or smothering sensation, butterflies in the stomach, dizziness, and the sensation of impending doom. None of these need a cortex or higher level brain function. That is one very important reason that words cannot cure it. It is basically visceral and subcortical. These manifestations are telling us that they emanate from a very primitive brain organization and from a time when there was only an inchoate cerebral structure (lacking a fully developed neocortex) to handle trauma. There is no insight that can treat it because it began its life long before we had words.

It is what we see in lower animals that are frightened by another animal. Their reactions seem like pure panic. We see this in some individuals who undergo MRIs. The minute they are enclosed in a steel and cement sheath, panic surges forth. The situation is approximating what happened originally. It takes the confines of such a machine to reawaken the primitive feeling. The patient may believe it is the machine that is producing anxiety, but it is the primal panic from a confined, enclosed space. What the MRI does is stimulate a resonating memory; not a memory in the way we usually think of it, because it sets off a bodily reaction. If we do have this kind of anxiety while having an MRI exam, we can be fairly sure that we endured a difficult birth; it is, in short, a differential diagnostic to separate out those with healthy births from those with traumatic births. I teach the technicians who perform MRIs on me to tap my foot at irregular intervals so that I cannot organize a full-fledged anxiety reaction.

It does take some kind of higher cerebral organization to produce an anxiety state. The concept of resonance is important because situations can resonate within us below the level of language. We can be stirred up even when we don't know with what the outside situation is resonating. Thus, in sex, a nude female body can resonate in a man with an early experience with his mother. She may have been seductive long before the child had any understanding of it. I had one white patient who had a very seductive mother; she French-kissed her son. Later, he could only have girlfriends who were black or Asiatic—a white girlfriend would resonate with that early seduction and scare him. Here "white" women resonated with a white mother, which is something to be avoided. I treated a lesbian woman who was molested sexually by her (white) stepfather. She could only have relationships with black men. Later, any man resonated with the early stepfather. She switched to sex with women. It seemed much safer to her.

When there is a life-and-death struggle at birth due to lack of oxygen (anoxia), for example, the existing reactive system is activated, but because it cannot fully respond due to the complete load of pain (to feel it completely would be to die, or at least to lose consciousness), it reacts partially within its biologic limits and then puts the excess part of the terror away for good keeping; it houses it until our system is strong enough to feel and resolve it. It lives behind our repressive gates.

However, we continually respond to this stored terror with chronically high stress hormone levels, a compromised immune system, misperceptions, strange ideas, nightmares, and chronic malaise. This high activation level gnaws away at the cardiovascular system so that we fall seriously ill at age 55, even though at the time we seem to be living a normal, relaxed life. Not surprisingly, one of the highest concentrations of inhibitory neurotransmitters—part of the brain's gating mechanism—is found in the thalamus, which is constructed so as not to relay overwhelming information. It needs to block pain when pain threatens the frontal cortex. During a Primal Therapy session, when a person has access to feelings and the connection is finally made between the left prefrontal cortex and lower brain centers, there is first great hurt and then great relief. In a Primal experience (reliving an early lack of love completely), there is such a rush of pain that the defense system is temporarily overwhelmed, gating weakens, and what sometimes gets through is compulsive coughing, feelings of choking or losing breath, and very rapid foot shakes (these shakes can go on for a full half hour, even when the patient is unaware of it). These are often deep-brain originated and are elements of what we know as anxiety or panic states. This is a nonconnected state.

When we do not face our internal reality, we also cannot face the external, particularly when that external reality triggers the inner feelings we are trying to avoid. In other words, the external and the internal form an integrated circuit in the brain. Ultimately, the external is internal. When there is an open sensory gate, information from both inside and out are accepted and integrated. When the gate is shut we see neither inside nor outside clearly. We are disconnected from ourselves. Repression keeps the inside from getting out and the outside from getting in. Love hasn't a chance to gain entry in this case. It is then that we suffer from any number of psychosomatic ailments. The energy cannot be connected and integrated. It continues to do its damage. Just imagine a battering ram knocking at the gates. Feelings are that strong, and eventually the gates give way; hence, anxiety and panic attacks.

> *During a Primal Therapy session, when a person has access to feelings and the connection is finally made between the frontal neocortex and lower brain centers, there is first great hurt and then great relief.*

What most of medicine and psychotherapy involves today is the treatment of fragments of a human being, fragments of an original memory that has lost its connection to the whole. So we have coughing spells, pressure on the chest, anxiety, phobias, and the need to escape, all pieces of an original imprint. We then treat the varied offshoots from a central imprint rather than the imprint itself; treatment then becomes interminable. What we get is a fragment of progress—a change in fragments of an early experience. We treat the phobias, the high blood pressure, and the palpitations, sometimes all with the same drug. Why? Because it is all of a piece, aspects of the same early experience. Inadvertently, we are treating the experience even though we may not be aware of it. There are "successful" cognitive and behavior therapies for phobias, for example. The phobia is now "cured." But its origin is not; it will continue to do its damage.

The thalamus and prefrontal cortex are a reciprocal information service. Sometimes the information sent upward and forward is so overwhelming that it cannot be accepted and integrated. The information is returned to sender. There is a certain nucleus in the thalamus that is the center for the perception and relay of pain. It is in this nucleus that pain can be blocked from its voyage to the prefrontal cortex. It is also the area, together with the frontal cortical centers, that helps integrate feelings, to make them understandable. The thalamus nudges the cortex to manufacture thoughts to keep us comfortable. When the neocortex is ready, a reasonable amount of pain will mount and become integrated. Our job in Primal Therapy is to turn vague malaise, panic, and suffering into specific pain; to produce integration. In other words, produce harmony.

If an individual has been overactivated from very early on in life, it becomes a normal state to the person. He then thinks he is normal. Therein lies the rub. He may be overactive, and believes that is normal because it is all he has ever known. This is especially true because we organize our lives around the imprint to make it rational and coherent; we fill our lives with projects and plans to rationalize the inner agitation. When we take the pain activation out of the system in Primal Therapy, he finally knows what "normal" is.

Ideas do conform to feelings and are integral to them. We react as a total system, not just with ideas. If we are full of rage, it might leak out as constant sarcasm, which may seem like normal behavior to the person. It is just part of her "personality." We say that she is sarcastic and cynical as a personality trait, but that trait is the result of anger and rage stored deep in the brain. It rises to affect what comes out of our mouths, but we need to treat more than what the mouth is doing. The mouth, in short, is following the imprint.

If we have terror stored in our systems, then certain phobias seem normal, or at least comfortable for the system. There are hand-washing compulsives who are comfortable that way and would not dream of changing, nor could they. The ritual binds the pain. Deep feelings rise to the level of behavior and drive compulsions. A prominent comedian who cannot touch doorknobs says he is fine the way he is and would not want to change. That compulsion (using a handkerchief to open doors) allays his fears (the origin of which he is unaware) and makes him feel comfortable.

Edith could never fall asleep easily. Her ideational system of far-out beliefs resulted from constantly surging impulses pushing against the left frontal neocortex, impulses that were created from the auto crash while she was in her eighth month in the womb. It was the same force that made her mind race at night. She needed those ideas to keep herself comfortable.

Ordinarily, the frontal cortex is engaged to steer and direct us into handling situations. But here the danger is hidden, so the cortex is enlisted to help but can only churn away with no direction. If we were to try to eliminate or extinguish those ideas with cognitive therapy, we would be tampering with key survival mechanisms. If we ignore those final weeks that Edith spent in her mother's womb, we can never appreciate the origins of her problem. She was scared and fragile from the start of her life; she literally had a shaky start. There was no way that the fetus could make sense of what happened from the auto crash; consequently, senseless hurt and vague terror became the imprint. It is the kind of thing that bubbles up when defenses are weak and forces the person to adopt all manner of phobias or strange beliefs that may make no sense to others.

When Edith retrieved that memory, it began with a crushing sensation, which was a mystery to both her and the therapist. But the trail led to higher brain structures and finally to the thalamus and then to the neocortex where she was aware of the crushing sensation, the terror, and the fragility. What was missing was the "why." Finally, her mother told her what happened in her eighth month of pregnancy.

It would be impossible to deprogram her away from her strange ideas; they had roots that trailed all the way down to the lower reaches of the brain and to the beginnings of her life. Edith developed a phobia where she couldn't leave her bedroom for very long, even to go shopping. A trip away from home made her anxious. The terror had found a focus, but it was only a focus. She went to a behavior therapist who went outside with her; first one block, then another block, then to the shopping mall. He held her hand and soothed her when she became more and more anxious. He did what a good father should have done early on. But clearly, it was only a temporary solution because the real terror was so deeply hidden as to be unimaginable. Once she felt all of her terror, the little fears did not have to leak out here and there. She connected to a hidden memory. Failing that connection, the fears will continue.

Let us suppose those fears were channeled into elevators, a fear of being enclosed, as the object of terror. The terror is deep brain; the focus is higher brain. Psychotherapy cannot cure a deep brain terror by a discussion with the higher brain; it is not where the wound lies. There can be circumstances in life that could create such a phobia, such as being stuck in an elevator or another enclosed space as a young child, but real terror—a life-and-death event, only rarely derives from happenings in late childhood. The imprint is the origin, terror becomes the reaction, and phobia becomes the focus. We need to separate each so we understand the problem, and then address the imprint with its reaction. The imprint generates all of the rest.

To control her phobia of going out, Edith had to return to where she felt safe—home. This stemmed from the accident, but gradually, with time in Primal Therapy, her phobias disappeared without our ever discussing them directly. The world was dangerous for her and she never knew why; it was dangerous before she even took her first breath. Safety, for her, lay in her cocoon of her home, which was the womb. She felt comfortable in not going out. She kept trying to go back to a safe place, such as the womb was before the accident happened. Being out in the world reawakened the accident and the unconscious terror. She was always afraid that something terrible might happen away from home. Something terrible already happened; it lay as a memory in her whole system. Because it was inaccessible, she had to focus in the present. She did what Freud called "projection." She projected fears from an early experience onto the present.

Our ordinary frame of reference for understanding the world should be ourselves. But if we don't have ourselves, don't have access to our feelings, we lose our personal frame of reference and then have to rely on outsiders, gurus, therapists, and so on. Until we have access, their judgment and perceptions become ours. They can download their ideas into our frontal cortex and their feelings into our limbic system. We lose the ability to see if what they say feels right because we have lost access to that limbic system. We then go by the words and not the feelings.

When we don't have access to our feelings, we tend to choose the wrong partner based only on their external behavior and not on what lies underneath. We cannot sense nor see what people are really like. Words and behavior, the front, become all important.

Generally, what we see in others is the fulfillment of our need—someone to guide us, take care of us, protect us, be kind to us, be aggressive for us—or to do all the social things that we cannot do. We see fulfillment of our needs in others. We like other people when they offer what we need. We don't like them when they don't. For example, a narcissist who needs constant attention is not going to like someone who not only does not listen but also wants all the attention for himself. Most of us spend our lives seeking out symbolic fulfillment—finding someone who is critical and trying to make them approving—the struggle recreated with hopefully a better ending. Or finding someone cold, such as our mother, and trying to make them warm. We always seem to start at zero, recreating the original trauma and trying to have a desired resolution. We never give up trying.

We must not just examine brain chemicals or structures for explanations about behavior and symptoms anymore than we should concentrate on psychology for it. The brain and body are unified. We must not consider the standard for wellness as cortical normalization without regard to other sectors of the brain, as do some of those who conduct brain biofeedback sessions. Conversely, we must not depend on psychology to determine normality. That is, we must not be satisfied with patient reports nor how they do on psychology tests. Our bodies speak a language, and we can understand that language if we know where to look and how to listen. We must continue to probe ever more deeply.

4

The Imprint: How It Runs Our Lives

One of my patients had parents who tried to stop him from doing anything. From the start they didn't want to be bothered with him, and they told him to sit in his chair, not move, and not talk. This was on top of a birth that was blocked and resulted in great difficulty for him to get out. These two traumatic experiences during the critical period for him became an imprint, which combined to make him unstoppable once he got out of control. He did not know it, but he was reacting to events that had occurred long ago. To be stopped originally meant death; if he could not get out at birth, he would have died. He had to force his way out, and, when later faced with obstacles, he became overly aggressive. He was fighting birth and parents who never let him have his way. His only solution to problems was to charge ahead, never knowing when to back off.

Another patient had very different key personality-shaping events during the critical period. His mother was heavily anesthetized during childbirth. The anesthetic entered his system, depriving him of oxygen. In order to survive, he had to conserve energy and not use too much oxygen. To save himself, his system slowed down to a passive, waiting state, a physiology of defeat and despair, as there was nothing he could do about what was happening (the anesthesia). This was later compounded by his childhood treatment by his parents, who never let him express his feelings or object to anything. There was no use in battling at birth, and later no use in struggling for anything with his parents, which would have only made them more dismissive and unresponsive. In both cases, he was dominated by outside forces over which he had no control, and he had no choice but to give in and give up. Passivity was the appropriate, and in fact life-saving, reaction. And from then on, when faced with even minor obstacles, he would give up, as he did originally and later with his parents. In effect, he would go into a "defeat" mode again and again, just as he had from the start.

Both patients are victims of events, as many of us are. Early experiences during the critical first three years of life largely give shape to our personality and our health. The Catholic church used to say, "Give me a child til age six and he will be a Catholic forever." It turns out that they only need the first three years. This is almost the end of the critical period when we become pretty much what we will be for the rest of our lives. We either become optimistic or pessimistic, concentrated or dispersed, active or reflective; or we try or give up, reach out or reach in, overcome obstacles or are overwhelmed by obstacles, look ahead or look back, are goal-oriented or floundering, are aggressive or passive. There are those who are always helpful—denying their need for help—versus those who always want to be helped—acting-out being helpless. Remember, the act-out is automatic and unconscious because the driving feeling is. So if we never had a mother who helped, we get others to do it, and then we are not even grateful because we expect it. There are those who go through life trying to fill old needs, as opposed to those who give up. The need is the same for everyone, but early life circumstances twist us in one direction or another. Because we are largely feeling beings during these critical years, without the cognitive powers that come later, the core of the self is largely shaped through the warp and weft of preverbal and nonverbal processes. Moreover, what diseases befall us also begin here. There are, of course, genetic factors to be considered in every disease, but I have found that environmental factors are the pre-potent ones in most cases. To repeat: because we have neglected womb-life, the most important nine months of our lives in terms of shaping personality, we have forcibly ignored key events that changed us. We therefore have painted ourselves into the genetic box where we must incorrectly assume genetic factors for what is most likely womb-life, birth, and infancy caused.

The concept of the imprint has been central to my work for several decades. When early trauma during the critical period of development is great, it becomes an imprint—a permanent state. The suffering component, the part that cannot be integrated, because it is too much to bear—is sheared off and stored. This is the imprint, and it takes on a life of its own in our nervous systems.

It becomes an alien force, not truly a part of us, detached yet seeking ways of entry into conscious-awareness. It is that alien force that shapes our thoughts and behavior. Some people perceive "alien forces" in the world; these are no more than their own terror, projected externally. The traumatic imprint most commonly happens because of two important causes. The first is a difficult birth, while the second is a lack of loving relationship between two people—between a mother and child, and, obviously, father and child. It is usually the mother who stays home and provides care, however.

Earlier I discussed the importance of a mother's brain being in synchrony with her child's, and what forms is a kind of mutual cerebral resonance. The more the mother is in synchrony with the baby's right brain, the better organized the right brain of the child is. When their relationship is out of synch, the stage is set for an adverse imprint.

There are many ways to imprint the feeling of not being loved. For instance, in a situation where the child is not attended to just after birth, not held or caressed, he may be imprinted with "I'm all alone," a feeling not articulated until years later. Sometime later, a girlfriend leaves, and he tumbles into a deep depression. Why? She has set off the imprint "I'm suffering from terrible aloneness" from just after birth. If he has no idea what is wrong, he may suffer depression or suddenly feel alienated in a crowd with an ineffable loneliness. The feeling of total abandonment can overcome someone who is left alone even for an afternoon. He cannot be alone, cannot feel the primal aloneness, which was and is devastating. Is there a "good" imprint? There are good memories that shape us and allow us to develop normally. They are not stored in the unconscious as bad events are. They are accessible because there is and was no reason to repress them. Early love simply becomes part of us, whereas bad events become alien, and then are stored.

Research at UCLA and the University of Toronto concluded that depression may be caused by malfunction of certain neural circuits that connect the limbic system with the prefrontal cortex. And, of course, in our work with patients we find this too; only the reasons are different. It is not a malfunction but a crucial function so that we can remain unconscious. That is, there is a disconnect between the two systems to help us from being overwhelmed by pain input. It is a survival mechanism, not a "malfunction."

Simply not coming when a child calls conveys the message that he is unimportant, that nobody cares. Letting a baby cry it out in the crib hour after hour finally induces a sense of defeat: "What's the use? I can't try anymore." That feeling may exacerbate the already established tendency to resignation and despair stemming from birth trauma. Each new experience builds on imprints and shapes personality. We see corroboration of this in research on rats. Those rats never touched or groomed early on, never handled during their first 21 days, experienced lifelong effects of this deprivation. They could not deal with stress as well as those rats who were handled.

Once the imprint of "unloved" exists, no one can ever make us feel loved. This is one key fact of our lives that all of us are in a mad scramble to avoid. We try to feel loved by friends, family, children (above all, our children), and even the usher at the theater. If the pain of not being loved during the first weeks and months of life is very deep, we can later join cults and believe in the most bizarre of ideas, all in the search for the love we did not have. The imprint of hopelessness might generate beliefs in a deity or guru who offers hope. One patient began to relive an incidence of incest. At the apex of his feeling, he sat up and said he found God. He said he was saved by God. Actually, he was saved by the *idea* of God—an idea that helped block the terrible feeling he was about to undergo. He was "saved" by the *idea* of being saved. Here is the disconnect I mentioned between prefrontal ideas and feelings held in the limbic system. It is an example of the evolution of beliefs. Lower level painful feelings cause the higher level production of ideas and beliefs, just as in the evolution of mankind adverse events helped to produce a frontal cortex that could eventually develop ideas to flee from *internal* danger. This is based on the assumption that ontogeny (our personal evolution) recapitulates phylogeny (the evolution of the species). With the development of the prefrontal area, we could at last flee from internal danger, which, in animal life, we could not.

We walk around each day in the grip of our unconscious memories ("No one wants me," "Trying to get love is useless"), and our adult behavior is the analogue of the imprint. It is in our posture, facial expression, and gait. Above all, it is in the decisions we make, in the hobbies we have, in the profession or work we choose, and the people with whom we get involved. The physiology of hopelessness is the bottom rung of a whole chain of feeling that ultimately results in depression. We can feel defeated long before we have words for it. Many of my patients report how they gave up trying in school as a result of that feeling of defeat. Or they gave up trying to find a partner in life if they encountered the slightest obstacle. Many of the choices we make in life fall within the confines of such paradigms.

If a person's desperate need for his mother in the first months after birth is thwarted, he may forego any chance of love as an adult because he is still stuck in the needing-mother mode. No one woman can make him feel fulfilled because the imprint is feeling "unfulfilled." He will go through woman after woman, never feeling satisfied, always thinking that another woman will be the ideal one for him. After all, what is a "womanizer"? Someone who needs one woman after another, and it is never enough.

The lack of a loving mother profoundly affects the little girl who, years later when she is an adult, finds that she does not have the milk she needs for her own baby. This is because lower levels of the hormone oxytocin produced during her infancy have seriously diminished the now-adult mother's ability to love her own child and produce milk. It is not a matter of will that makes a mother return to work prematurely and neglect her child. She is driven by the same lack of love from which her baby will be suffering. It is so difficult to believe that it may all stem from prebirth events or the first weeks and months of life. We just obey those memories, and run them off as if we had free will; as if we made conscious decisions to do so. Alas, it is slavish obedience to unseen and unknown primal forces that hijack our lives interminably. Most of our adult lives are but a rationale for the imprint. I had one patient who never voted because she thought that what she wanted never mattered. And this was true with her parents, not even what she wanted for dinner. So she was sure that her vote, who she wanted, was of no consequence.

Imprints and Neurophysiology: How Memory Is Inscribed

The concept of the imprint is being confirmed by new research, which demonstrates that extreme, early emotional trauma is inscribed in and locked into our system as a physiological event, with continuing physiological effects. It is for this reason that preverbal trauma that occurs before the frontal, thinking area is mature is critical to our development, and continues to affect our personality, behavior, and health for a lifetime.

James McGaugh, of the University of California, Irvine, points out how heavy emotion catecholamines (alerting chemicals, the neurojuices of vigilance) are secreted, which tend to seal in the memory; in effect, inscribe it in the brain. It becomes, in my terms, *the imprint*. It means that extreme emotional trauma is locked into our systems as a psychophysiological event. It is not just psychological or physical, but rather both at once, and it can last a lifetime. "No one wants me," for example, endures because it was too much to feel and integrate at the time. The imprint changes our brains and drives our behavior.

Researchers have identified both the location of these traumatic imprints in the brain and the mechanisms by which they are stamped in permanently. Remember, there is a cascade of physiologic reactions that stem from the central hub of an experience. The imprint continues until we are able to return to that hub, relive those reactions, make them conscious, and finally integrate them. Thus, there is no longer a need for the skewing and dislocation of physiologic processes. High blood pressure is held intact by the memory of a trauma, which originally included changes in blood pressure. It was part of the galvanizing apparatus to fight the intrusion of a trauma—strangling on the umbilical cord, for example. Reliving the choking, suffocating event, and integrating it means it is no longer necessary to fight the imprinted event. The earlier a trauma occurs, the more the incipient, inchoate brain is being restructured, and the more difficult it becomes to change it. It is why panic attacks are so obdurate: they are set down early in gestation.

Imprints during the critical period are engraved in the brain's right hemisphere, particularly in the right limbic system, the "feeling" brain. The right brain develops earlier than the left. At birth, the right amygdala, which appraises crude information, is active among limbic structures along with the brainstem, which goes on developing from early in gestation until the first six months of life. The rest of the limbic system becomes active soon after, and the right limbic system is in a period of accelerated growth until the baby's second year. The hippocampus, another limbic structure, which registers what happens to us very early as fact, is mature by age 2. When there is traumatic experience during the critical early years, various brain structures that deal with vigilance, such as the locus ceruleus, help organize the chemical secretions for the imprint. The hippocampus helps consolidate the imprinted memory, while the guts of the feeling are supplied by the amygdala. For example, it is the right amygdala and brainstem that will engrave whatever upset state the mother is in. Incidentally, this idea of the "guts of the feeling" is my assumption based on an ensemble of various research studies. It is inductive logic, not an established fact. It may be simply a metaphor, but there doesn't seem to be any other structure that could fill the bill. Certainly, feelings are the property of the limbic area, and the amygdala becomes enlarged when there is preverbal trauma. It bears the brunt of the trauma and seems to be bursting at the seams.

One also has to ask why the alerting neurochemicals aid in the imprint. Clearly, because great danger needs to be remembered as a guide to the future, of what must be avoided. And when we are in danger later on, the brain scans its history for the key early imprints to use as guideposts.

Imprints Bend Us Physiologically

Our emotions affect our system far sooner than our thinking processes. It's on the right side that we cope with stress early on, and this may determine how the whole system will react. The prototype "bends" our physiologic processes globally. It is the network of right limbic/brainstem cells that affects hormone secretion and other physiologic processes; this is where our feelings are directly translated to our biochemistry. In this way our early experiences can determine which hormones are over-secreted and which are under-secreted, and whether levels of neurotransmitters are normal and balanced or not.

For the "sympath" (mobilized by the sympathetic nervous system) prototype, there seems to be an excess of secretions. Someone may be "wound up" a lot of the time due to over-secretion of the hormones of aggression, more noradrenaline, for example, due to first-line imprints. This may also later play a part in the development of jingoistic attitudes: "We've got to get those bastards!"

> *Being aggressive may not cause higher noradrenaline, but a trauma early on may produce aggression as a style, and with it higher levels of activating hormones.*

The parasympath (dominated by the parasympathetic nervous system), by contrast, remains in the "hypo" mode. Many of his essential hormones and neurotransmitters are below normal output: hypothyroidism, less testosterone, low levels of serotonin, and so on. Though we found low testosterone levels in parasympaths, the opposite was the case for the sympaths. As a result of these prototypes and their systemic effects, the parasympath may tend toward impotence; the sympath may have a problem with premature ejaculation. (Six males that we studied with testosterone levels of more than 600 nanograms per deciliter had a decline of between 15 and 35 percent after 26 weeks of therapy. Those with low starting levels showed a 20 to 35 percent increase.) All of this stemming from chemical set-points that may have had their start way back in infancy or before. The personality and hormones proceed apace, they accompany one another. Thus, those high in testosterone and noradrenaline may tend to have more aggressive personalities. Being aggressive may not cause higher noradrenaline, but a trauma early on may produce aggression as a style, and with it higher levels of activating hormones.

Early alterations in hormones and neurotransmitters are not transient affairs. They are part of the way memory is inscribed. There is a danger: lack of fulfillment. And that danger of needs not being met is accompanied by an inordinate secretion of stress hormones. Trauma to the fetus and infant causes the sympathetic system to gear up, producing more adrenaline, dopamine, cortisol, and noradrenaline. Once need remains unfulfilled, we are activated. Being vigilant is a matter of survival; the flight, remember, is from ourselves, from our conscious/awareness. The whole system is on alert, and stays alert as long as the imprint is fixed in the system and needs are not met. It is not that we have a memory and then there are hormone changes; those changes are part of the experience. And, in turn, the changes in biochemistry influence our ideas and attitudes and behavior. Because alterations in neurojuices and hormones are part of the experience, in order for them to change, there must again be the full original experience.

For instance, feelings affect the hypothalamus, which governs the output of oxytocin and vasopressin, the "love hormones." These hormones help us establish loving relationships, and they also function as partial painkillers. Love can do that. Love is the major painkiller for a young child, so it is not an accident that with early love our "love hormones" are more in abundance. But if no one came to love us early in life when we were lonely or felt neglected, chances are we will suffer from chronically low output of these hormones. The underlying feeling will be "No one wants me" or "No one loves me." It was, and is, hopeless. The feeling of "No one wants me" governs our lives. It makes us shy in social situations. It can also make a child so angry as to become violent. What is a gang but a real family with leaders, a place to belong and gives outlets to the anger. It provides brotherhood, acceptance, approval, and camaraderie. Eventually, we may need tranquilizers to hold down the feeling that "No one wants me." That feeling hurts—any thwarted need hurts.

Evidence for what I am discussing is found in the research by Johannes Odendall of South Africa (Pretoria Technikon), who studied owners and pets who relaxed together, and where the animals were petted and stroked. Blood samples of both humans and animals were then taken. The result: blood pressure fell while oxytocin doubled. Not only did it double in the dogs, but also in the loving humans! It is quite clear to me that early love helps us relax—for a lifetime, and it may do the same for the mother.

Deficiencies in hormones or neurotransmitters can also set up vulnerabilities so that later trauma creates full-blown afflictions. We do not see any apparent disease when the child is 5, but the seeds have already been sown. We may say later on, "Anorexia is caused by...too much noradrenaline," or too little of this or that. However, these are not causes; they are accompaniments to the original trauma—fellow travelers to a trauma we can no longer see and cannot imagine in a person who is 40 years old. The imprint produces deviations in personality and physiology, which ultimately end in specific symptoms. Thus, the aggressive sympath may have an excess of noradrenaline. It doesn't *cause* anorexia; it is part of the ensemble of reactions to the original event.

Likewise, it is not that someone who is depressed is repressing her anger, as the Freudians would have it. It is that for a parasympath, the chemicals that make for anger are diminished in her, whereas those that make for depression are elevated, while her neurotransmitters tend to drop in the fight against her pain. Chronic depressives have low serotonin levels, for example, and they use up precious supplies in the battle to repress.

Migraine for the parasympath is another example. Lack of effort at birth was life-saving because of the relative lack of oxygen, but now any stress can activate the symptom. The person remains in the energy-conserving mode due to the imprint of lack of oxygen. Any current adversity can set off the old memory of reduced oxygen and the migraine.

Think of the imprint as a conductor. Because experience affects almost every one of our systems, from the muscles to blood to brain cells, the imprint is bound to produce effects everywhere. Each system plays a different instrument, but all together they form a unified entity. If we only pay attention to the violin section, we will never understand the whole piece, nor will we see the interconnection of the various instrument sections; the same is true if we only study blood pressure to the neglect of the human who owns the (blood) vessels. The same imprint can, and does, affect the central nervous system, heart, and blood sugar levels, and can create chronic sweats. It can alter all of the survival functions because survival was at stake. Compounding our early pain with later experience makes symptoms manifest, giving rise to high blood pressure, diabetes, migraine headaches, hypothyroidism and/or Parkinson's disease.

The simple fact of chronically high cortisol set up by the imprint can impact memory later in life, not to mention making us more vulnerable to cardiovascular disease. When the stimulating stress hormones become overactive, as they do with chronic pain, they can affect brain cells and produce cell death, perhaps not immediately, but over time. For the brain, extreme pain experienced early in development is truly a matter of life and death. Nothing alerts us as much as pain—a pain we do not feel. Interestingly, a study published in *Neuron* found that amyloid plaques, a key culprit in Alzheimer's disease, is increasingly manufactured in mice when there is a hyperstimulation of neurons in the brain.[1] This is particularly true in those areas involved in memory retrieval (according to a study on humans published in *Science News*, January 2006).[2] There is just so much stimulation any organ, including the brain cells, can tolerate, particularly when this stimulation goes on over decades of our lives.

One way we know about the imprint's role in orchestrating changes in the functioning of multiple systems is that after a reliving of the imprint, there are key and beneficial changes in many psychophysical systems—not excluding the survival functions of heart rate and blood pressure. In other words, the reliving is key to survival, in many cases. In our research some years ago, we found a dramatic drop in heart rate after one year of therapy. It would seem that the whole system is geared up against memory. When there is a reliving of the memory, the body no longer has to be mobilized, hence the drop in heart rate. It is one of many indices for how memory is stored and combated permanently. It seems to me that slowing the heart rate affects longevity in no small measure. Given that the set-point tendency for heart rate can be set down even before birth, we need to pay more attention to pre-birth life of our babies. A mother who drinks caffeinated soda and coffee while pregnant may be resetting the heart rate speed of her offspring.

Talking Therapies: No Match for the Imprint

We have seen how the system will return again and again to the prototype, which most typically is one of either aggressive striving or easily giving up in the face of life's challenges; how those who are detached emotionally from others begin with detachment from themselves; and how the imprint inscribed into the system early in life will drive act-outs such as repeated failed relationships, drug use, or fervent religious belief for a lifetime. The latter are not simple adult behaviors to be redirected in cognitive or behavior therapy; their roots are deep in the history.

The prototype, which is stamped in during preverbal life, cannot be reversed by verbal means. The prototype is engraved largely with the right brain; the left brain ideas will be of no help in making any change (except, of course, when the left brain participates in connection).

To feel defeated is real—a real reaction to a real event of being deprived any struggle at birth due to a heavy anesthetic administered to the mother, not some neurotic aberration.

When someone is detached and distant, we can sense this; we can't really get through to him. His defenses cannot be penetrated. His seeming aloofness is part and parcel of the imprint, not something to be reconditioned or argued away in cognitive therapy. When someone goes lifeless—shuts down—when sexually excited, it is not anything she or he can help. It may be an analogue of a birth where there was excitement and struggle followed immediately by anesthesia to the mother (therefore, to the fetus) and shut down. The birth sequence is a prototype that dogs us all of our lives. In therapy we see this in patients who try hard in the first minutes of a session and then give up and feel hopeless. Similarly, to feel defeated is real—a real reaction to a real event of being deprived any struggle at birth due to a heavy anesthetic administered to the mother, not some neurotic aberration! If we try to remove that attitude ("What's the use of trying?") without the imprinted memory, we are only cutting off the top of the weeds, and depriving someone of key aspects of the memory of survival.

Some cesarean birth patients we have seen have this struggle-fail syndrome, never having been allowed to finish the birth process. One patient always felt "unfinished," as if there were something she had to do but she never knew what until she had the prototypic experience. The prototype is dictatorial. It allows no current mercy because it already was merciful at the start by allowing unconsciousness of key pains. We can't have it all.

In terms of the prototypic frame of reference, the parasympath's shyness, timidity, and passivity are defenses, not bits of caprice. They were designed originally to keep the pain away. We are neurotic (deviated) for a good reason: adaptation. For the parasympath, his whole system veers toward less—less dopamine, testosterone, noradrenaline, serotonin, thyroid hormone, and so on. The parasympathic reactions stem basically from the prototypic "freeze" response; the inability to react fully. That is, freezing was one option for survival, an option directed by the parasympathetic nervous system. From the beginning, the whole system has tilted toward this "hypo" mode as a mechanism for survival. It makes us inward, introspective, diffident, hesitant and conservative. The other option is the impulse dominated person who plunges in and tends to be far more spontaneous.

Because the imprint orchestrates a cascade of alterations, we can attack the problem with thyroid or any number of other medications, and they will all help. For example, adding any one of these ingredients to the deprived system may help feelings of depression and defeat. This is why giving thyroid to a depressive, or a drug that enhances the work of serotonin, often helps. But they are not cures. Hypnosis works on smoking, but there is still the person there who needs to smoke (someone who needs), and there will be more adverse reactions in the person's area of vulnerability. Hypnosis helps suppress wants but not need. Those wants are the act-out of needs. "I want a cigarette" can be the act-out of the need to suck from very early on. To say nothing of the need to suppress pain.

We have a choice: alleviate symptoms or cure people. Either reregulate each physical change (add a bit of thyroid here, a dose of Prozac there, a nicotine patch to help a smoker break the habit), or address the orchestrator and change all of the physical alterations together.

When someone is a chronic smoker or a depressive, or is sedentary and avoids people, his whole system informs his behavior, and his system is a function of history. Our therapeutic task must always be historical. History is one essential difference between cognitive and feeling therapies. If we treat a person as ahistorical, we can only change his current presenting symptom, not his personality. Modern cognitive psychotherapy stops with the mental. It is confined to the left frontal brain. However, as we will see, the right/feeling brain is dominant in infancy, and it is early right-brain imprints that continually activate the brain. That is where we find "defeat." We must go to combat with that important feeling that governs so much of later life. The only way to go there is with the right brain and the right limbic system, ending eventually at the apex of that system—the right orbital frontal cortex (the right forward part of the top brain).

The cognitivists have confounded brain hemispheres and attempt to get there with an appeal to the left side. We cannot get there from here. The left frontal area only comes on line after the key imprints are set down on the right side. If anything should prove that ideas follow feelings, rather than vice versa, it is that the feeling/sensation areas of the brain are in force long before ideas; moreover, the feelings militate upward and forward to create resonating ideas, thoughts that "rationalize" the feelings. That is why we can take an idea in a therapeutic session and help the patient follow it down to early feelings. For example, "They don't like me" becomes the mother who detested the child ("Please don't hate me, Momma. Want me!"). Cognitive therapy deals mainly with the results of feelings on the left brain, when feelings on the right are importuning at all times.

> *We have a choice: alleviate symptoms or cure people.*

When someone's entire being is permeated with the sense that "no one wants me," to the degree that he needs drugs to kill the pain, this is not just an idea we have to change; it is an organic part of that person. Ideas are not something we produce willy-nilly. We don't just have differences in opinion; we have differences in total personality, which gives rise to opinions. Likewise, when a person's "default" mode is to give up in the face of obstacles, he is responding to the sensation deep in his brain of

"What's the use of trying?" Because it lies so deep, it has a profound impact. The words to describe his state are a late evolutionary development. They are not to be confused with the biologic state; the physiology of defeat.

In the hierarchy of valence or strength, words are the weakest when compared to the force of these first-line nonverbal imprints. We must not believe that if we treat the patient with words, changing the labels, we can make a profound difference. We can plaster on new (false) ideas to old feelings, but the feeling does not change at all. All that happens in this case is that the further suppression of the real feeling creates more stress on the system. Imprints are not conquerable nor can they be convinced to change. We may be able to convince someone to change her ideas, but never out of her physiology. Our job is to align the ideas with the feeling. I should say it is the patient's job, because her feelings, when felt, will do it all by themselves.

No patient sitting up in a chair in a comfortable office can feel the kind of terror he can only feel in a darkened, padded room. Yet this sitting-up framework prevents the cognitive therapists from taking patients back in history. First, their theory does not account for it, and secondly, the very office setup prevents it. The organization of an office follows from the theory. It is all designed to keep the focus in the present—often on the words of the therapist. Sadly, one of the greatest dangers we face is from our past and ourselves, a memory informing us that we are not loved by our parents, that we never will be, and that all is hopeless. This forces us into all sorts of behaviors to avoid feeling hopeless. The problems we have may be between people, but the solution is within. The closer one is to oneself, the closer one can be to others.

Reverberations in the Brain

Imprinted feelings form reverberating loops of neural networks within the limbic/brainstem circuit. Every time Eva felt powerless in a situation, she would pack her bags and start to leave—so she wouldn't feel helpless; feeling that there was nothing she could do. "Helpless" was a constantly reverberating circuit in her brain. The idea of staying put and tolerating great frustration was too much for her. The need to feel safe, born of a feeling of being unsafe, could make us act in constrained, constricted, non-spontaneous ways as an adult. A therapist can exhort the person to try to act spontaneously and be creative, as the Gestalt therapists do, but her whole system will militate against it.

The fear of making a wrong move may begin at birth and continue thereafter. Contrived behavior (Gestalt therapy: "Be free; act like an ape") won't change that. We are already apes; we just have lost touch with it. The feeling of being wrong is behind so much inability to accept having made a mistake. One woman who was born breech always had a feeling that something was wrong. She never knew what, but it was just a sense that things were going to go wrong, which she managed to make happen. Any criticism telling her that she did something wrong lay on top of that birth experience, which was compounded by parents who criticized her unmercifully. She immediately deflected blame on circumstances or others.

Another patient was criticized slightly at work. She became quite anxious and suddenly felt like a failure. We helped her into the feeling: "I'm not going to make it." It started with cesarean birth, where she almost did not make it. This set up the physiology of defeat. Layered onto this was the constant criticism by her father. The anxiety from the slight criticism by her boss was first-line terror from the birth trauma. It was compounded by her childhood. This newborn girl was born without a pulse and did indeed almost die. It was an indelible memory. Thus, the inordinate reaction to the criticism was not irrational. The slight criticism raced along the nerve pathways, reaching down and triggering origins, which made the present excessive response so great.

Those pathways become grooved over time, like a well-trodden path that directs feelings in specific directions. They account for why a current event, "Take out the garbage," can suddenly travel down to basic prototypic events at birth and evoke the feeling "I don't want to work anymore. I've done enough. I am not going to do it." Above all, it explains why discussing something in the present in a therapy session can suddenly provoke an old feeling that needs reliving. It is why the most neutral of remarks can abruptly set off an emotional explosion. This is someone who has very weak gates. Weak gates are usually the result of terrible pre-birth and birth, compounded by a loveless early home life.

> *The imprint is really an ensemble of reactions that is impressed simultaneously into the whole system.*

Keep in mind that each higher level of the brain is an elaboration of lower level events. When we start in the present in a session, given the right techniques, the patient will be automatically taken to the past. When the gates are weak, compounded by a good deal of childhood trauma and lack of love, the descent is too sudden. Here is where we need to use tranquilizers for a short time to help gating. In psychosis the gates fail, and the first and second lines penetrate the third. The person is immersed in his past and doesn't know it.

One patient came in just after his girlfriend left him. He started to feel abandoned and then abruptly sat up and said he could not go on with the session. He was too anxious. He was put on tranquilizers for a brief time to push back an early abandonment—his mother ran off with another man when he was 5. He was left with a depressed father too shattered to pay attention to his children. Effectively, his life was over at that point. It was agonizing; something he could only feel a bit at a time. When his girlfriend left him he started stalking her. She had to get a restraining order to keep him away. He could not take the abandonment now or then, and he became paranoid. His prefrontal area was overwhelmed and he began to imagine a scenario that was only a product of his own mind. As so often happens, a patient can feel a current abandonment so long as there is no great past of neglect.

The imprint is really an ensemble of reactions that is impressed simultaneously into the whole system. It is a total experience, unlike recall, which is largely mental, meaning a left frontal cortex operation. We may not be able to recall an imprint. We can only remember it with our entire system—with our muscles, viscera, and blood system—because all of each of us was involved in the original experience; therefore, it must be relived with all systems involved originally when it was set down. Not only that, but it must be relived with the same intensity in which it was impressed, which is why it has rarely been seen in conventional or cognitive therapy where the emotional level is rather subdued. It is why early in our therapy the patient rarely retrieves memories of high life-and-death valence. We have found a way to access the depths of the unconscious in an orderly, methodical fashion so that the patient is not overwhelmed by pain. We know that the heavier valence pain is located deep in the nervous system, and therefore we skirt any foray to that level early in therapy. I call Primal Therapy "neurosis in reverse," because we go back along the evolutionary chain to where it all started. We revisit the past in measured steps:

childhood events are felt before infancy, infancy before birth, and birth before gestation. The physicist David Bohm noted that man is a microcosm of the universe; therefore, what man is, is a clue to the universe.

That is exactly our point. What man is, is what man was, and inside the human brain we can find remnants of the fish and reptilian brain. What this means is that what we are is built on the most successful adaptations of what we were. When our patients go back to the most primitive brains in their reliving, we see those ancient brains at work. And, I might add, there are never any words in those relivings. The role of the therapist is to "speak" the language of the nonverbal brain. To be quiet for a long time while the patient slips down the chain of pain and merges into his infancy. A touch here or there when appropriate, pressure on the head when the signs are there. Nerve circuits are related through feelings. So to feel abandonment in the present dredges up an earlier experience, then again perhaps just after birth when the newborn was left unattended for hours. The latter is the kind of feeling that is stamped in unmercifully and makes us overreact to a current situation. The problem is that too often the paranoia becomes reified, set in cement, and is unyielding to any outside pleadings.

> *We have found a way to access the depths of the unconscious in an orderly, methodical fashion so that the patient is not overwhelmed by pain.*

When we consider the nature of consciousness *we must* take into consideration the brains that went before us, the brains that still reside within us. They help make up our consciousness. After all, the lower animals had to be very aware of where food and enemies were. They certainly had an awareness, and that kind or level of awareness still exists in us. Those "awarenesses" certainly make up modern consciousness. To think otherwise is to adopt an anti-evolutionary stance, to think that the late-developing neocortex is the be-all and end-all of human consciousness. If we want to understand the origins of the universe, both personal and phylogenetic (of humankind), it helps to delve deep into our internal past. Do animals feel? We descend down into the old limbic system, part of which we share with animals, and find that they do. Are dogs feeling? Absolutely.

We redo and recorrect the deviations forced upon us by early trauma by living the events that caused the key deviations. *The imprint is the problem and the solution*. It is an ineluctable force. The seeds of resolution lie in the pain, and only there. Going back and feeling unloved by our parents means to feel; only when this is done can we let love in. Events held limbically allow us to retrace our childhood—smell father's aftershave, sense the feel of his beard again, see our childhood home, and recall how we used to feel at home at dinner. We see the scenes of family battles, of early fears and terrors. When we descend to lower limbic levels, we see the color of the carpet clearly, we see the look on Father's face, and we sense Mother's indifference and lack of interest. We are again the vulnerable, sensitive child. Patients in a Primal Therapy session can recall in minute detail scenes when they were 6 years old or earlier that they could never have recalled otherwise. All that was outside is inside; all patients need is accessed. I find it astounding that somewhere in that brain of ours is the smell of father's pipe and our childhood need for him to turn and talk to us just for a minute; some acknowledgment that we exist and are important to someone. If it never happened, we stop expecting it to happen. We go on about our loveless business.

It is not enough to feel pain in therapy, for we must understand that inside the pain lies the need, the need that was first converted to pain when it was not fulfilled.

What is most remarkable in our therapy is that biologically, it seems no different to love the child early on or to relive the lack of love later on. There is a normalization of the system. What happens during Primal Therapy sessions is an analogue of our evolutionary history. As a patient plunges into the depths of hopelessness, to the base of his deep depression, there will be a shift to dominance by the sympathetic system, with frequent urination, high blood pressure, rapid heart rate, stomach cramps, and muscle tension. The system, reacting to the imprinted pain, is in high arousal. *The adult system can now handle the pain, whereas the infant's could not.* The pain can be experienced because the critical period is over.

It is not enough to feel pain in therapy, for we must understand that inside the pain lies the need, the need that was first converted to pain when it was not fulfilled. It is need that ultimately must be fully experienced. For instance, the need to suck is there, unarticulated, as soon as we are born. When mother offers the breast, there is fulfillment and relaxation. Without fulfillment we may be left in a sympathetic dominant state with accelerated functioning, and still have the need to suck. There is nothing in the environment that will allow the parasympathetic nervous system to step in and diffuse that need. Needs are hard wired; they always involve survival. They are not meant to change; nor should they. The act-out, which in this case may involve getting women to mother us over and over, taking care of every chore, putting meals on the table at the right time, is a constant reminder. When it is not fulfilled, we then act out the need symbolically. Because the fulfillment is symbolic, it is never fulfilling nor resolving. Cognitive therapy is about treating the symbolism. The need to smoke is a symbol of real need. Too often the wrong need is being addressed. And when the wrong need is diverted or suppressed in therapy, it is considered a success. Remember, we never overcome need no matter what age we are.

Feeling need is the bottom line because it is converted to pain as a warning. Feeling need means feeling the need for oxygen if it was lacking at birth due to anesthesia. The patient may gasp, gag, and turn red in the reliving. She is reliving the need without speaking any words. That is sufficient. Pain won't let go until basic need is felt. So yes, we must feel pain but that is a way station to need. Feeling "Help me, Momma" over and over will stop the act-out of having women mother us. We cannot just feel it once and expect change; we must feel it often and with the strength of the deprivation at the time. To be clear, we relive pieces of the suffering a bit at a time so that it can be integrated. If a patient tried to do it all at once, she would be overwhelmed and take off in the symbolic stratosphere—into past lives, for example. It is the same memory, but different aspects of the pain.

We must experience the feelings with the strength of the imprint; there is no shortcut to that. The need was deprived and that deprivation is reinforced year after year. It becomes almost monolithic. If anyone attempts to feel it in its entirety through the use of drugs, he will almost certainly fail. The system is not designed to connect to overwhelming feeling. It is designed to shunt it and convert it into symbolism; consequently, a girlfriend becomes a mother.

After connection, after feeling "No one wants me. They never wanted me," the system can shift to a parasympathetic-dominant state. At long last, the system can now rest because the danger is past (and in the past is where it belongs). When we connect the suffering component of memory, and the alien force becomes integrated, the "cascade" of deviations in multiple body systems begins to normalize. To relive pain and need fully is to produce a physiologic system that functions as if that need had always been fulfilled. It will free the parasympath to widen her vision and take more chances. It will allow the sympath to ease off the incessant struggle that never lets him relax. Finally, it puts our systems back in balance so that they can find an equilibrium. We are no longer prisoners of medication after medication, drug after drug. A balanced system means the parasympathetic male's chronically low level of testosterone is normalized—something we have found after one year of therapy. It means he is now more assertive and less depressed. A balanced system means not having to drink five cups of coffee a day or being hooked on cola. It means not having to smoke, which ultimately will shorten our lives. It is the true meaning of being free.

Nearly all of us are prisoners of our prototype. Cognitive therapy assumes we have an ample amount of free will. I am not so sure. We can make choices within the prototype, but it tends to be a narrow range. What we are free to do is go back and find out how all that got started. That is what will ultimately widen our range of choices in life.

Depression, or the Physiology of Hopelessness

Depression is an example of the effects of the imprint. Diminished oxygen at birth and before (a carrying mother smoking at least 10 cigarettes a day plus anesthesia at birth) establishes a physiologic record. This record orchestrates a large variety of reactions; each reaction is an adaptation to the threat against survival. Thus, there are lowered oxygen levels as expressed through chronic fatigue syndrome, for example, and many phenomena governed by brainstem functions, such as butterflies in the stomach, dizziness, spaciness, and a vague terror. All of the visceral reactions can be included here. Those reactions are controlled by our primitive or ancient nervous system. When terror is set down early, the fetus or newborn has no cortical capacity to dilute its impact. The nature of deep terror is so profound that in the reliving it decades later, it is only possible to feel it for moments at a time.

Hopelessness, helplessness, despair, and resignation can be imprinted through diminished oxygen; all of the true sensations accompanying the memory. It is later called depression, a state that was compounded by an unfeeling, dictatorial home environment where the child had nowhere to go with her feelings. It is not that parents necessarily suppressed the child's feelings but that they may not have been present emotionally. The result is the same: there is no one to tell our feelings to. We are again helpless and hopeless. Not making a substantial effort, not struggling to succeed because struggling at birth meant the possibility of death, is also part of the adaptation process—conserving energy for survival.

In the original context, any struggle, perhaps against a strangling umbilical cord, could be fatal. Massive drugs given to the mother at birth suppress the newborn's system, leaving him with a physiologic memory of hopelessness and powerlessness. Hopelessness is then installed as part of a survival syndrome and is exacerbated by cold, distant parents. It may not be conceptualized for decades. We can feel hopeless without a label, give up trying without having a concept about it, and be dominated by it long before recognizing what it is. I remember in my psychoanalytic days telling patients they had a "masked depression" because they didn't even know they felt depressed and hopeless. But they did. Now I don't have to tell patients anything. They figure it out for themselves. They feel the early hopelessness, nearly always signaled by a very low body temperature, and they slowly come out of their depression. Now they could look forward to living a feeling life.

Case Study: Kiki

When I was 15 years [old] I had surgery. A cyst was removed from my right ovary. When I woke up from the operation I felt so cold. I shivered and the blankets brought about by nurses couldn't make it stop. The first night after my operation, I was scared to move, because my tummy felt open, as if they had forgotten to sew me up again. I felt if I ever was to move, then all my intestines would fall out of me. I forgot about the operation. It became one more of those black holes.

Two months into Primal Therapy my previously very painful periods worsened. The pain was diffuse in my pelvis with occasional sharp abdominal pains. Although the pain was almost unbearable, I would not make any serious attempt to soothe it with painkillers. I suffered through that month after month until about a year into Primal Therapy. Then I began to [P]rimal about my surgery. The surgery memories are triggered if I feel utterly rejected by people I am close to in my present-day life. Immediately my scar starts to hurt, my uterus cramps, and I begin to bleed.

When I drop into the feeling, I have sensations about how my organs inside are roughly handled and pushed aside. I feel how something very cold and hard is inserted into my vagina. I feel a cut and then tremendous pain spreading everywhere in that area. It feels like something or somebody puts tremendous pressure on me there. I feel as if air is blown into my insides and I'm going to burst inside.

I also sense an awful atmosphere around me: that kind of atmosphere that arises when people are very stressed and work without any sense or feeling for the person they do surgery on. I feel very cold and start to shiver. The feeling is of utter rejection, the most awful I ever felt. I think current rejection sets it off. All the time I feel how everything that happens to me is entirely wrong and how I cannot do anything. This feeling, "I can't do anything," I acted out in the reliving for a long time by not even getting the idea that I could do something like take pills to dampen my pain.

My major insights from the surgery [P]rimals are:

1. *How much I would have needed to be kept warm just physically (clothes or higher temperature in the operation room).*
2. *How much I would have needed the surgeons to handle me carefully, to move my organs inside of me gently.*
3. *How much I would have needed a person to be with me although I was sedated. I would have needed somebody to touch me gently, to talk softly to me, and to soothe me by just being there for me, close to my head. All the time I was sedated I assume that my thinking mind was asleep. But down low in my brain it was alive, sensing all what was going on, remembering it in distinct imprints that I now remember and that I would have loved to never have experienced.*

Here we see that anything that triggered the original cold sterility of the operating room, a rejecting, indifferent, cold atmosphere in the present, could set off Kiki's surgery experience, which she did not relive until many months into her therapy.

5

The Left and Right Brain: Balancing the Human Being

There are several primary systems at work in the brain. These systems run from bottom to top (which we'll discuss later) and also from right to left. The brain has two sides, left and right. Each side, or brain hemisphere, has different functions. Broadly, we might say the right side is responsible for feeling, while the left side thinks, plans, and schemes. The left hemisphere manages the external world, while the right brain manages our inner lives. One is the scientist and the other is often involved in mysticism. The right brain forms much of our personalities, governs many of our biochemical processes, and directs our later lives beyond what most of us realize. This means that feelings govern our choices, interests, professions, partners, and loves. The left brain, by and large, deals with the quantity of things; the right, with quality.

When we speak of "quality of life," we are dealing with feeling. So we have one brain that is fragmented and the other that sees the whole. To become whole we must manage to recruit the fragments of our lives into a complete picture; for that we need both brain hemispheres working in harmony. That is one definition of consciousness and its differentiation from awareness. In therapy we see how this works when, after a feeling, the patient will begin a litany of, "That's why I did this and why I did that." The fragmented behavior begins to make total sense. It has a gestalt context—consciousness out of unconsciousness.

The right side creates images and rhymes and makes spatial connections, whereas the left is more literal. It looks to the future and sees the consequence of our actions. Left side intellectuals need order and reason to explain their worlds, while artists working with the right disdain such order. Those who don't "get" a joke are often more left-brain oriented, because they miss the nuance, the underlying feeling or humor. They also react less to music, to rhythm and tone. Those who can't "sense" someone's insincerity or psychological subtext tend to be left-brain bound. They often take people at their word and are fixated by words. By contrast, those who feel can sense the tone or subtext in what others say. They respond beyond the phrases to their hidden meaning. They also sense what their children need. Whole human beings have a balance between right and left; they are sensitive, feeling, and perceptive. By whole in this context, I mean connected, hence conscious.

As I noted in the previous chapter, feelings by the mother sculpt the baby's feeling centers. A baby who is loved will develop a good balance between the left and right hemispheres, have healthy access to her feelings, and can use them to make good decisions. She will be able to see herself "objectively." We see this in therapy when patients who connect the right and left prefrontal areas see right away the mistakes they have made with their children or their spouses. She will also be more sensitive to the feelings of others. The right side remembers love and no love, and tries to communicate this to the left prefrontal area. It speaks in chemical terms: "No love, that's terrible. Send in the stress hormones." Closeness, love, and emotional attachment—or their absence—affect the right brain of the infant during fetal life and for the first three years of its life more than in any later period. It is the key critical period. For this reason, receiving love early on from the mother, including during pregnancy, is so important in determining a baby's overall health, because the mother's love is actively regulating the development of the baby's brain. Events during this time alter the brain, both functionally and structurally.

When we consider that the right emotional/limbic brain is in a growth spurt in the first years when touch and love are absolutely crucial, it is clear that a lack of it will have lifelong consequences on our emotions. The brain's neurochemistry, the levels of stress hormones and other activating chemicals, are mostly under right brain control. When these are altered, they influence how we relate to others and to ourselves.

What transpires between mother and child is a conversation between their right-side limbic systems. When the mother is attuned to the baby's feelings, her right limbic system is in tune, and she can feel what the baby is feeling and respond appropriately. The more parental love there is, the more the dopamine neurons in the right brain activate, giving the child a feeling of wellbeing. The better the baby feels about its environment, the more optimum the dopamine activation in the right brain. What happens when we receive mother's love is that we feel good physiologically.

The right hemisphere is actually a model of what happened to us early in life. If we did not have strong emotional relationships with our parents early in life, the right hemisphere will become a template that may cause constant broken relationships in adult life. It is also the right limbic brain that determines our vulnerabilities to later psychosomatic ailments. If we don't receive sufficient love early on, we will suffer for it later; heart disease is but one of many examples. Why is that? Because very early trauma registered in the brainstem and ancient limbic structures have direct connections to various organs, not the least of which is the heart. An early imprint can set the heart slightly fast, which can erode its functioning over time. Later heart disease can begin its life before we begin our social life on earth. Love not only makes the world go round, it makes the brain function the way it was meant to. All this transpires during the critical period where experience will change the brain in numerous ways, often permanently.

The only thing that is curative is to go deep down in the brain and relive the prototype—the basic personality set even before birth, the crucible for the later neurotic superstructure.

No amount of fulfillment later on can replace an early deficit of love and caring. This means that no amount of caring by a therapist can produce any profound change in the patient. She is long past her critical period. To repeat: you cannot love neurosis away. Of course, caring in the present can act as a holding action, keeping the real deprivation at bay for a short time; it tranquilizes but cannot be curative. And it has to be tranquilized all of the time lest the pain surge forth. That is why many patients seek conventional therapy ad infinitum.

The only thing that is curative is to go deep down in the brain and relive the prototype—the basic personality set even before birth, the crucible for the later neurotic superstructure. In brief, to relive the no-caring by one's parents—there was no help, over and over again until repression of that pain is lifted, and then to relive the no-help at birth. Then one can let in love once again and allow oneself to be helped. The more pain that leaves the system, the less one needs repression.

Can one really relive "no-help" in a situation where there were no words? One can relive the later aspects of it that do have words, "My father never helped me," which will then transport the person back to where there was the sensation (not articulated) of no help at birth or just after.

Without harmony between the two sides of our brains, we cannot be whole and integrated. Because brainstem and limbic structures on the right largely make up the unconscious, the task is to bring the right brain into symmetry with the left. Remember, events are unconscious because early trauma impacts the right brain far more than the left, and that brain loses touch with conscious-awareness. It becomes disconnected.

I am not ignoring genetics, nutrition, or environmental factors. There is an ample amount of discussion of all that in current literature. Health sections in various newspapers are full of related discussions. What they lack is an understanding of the primal factors that I am writing about.

Mechanisms That Aid the Disconnection

One primary way that love, or a lack of it, sculpts the brain is in determining how well we are connected to our feelings. Our ability to connect to our feelings depends on a key brain structure that serves as a bridge between comprehension of feeling, which is a function of the left brain, and feeling itself, governed by the right brain. This bridge is called the *corpus callosum.* It is the most important of several highways connecting the left and right brains; 80 percent of feeling information traverses this structure. Early experience can effectively block this information "highway" from one brain hemisphere to the other. This means that the left side doesn't know what is in the right, literally.

With early trauma, the corpus callosum suffers, and its fibers are thinned out and rendered less efficient by fewer connecting nerve cells. With fewer nerve cells, this bridge impedes the right brain and left brain from interacting normally. For instance, premature birth can enfeeble the corpus callosum so that later there is effectively a disconnect. Other early trauma tends to prune the cells literally, creating a bad connection; one side can't hear the other and has no idea what it is trying to say. As a result, we lose contact with our feelings, which are then buried in the right "unconscious" mind. Nevertheless, we are driven by these forces without our ever knowing it. The left brain reacts to the pressure of the message, however garbled it seems. The great aloneness when a newborn is not attended to right after birth is imprinted, and later can drive us to phone friends incessantly when we are alone. The reason: being alone can bring up the original devastating feeling and therefore the drive to connect in order to keep the feeling at bay. The person is driven to make phone calls and see people not because she is social but because she is in a frantic rush *away* from the feeling of aloneness. Another example: a man had an early life that was hell, so he latched onto communism as the promise of paradise on earth. His beliefs—the need for an alternative to hell—were locked in by the feeling. It was hope derived from deep hopelessness that drove his beliefs.

A repeated lack of love experienced early in life can produce the illness known as post-traumatic stress disorder (PTSD). A key effect of PTSD is the damage that is done to the corpus callosum, which reduces a person's ability to connect to her feelings; or, literally, for the left brain to connect to the right. In an article in *Scientific American*, Martin Teicher of the Harvard Medical School describes his finding that young boys who had been abused or rejected had significantly smaller corpus callosums than normal children. In girls, sex abuse was found to be associated with a major reduction in the size of the middle part of the corpus callosum. Dr. Teicher makes a crucial point: "Our team initiated this research with the hypothesis that early stress was a toxic agent that interfered with the normal, smoothly orchestrated progression of brain development. Exposure to stress generates molecular and neurobiological effects that alter neural development in an adaptive way that prepares the adult brain to survive and reproduce in a dangerous world."[1] Dr. Teicher adds that a smaller corpus callosum leads to "less integration between the two halves of the brain," which corroborates our clinical observations. The person cannot "get himself together," literally.[2] Whether the corpus callosum can grow to normal size following Primal Therapy is an area of research we hope to pursue. Damage to the corpus callosum is a key impairment to the brain, and affects learning, coordination, and emotional stability. We will see later how the left side can "act" normal when the right side is a mess.

Clearly, stress and neglect in early life changes the brain. Because of this, we grow up with a different cognitive apparatus, not as capable as "normal" brains. We think that this brain is maladaptive but, in fact, it is altered to adapt to early trauma, now lodged in the lower brain system. The resulting gap between the brain's left and right hemispheres—I emphasize—is a literal bad connection in the brain, a measure of disharmony in the system. The left brain is not attuned to the right.

This disconnection is adaptive in the sense that it shields one from agonizing exposure to blocked pain. Yet, one must react to the pressure of its message. "You are not loved" drives one to imagine love where it doesn't exist. The belief in a loving deity is one example. The left brain will fabricate all sorts of rationales for its behavior. This is what happens in split-brain studies. For example, a funny scene delivered to a severed right brain can make the person laugh. When asked why he laughed, without being aware of the funny material that was fed into the right side, the subject remarks that the doctor is wearing a funny coat. In brief, the left side fabricates and rationalizes input of which one is unaware. This is a paradigm for neurosis. There is input from below that rises to the right frontal cortex but cannot traverse the callosal bridge. The person makes up a reason for his behavior. "I wouldn't get mad if you didn't ask me that question a hundred times," he may retort to a mild question, when in fact the anger is generated by deeper feelings to which he does not have access. Someone harassed by one's parents to do his chores will not look kindly on another person's insistence that he perform a certain task. The left brain is, by and large, the interpreter of experience. If we want a truer account, we must address the right.

The dangerous world that Dr. Teicher talks about, I submit, is the danger of imprinted feelings, left there by the "toxic stress" (trauma) he mentions. In his piece he found that in abused patients, the right hemisphere was fully developed, but the left hemisphere lagged behind. He wonders if mistreated children store disturbing memories in the right hemisphere. From our clinical experience, and nearly all later research, that would seem to be correct.

Teicher's work is important because it verifies that early stress leaves an "indelible imprint" and induces a "cascade of molecular and neurological effects that irreversibly alter neural development." As we see, the imprint is not a theoretical concoction, but a neurophysiologic fact. The imprint is the overarching fact. The changes in neural structure and biochemistry are aspects of this fact; the context that makes sense out of it. Neurologist Dr. Bessel van der Kolk has also supplied evidence that repressed trauma has specific neural (nerve circuits) in the brain.[3] Trauma is likened to an event that is "flash-frozen" in a nonverbal neural stream. Once frozen in time, it secretes the hormones of stress in response to inner terror. Our goal is to bring memories from the nonverbal to the verbal areas of the brain, to connect and integrate them. Helplessness is a good example, and "Can't make it" is another. One patient felt he could not make it in class until he felt "I can't make it" in its original context. The patient was able to give words to the ineffable feeling. Those words explained the feeling on all three levels of consciousness.

The Problem With Left-Brain–Centered Psychotherapy

Unfortunately, we tend to glorify left-brain activities to the neglect of the right. We expect the left brain to fight our battles, particularly, the internal enemies. We do this without taking into account that left-brain development came into being much later in evolutionary history than the right brain, and in each of our individual lives, in part as a means of disengaging us from the other side. One kind of brain tissue cannot do the work of another. The left brain developed different abilities to avoid a redundancy between left and right. The left brain's activity helps soothe and calm us. It allowed and continues to allow us to defend against feelings that were too much to bear. We use the left hemisphere to rationalize a hurt or insult so it won't create so much pain. Or, at the mercy of needs of which we may be only dimly aware, the left brain can superimpose all kinds of needs onto a romantic object and imagine her to be wonderful, only to be disappointed two years down the line because the left brain didn't perceive reality. It didn't listen to the right because communication was either reduced or nonexistent. When perception is detached from need and feeling, we misperceive. For instance, if we need a strong protector, we will overlook the other person's weaknesses and ignore his flaws. We "see" protection where it may not exist, or we get protection accompanied by total domination.

The left frontal area is also where we conjure up or embrace beliefs. Insights given by a therapist are ultimately beliefs to soothe and ease pain. Indeed, the words of a therapist, no matter whether right or wrong, can be soothing to our agonies. It is not only the content of what the therapist says, but just his words offered in soothing tones. Oddly enough, that tone affects the right brain, not the left. The content of the insight remains in the left. We can be fooled into thinking that the content of an insight is what makes us feel better, but in reality it is the reassuring tone, all along. It dampens right-side pain—the pain of a father who never cared, was never soft, and whose tone was unrelentingly harsh. The therapist's presence says, "I'm here now. It's going to be all right." Just being in his office can make us feel better. In other words, the left side allows us to be partially oblivious to ourselves. This is particularly egregious when it comes to psychotherapy, which traditionally has been left-brain focused for more than 100 years.

> *It is difficult to know what is real about humans if we take words alone as a sign of reality.*

It is now apparent, due to an abundance of new research, that psychotherapy must address the right brain and consider how to affect right-left brain connections—as this is the way feelings become integrated. Psychotherapy must work to help not only our mental state but our entire neurophysiologic system. This is the difference between dealing with words (left brain) and the use of images, scenes, and feelings (right brain). The former is what occurs when we "reflect" on our past, while genuine emotional retrieval, which is what is needed for integration and genuine healing, requires access to the right-brain feeling structures. Once again we see that it is not possible to use ideas and thinking processes, which literally came along millions of years later in brain development to affect what is lower in the brain, and developed millions of years earlier.

The different functions of the left and right brains are apparent when we say, "I am trying to convince myself to stop smoking." What selves are those? The left is trying to smother the need on the right, but is never as strong as either of them. The right brain only knows about its internal universe. It "tells" the left in a coded message to pick up a cigarette, and the left obeys. It commands the left to believe in reincarnation, past lives, and other supernatural events, and the left obeys. It commands from its fortress, say, of being abandoned in infancy—the terrible isolation, loneliness, and fear. Here we see how our reality constructs unreality, an unreality commensurate with the valence or force of the hidden reality. Thus, the scientist and the true believer can exist at the same time in the same person, a seamless conjoining of the two halves of the brain, each unaware of the other, or at least indifferent to the other. What is diabolic about the belief in past lives is that there is a reality there—a real past life that drives the cortex to invent beliefs. The person has simply skipped over reality because of its heavy valence. Each of us gets but one life, but when death feelings threaten, we opt for more lives. It is possible that there is a contagion of feelings and beliefs in a culture that tends to circumscribe the kind of beliefs one will adopt. The content matters little, because the brain cannot tell the difference between Allah, Buddha, and God. It just needs to believe. The prefrontal cortex conjures up beliefs to accommodate the need. The feeling inside the belief, however, is hope—for a better life, guidance, and protection.

The basic laws of nature that apply to feeling exist; our job is to discover them. That will be very difficult if we do not have deep, right-brain access. Even more difficult if we are not aware of the imprints is deciphering how and where they are laid down. It is doubly difficult if we are unaware of the different functions of the two hemispheres. We don't have to invent intellectual theories about human behavior; we have to discover natural law. That should make our job easier, once we leave the intellectual behind. It is difficult to know what is real about humans if we take words alone as a sign of reality.

When an animal hears the distress signal of an offspring, the right springs into action. Many mothers report experiencing tightness in their nipples or a flow of breast milk when they hear any infant cry. The very early pain we undergo in the womb is going to be registered largely on the right. Thus, in order to understand the insincerity of someone or the hidden meaning behind their words (think politicians), we need right-side access in the same way that we need it to understand sarcasm or the humor in a joke. Above all, if we want a good therapist, he must be someone who understands what people are secretly feeling. He must see the implicit in people's behavior and statements. The right gives us an overview of our internal/emotional world; the left side is largely confined to the cognitive world. The cognitivists remain on the level of the overt and obvious, and neglect the unconscious and its forces. At least in the Freudian world, the unconscious is recognized, but there is no royal road into it. Because the cognitivists tend to miss the context of events and treat the presenting problem as *the problem*, they are forever bereft of generating causes. This is fine for counseling therapy where a couple needs some direction, and I often refer couples for counseling, but it is not fine for treating deep problems.

We need the left and right working together to tie disparate pieces together to make sense out of symptoms. Deep fears may be creating a phobia, say, of enclosed spaces. When the original imprinted memory is made left-brain aware, the fear can stop its diversions into phobias and connect with conscious-awareness. Phobias here are diversions, way stations, and detours because the fear cannot go to where it has to.

There are therapies of the body, the Alexander, bio-energetics approach, and the so-called feeling therapy of the Gestalt school, that in decorticate fashion concentrates only on feeling; and then there are the cognitivists who focus in cortical mode on ideas and beliefs. Both areas of the brain are essential in a proper psychotherapy because we are made up of two hemispheres, not one. We need text and context, past and present, feelings and comprehension. The neglect of any of that will compromise any therapy we do.

A precise person is usually left-side dominant. Those who learn languages easily later in life have right-brain access; they sense the nuance and differences in tone and are more feeling. They feel the cadence and accents of a language. That doesn't mean "more normal." Right-siders can be hysterical messes with no left-side control. They may have rages, screaming matches, and act out and be out of (left-side) control. The left-siders learn the words but little else and usually never learn the accent and tone of a language. Yet, left-brained people are crack in terms of grammar. Again, it is all about the subtleties in others and in language. It is what makes us sensitive to other's feelings and their needs and desires. It is what makes a parent a good one—not child-rearing manuals, but out of feelings, sensing the child's needs, because one is in touch with one's own. What happens in some right-brainers is that they are loaded with input from below, so that when there is too much input from outside they get overwhelmed and often hysteric. The first line comes bursting forth and they are all awash in feelings. Thus, the outside stimulation (for example, too many people at a party) can, combined with the internal stimulation, become far too much. They cry, explode in rage, and so on. This is part of the basis for social anxiety. The need to diminish outside input in order to keep oneself in equilibrium.

What is important is that right-deficient individuals cannot change with the change in context. They continue to act out the past in the present and have a hard time adapting to the new. They are therefore (in general) more rigid in approach. Change is threatening. There are those in neuroscience who understand this point yet use a variation of cognitive therapy once the patient discusses feelings. There is still this focus on discussion, still a concentration on the relationship between patient and doctor, rather than on the relationship between the patient and herself. *We go to cognitive therapy to enlist the armies of the word against the ranks of feelings.* With this understanding, we can see how futile it is to use ideas in treating the effects of deeply ingrained traumas. It is not just ideas that are involved in therapy. The therapist is not only the purveyor of ideas, she is also the filler of needs (symbolically) and in that way we can only get well symbolically; therapy is yet another form of act-out. What is real is the patient's unresolved childhood need and the dislocation it caused long ago. No current therapeutic caring can undo childhood deprivation.

Remember, insights are a set of belief systems. They are different with the Jungians and the Freudians. What a therapist tells the patient is often part of his own apperceptive mass, of his own beliefs that the patient must adopt. Insights are not neutral; they are multi-determined. There is a theoretical frame of reference behind them, a system of beliefs, which is inculcated into the patient. Often, the cognitive therapist is using words to activate the patient's left prefrontal area, thereby strengthening the defense. The Freudians don't call it cognitive, but they rely heavily on words to accomplish their goals. They want to reorient the patient to more rational ways of thinking. So here we have a paradox: the therapist's words strengthen the left-brain defense while the tone calms the right brain; together they seem to help. It is not the content of the insights a therapist gives, but the *fact* of the insights; proffering ideas as a balm to soothe those inner wounds that do not bleed.

What is the meaning or subtext of the therapist's insights? "I care. I listen. I want to help. I talk to you with empathy. You are worth talking to." All that is the "healing" subtext, which is symbolic. Whatever reinforces our defenses tends to make us feel better. It puts an ideational salve over the hurt so we won't feel it, when it is the opposite that must take place. No psychotherapy can alter our unresolved childhood needs and the act-outs they drive once they are sealed in. We can beat or exhort smoking and drinking away, but their motivating forces remain. Or we can go to psychotherapy where the therapist encourages us to understand and forgive our parents for their weaknesses even while our systems are in agony from deprivation. It is the left brain that forgives while the right suffers, and forgiveness will never change that suffering. Forgiveness is a religious notion, not a scientific one. Forgiveness is best left to the church.

We tend to think that ideas change our behavior when in fact it is our feelings. It doesn't matter whether our feelings are conscious or not; they still affect all of our biological mechanisms, including hormones, our circulatory system, muscles, and so on. Left-brain insights decades later in therapy are not going to change those physiologic imprints, our memories, our critical right-brain history, because they are not directly connected to that history. Indeed, they are disconnected from that history.[4] The real challenge in therapy lies in how to address another human being's right brain without words. The right side always tells the truth because the imprint leaves it no choice; yet that truth often forces the left to lie, mostly to ourselves. In the October 2005 issue of the *British Journal of Psychiatry*, there is a study indicating that the ability or facility for compulsive lying lies, not surprisingly, in the prefrontal cortex, away from the feeling level.

> *We go to cognitive therapy to enlist the armies of the word against the ranks of feelings.*

Without right-brain access we are not going to solve many of the physical symptoms, to say nothing of mental problems that are derivatives of early hidden feelings. Every mental problem has its somatic counterpart. We can separate them for study and treatment, but we are, after all, organic beings. Thus, we go to three different specialists for the three different ways we react to the same early trauma. The internist deals with ulcers, as he should; the psychologist deals with phobia, as she should; and the psychiatrist deals with attitudes of despair by offering tranquilizers, which sometimes are necessary. In Primal Therapy we deal with the whole person, observing how the resolution of trauma seems to dissipate symptoms on every level of representation. This is not to say that each symptom must not be treated. It must. Continual symptoms always pose a danger. If we want the truth behind someone's behavior we have only to access the unconscious, the deep right limbic/amygdala areas, and we will find it.

> *So many of our patients had all kinds of symptoms before therapy that were a mystery, not the least of which was depression. Once connected, none of those symptoms are a mystery; moreover, they no longer exist.*

To reestablish equilibrium, we need to return to the events that caused the disequilibrium. Fortunately, we can take the person back to where some of the circuits got rerouted and rewired. The right side offers us a chance to recapitulate our past, relive it, and change it; a Herculean task, but very possible. We don't have to rely on theories from the left side to understand. Above all, we no longer have to superimpose our theories on our patients; we can develop our theories from the mouths of our patients. Their feelings explain what we need to know. Going back and feeling unloved by one's parents early in life is healing. It is the best chance we have at love because it means we are no longer closed down emotionally; we have opened up to our pain and emotions, and, hopefully, this will correct some of the damage.

When there is greater connection, our relationships will improve; there might be less divorce as each of us will see reality and stop projecting our needs onto others. We won't marry for the wrong reasons, because we will be more perceptive about our needs. To be perceptive means to integrate our feelings and to be in touch with our intuitive self. Good connections to the right prefrontal area of our memories helps us become well informed about our inner life so that as we age, we won't be surprised if we develop a bleeding ulcer or fall into a depression. In fact, none of that will happen because we will understand where our moods come from, be connected to them, and, therefore, can control them. That is assuming there will be unexplained moods.

Do I mean that if we are connected we will not have those symptoms? Obviously, not always or in every single case, but in the majority of cases—yes. So many of our patients had all kinds of symptoms before therapy that were a mystery, not the least of which was depression. Once connected, none of those symptoms are a mystery; moreover, they no longer exist. If we are connected to life-and-death events at birth that set our heart going with palpitations, and we experience those events fully at age 40 through a complete reliving (a Primal), such symptoms will cease to exist.

Once we understand that only the patient can transform himself, then we can move beyond trying to make him into what he is not. Reality lies inside of him, not in the head of the therapist. We need to help him find that reality.

Case Study: Nathan

I've been on edge lately. Actually, I've been losing it really, but with good reason. Everyone is conspiring against me, even the therapists. That is how I went into my session on Tuesday. So you think I'm smoking dope again, and you told all the other therapists and everyone now hates me. Valerie (my therapist) didn't respond much, except to say, "How does that make you feel?" I'm always getting screwed; somebody is always out to get me. I'm always getting blamed for something, and everyone always ends up hating me for some reason or another. As I'm saying this, I start to feel a knot of tension in my stomach and a deep sadness. My eyes start to get blurry, and it's hard for me to talk. What's happening? Valerie says that I feel that I'm not good enough, I can't do enough, and nothing I do will ever be enough! I can't please everyone. I can't be perfect! I start to break down and cry.

The feeling keeps penetrating and my crying becomes serious. I lose all sense of time, and then out of the blue, this flashback pops into my head. I'm in high school during computer class hiding my face in my arms and pretending to sleep while everyone else is busy doing their work. I was miserable back then, and I would usually spend my days in class sleeping or pretending to sleep. The teacher called me up to her desk, and I was thinking, "Oh shit, I'm in trouble again," or maybe she was going to ask me if something's wrong. That's what I wanted her to say: "Is something wrong Nathan? What's the matter? Can I help you? You can talk to me, I'll listen." But no, she asked me some stupid question about my homework, I answered and went back to my desk to sleep.

Now the tears are pouring because nobody can see how much I hurt, nobody wants to help me, nobody cares, and I feel worthless! My muscles start to clench and I start to cough. I cough and cough and cough, to the point where it feels like I'm going to vomit. But I don't. A pressure seems to release after these coughing fits and I just lay there limp and flooded with tears. I calm down a bit and Valerie says, "Ask for help."

"No, I don't want to!"

"Ask."

"No, I don't want to; they should have been able to tell. They should have been able to see how much pain I was in, how hurt I was."

"Ask."

"Help me! Please help me! I need help!" And I'm back in it, full-blown crying, spasms, muscles tensing up, and coughing. It goes on like this until I remember that phone call I made.

Just a few days ago, on Mother's Day, when out of guilt more than anything, I called my mom. "Happy Mother's Day," I said. But all I heard back was how well my brother is doing. He just bought a new motorcycle, he just got a new dog, he just did this, he just did that. And I feel like shit, because my life is shit, and I can't get it together. She just keeps rubbing it in, making me feel worthless. Nothing I do is good enough. I can't do anything right; I'm such a disappointment! Here come the tears again. I realize that these present-day feelings stem from this. These memories of being neglected and manipulated all my life. But not only that, as the session winds down, my therapist tells me that she didn't think I was smoking dope, and she didn't tell the other therapists anything like that. It was all in my head! The animosity isn't real, the conspiracy isn't real, everyone against me isn't real. It was all just a feeling, me acting out a feeling. And for me that is the hardest thing to take. Realizing that my feeling's distort reality so much that I can't even tell what is real anymore, and then realizing that I have been doing that my entire life. Repeating this vicious cycle over and over and over. I think of how much time I've wasted chasing these false ideas. All the untrue things my feelings led me to believe and how it has made my life a complete mess.

But I feel relieved as the session ends, like some weight has just been lifted. And that is what makes this therapy so amazing. It is what makes these therapists so amazing. They are able to pull these things out of you, things you didn't even know were there and not only recognize them but feel them so you can change them and rebuild your life, a real life.

6

Cognitive Therapy: Why Words Won't Do It

I have written a good deal on my perspective of cognitive therapy. To avoid any injustice, we should hear from the professionals in the field who practice it.

A 1996 casebook for clinical practice discusses many aspects of cognitive therapy. A chapter on recovery maintenance by D.F. O'Connell and Henry O. Patterson points out that, like Albert Ellis's rational-emotive approach, "Several dysfunctional beliefs are identified for the patient. We offer these to patients to help them dissolve the following beliefs and help them substitute more rational ones. 'I need others approval to prove that I am worthy.' 'I am powerless to get what I want.'" They go on to say how these beliefs can be counteracted by more positive thoughts that take their place.[1]

Now why would anyone feel that way—powerless and unworthy? Is it whimsy, or is it the result of life experience? No truly loved person feels either powerless (unless they are in a given situation with the IRS) or needy of others' approval. But here again in therapy we have a good daddy or mommy who is encouraging and caring. Of course that makes a person feel better—for a time.

The authors state that substance-abusing individuals often harbor these beliefs. Once these beliefs are brought to the surface, they say that the therapist "can employ the full spectrum of cognitive interventions to challenge them and supplant them with more rational assumptions." Basically, by cognitive interventions they mean that they redirect thoughts and behavior. They replace old thoughts with new ones, but they are still thoughts.

I never assume I am more rational than my patients. Luckily, I don't have to be. Their beliefs are rational and follow their feelings, which, I remind the reader, are adaptive. They are only irrational in the present context, because neurotic ideas are defined as neurotic because the reactions are out of context. Paradoxically, it is the feeling centers of the brain that remain rational while the so-called rational thinking brain is often irrational. The drive for rationality is a survival mechanism—to see reality and deal with it as it is.

The problem is that the therapist cannot know what those feelings are without going to origins directly. The therapist's left cortex is as busy as the left cortex of the patient trying to figure out something that is hidden in the right limbic or brainstem structures. It is a guessing game, sophisticated, but a guessing game, nevertheless. The cognitivists "supplant" bad ideas with good ones. But do they supplant the terrible need for a father who died when the child was 5 years old? Or the need for a mother who abandoned the children to run off with someone else? Do they supplant the inborn terror of watching one's parents die in an auto accident? These ideas do not need supplanting. Ideas come out of a whole system, not just a neocortex.

These authors go on: "Only the present is real, the past is over, and the future is not yet here." There we have it; there is no past to contend with. The patient is ahistoric. This certainly simplifies the therapeutic task. And this, by the way, is what the new ego-psychology, the darling of the insurance companies, is about. The here-and-now is what counts and what must be discussed, and must be accomplished in very few sessions. Forget incest, orphanages, broken homes, and alcoholic mothers. These are all reflected in internal states—memories that cannot be seen directly.

The problem is that the cognitivists see reaction in terms of "mind" reaction, not as a total physiologic response. So when we are beaten by a tyrannical father throughout our childhood, is it just how we see it—the ideas we have about it? Not the reality and the terrible pain of it?

The drug addicts I have seen often have had the most horrendous early lives. I am thinking of one of my patients born on an army base where his mother killed herself just after his birth. The father was transferred, and he was then left with a cold and indifferent nanny for the first three years of his life. He effectively had no parent for that time. The father, a major, was unaffectionate. This child suffered terribly. As an adolescent and adult, he needed drugs to kill the pain; it was not a simple choice. His system drove him to maintain a balance and to try to make it in life, to function at a job. To convince this person that he does not need drugs is a double mind twist. He will stop the drugs and suffer. What is the virtue in suffering? Ah, I have asked the wrong question because religious tenets do see virtue in abnegation and suffering. Theoretically, it builds character. Suffering also builds misery.

But that is his choice, they say; "The homosexual chooses his lifestyle." I have treated more than 100 homosexuals, men and women; it is never a simple choice on their part. Indeed, if they had a choice, some would not be homosexual. Their early lives dictated it. The view that there is no reality for which we are not responsible has taken various directions. Werner Erhard and his "est" promoted this idea. The view became so insular that reality became skewed.

In this view we choose our feelings, and therefore can "unchoose" them. Feelings are essentially capricious in the cognitivists' estimation. It is tantamount to the position of the anti-Darwinists who believe there is no evolution. These therapists deny evolution and its effects both phylogenetically and ontogenetically; thus, there is no evolution of the brain. The thinking cortex is all that counts. They begin and end with that.

Therapists still function as the kindly parent, offering suggestions and ideas. The subtext is "I care about you. I want you to succeed." It is very personal. The therapist is too sophisticated to say "I love you" overtly, but his attitude conveys it very well. When a parent looks us in the eye with love, listens attentively and cares, we call that love. It is the same with a therapist. My guess is that if the patient came every day of the week, and the therapist was very concerned every day but gave no insights, the result would be the same. It is not the need for insights that drives a person into insight-based therapy; it is the need for love. Insights are the price one pays.

> *Suppression of feeling seems to activate the thinking, believing areas as a kind of defensive maneuver.*

Insights, the currency of many current brands of therapy, are a form of beliefs. They help provoke the secretion of the inhibitory neurojuices that makes us feel better by quelling indwelling pain. Because no one really knows what is in someone else's unconscious, insights have to be personal constructs—belief systems imparted by the therapist. One of the basic insights the cognitive therapists encourage patients to have is to identify what negative sentences "you are saying to yourself." The idea is to pick out the negative thoughts and then counter them with more rational thoughts. For example, in cognitive therapy, the patient is to take more credit for the good things he does. Think the good thoughts! As I stated earlier, what self is repeating negative phrases to what other self, and what does this mean? Who is convincing whom of what? The left brain must be responding to feelings on the right and trying to convince the right of the error of its ways. The right is trying to tell the left of its feelings of never being valued, always criticized and minimized, and is saying, "Nothing I do is worth anything."

"Nonsense," says the left. "You are just indulging in negative thinking. I will help you change those thoughts to something more positive."

"Not so fast," claims the right side. "I am just doing the bidding of my feelings. I am not being irrational; on the contrary, I am responding realistically to those feelings that you cannot even see. It is you who are being irrational. You want me to deny my inner truth. I can't do that in good conscience. Speaking of conscience: I will leave it to you to perform that function. I've got impulses to deal with."

The right goes on addressing the left: "You see, I am a good deal older than you, and I know more about what's going on inside. I am bound by our feelings. I mean, they are ours, you know. I have no choice. I've got attachments and commitments I've made that I can't leave. You think you have a choice because you have more freedom to wander the intellectual landscape, but you don't. Your freedom is illusory; I control the game. Even though I can't solve problems as you can, eventually, I am going to prevail. I run your life. You're aware of all that stuff outside in the world but you haven't a clue about what I have to deal with all of the time. When you open yourself up to me, we can both relax. We need to be together more often. Will you agree if I tell you the truth little by little?"

There is now experimental evidence for how repressed feelings leak their energy to the orbitofrontal cortex (OBFC), resulting in all sorts of beliefs and strange ideas.[2] In an experiment where feelings were stimulated and the subject was then asked to hold down the feeling, the output of the amygdala was diminished almost completely while the activity in the left OBFC increased considerably. In short, suppression of feeling seems to activate the thinking and believing areas as a kind of defensive maneuver. Almost every defensive maneuver is designed to protect consciousness. That means that we do not want to become too consciously aware when pain lurks. It has to be achieved in slow increments; that is why rebirthing or the use of hallucinogenic drugs is so dangerous. There is no such thing as a weekend enlightenment where a new kind of consciousness can be achieved.

Now we see how someone can give up booze and drugs and find God. Feelings start their rise, and ideas take over to set in motion our inner drug factory. If the addict is lectured about the evil of drugs, activity in the amygdala goes down while at the same time activity in the OBFC goes up, responding to the words and beliefs of the lecturer. So ideas take over from feelings and aid in repression. It is a sine qua non that if one wants to give up addiction, one must adopt a set of beliefs that will form another addiction just as tenacious, which will boost internal painkillers. It is not that one is giving up a drug for ideas; it is that one is giving up an external drug for the very same internal one.

What this experiment and our clinical observations point to is that energy from below can reach the prefrontal area of the brain and drive obsessions, a racing mind that can't sleep, constant worry, or fervent beliefs. The pressure has to go somewhere, and if we block it in the limbic system, it will go to the next evolutionary stage—the prefrontal cortex. It is like a river that is blocked in one outlet that is forced to seek yet another. Defenses form a hierarchy; first-line pains can be blocked by the limbic system with its images, and then blocked on higher levels with ideas, beliefs, and concepts. Each level has its own gating system, but when it falters, higher level gating takes over.

What Are the Cognitivists Really Doing?

David Burns, M.D., is a well-known writer and practitioner of cognitive therapy. In his mass-market bestseller *Feeling Good: The New Mood Therapy*, and in other books, he explains the leitmotif of this approach in a nutshell. To paraphrase: Number 1: You feel the way you think; you will discover that negative feelings like depression, anxiety, and anger do not actually result from the bad things that happen to you but from the way you think about these events. Number 2: Most bad feelings come from illogical thoughts. Number 3: You can change the way you feel by changing the way you think.[3]

Basically, there is no reality; there is just what you think is reality. Reality is whatever you make it. It is all a matter of interpretation. Change the interpretation and ergo, all will be well. This, at bottom, is the essence of all cognitive therapy, including insight therapy. The cognitivists want the patient to respond to reality when she already is. It just cannot be seen.

On the back of one of his books, Burns is quoted as saying: "You can enjoy greater happiness, productivity, and intimacy without drugs or lengthy therapy." He says this because he's never seen the pain in all its early manifestations, including incest. He calls these "negative feelings" when they're real feelings. We must get over the notion of "negative" feelings. Our feelings correspond to key realities; they are neither negative nor positive. They are what they are. The key is to join the so-called negative attitudes to the original context that gave them life, not to deny and change them.

> *It is no more logical to think that ideas can change instincts, a survival system, than to believe a simple change in ideas can alter feelings, yet another survival system.*

A child who is unloved early in life will have an embedded feeling: "There is something wrong with me." This is a recurrent theme among most of my patients. She doesn't know that she is unloved; having never been hugged and kissed from the start of life, she doesn't know that she is missing something. She doesn't choose to feel or think that way; she is reflecting reality on an unconscious feeling level. (In our therapy, it remains a mystery—until one day she feels, "They don't love me.") As she grows older, she has a nagging feeling that something is wrong or that something is wrong with her. She goes to cognitive therapy to have her ideas rearranged; she is helped to look on the bright side, believing that those "negative" thoughts are dragging her down.

Therapists can dress this up, but it is still the "power of positive thinking." It is YMCA counseling writ in scientific patois. It is, "Put a smile on your face and you will feel happier." As simplistic as that sounds, it is essentially what behavior and cognitive therapies are about: behavior changes feelings, as opposed to feelings driving behavior.

Yes, the cognitivists can try to help patients develop a more positive attitude, but the patient's whole system may well be enmeshed in a pessimistic one, ingrained from birth—an engraved physiology of pessimism. The worst *did* happen early on, and expecting the worst is a natural attitude given that history. Nevertheless, even temporary help and encouragement in the face of catastrophic illness can be helpful. And if the sufferers meet once a week to help each other, all the better. Nonetheless, pessimism is not just an attitude; it is a physiologic state that churns out attitudes. We can try to change it with support in the present, but that effort has to be kept up continuously. If we can get that support, we can function, at least. It is helpful in the most human sense. But we are fighting against events during the critical period. That is why efforts have to be continual. Once an event is sealed in during the critical period, resulting in an imprint, change is unlikely.

Remember, we feel long before we have ideas. Feelings precede ideas in evolution and the structure of the brain. It is no more logical to think that ideas can change instincts, a survival system, than to believe a simple change in ideas can alter feelings, yet another survival system. It has to be automatic and immediate to help us adapt and avoid danger. Yes, it is possible temporarily to override feelings, but it cannot be a permanent condition. And it can in fact be dangerous and threaten survival. We can neglect the signs of a coming heart attack or stroke, and there are often signs, telling us that there is nothing wrong with us, but that will certainly not prevent the catastrophe.

There is a book called *The Blank Slate* by Steven Pinker.[4] Dr. Pinker is a well-known writer on matters of the brain. His specialty is cognitive neuroscience. ("Cognitive neuroscience" seems to be one more oxymoron. If neuroscience limits itself to the study of the thinking brain, the rest of the central nervous system and its interrelationships with the thinking area are likely to be ignored.) Pinker claims throughout his work that nurture, the environment, is never a match for nature—what we inherit. He points out that criminals are rarely rehabilitated, which is proof, he believes, that criminal tendencies must be inherited. What he does not consider is first, the impact of early life shaping future criminals, and second, that perhaps our treatment of criminals is what is wrong, particularly when he is an advocate of the cognitive approach, which is bound to fail with criminals. The logic then continues: because we cannot make the criminal well, it must be because it is an inherited tendency. Naturally, this reasoning doesn't put his therapeutic approach into question. Few, if any, professionals have seen the depths of the unconscious and observed the pain imprinted there. Therefore, they cannot know what nurture really is and what it can do *to* us. This is doubly true when the months of gestation and the first months of infancy are ignored. Because there is hardly any cognition going on, to speak of, in the first three years of life, when cognition is the focus, one is bound to ignore the most crucial formative times in life.

Ideas are fabricated to shield us from feelings such as, "My mother was never there for me." The feeling could be rationalized, "She had so much to do." But the need/pain remains. The result is, "I do not matter." If we want to know about so-called "self-esteem," we can find it here. The mother did have a great deal to do, but for a child it is devastating. When this occurs, the mother's ideas impressed into her child's neocortex never change the child's feelings or needs. "She had so much to do" now covers the need. I have never heard a patient cry about "esteem." That is someone else's idea about us, not a proper feeling. It is strange: we can feel unimportant (unloved) but not important. If we were important to our parents, we will feel solid, good, and capable but not important because that is not a feeling; it is someone else's idea of who and what we are.

What Albert Ellis in rational emotive therapy told his patients was, in effect, "Who says it's important that you must always be loved? You constantly say to yourself, 'I need love, I need love.' Instead you need to repeat a different phrase over and over again. 'No, I cannot be loved by everybody all the time, I don't really need love like that.'" He believes that we are adults now, not children, and we still act toward others to get them to love us. I believe we do. But it's not the sentences we say; it is the leftover needs from childhood—the desperate unfulfilled need for love. We act out that need every day in every way, and it will not go away until we feel how much we needed love. We may grow old, but our feelings never do. Even when we deny that we need love, the act-out may go on.

The problem with any scientific data is the criteria that it is based on. If I give up drinking for six months, and that is a criterion of progress in the treatment of drug addiction, am I well? It may be a first step, but it is not being well. There is a whole neurophysiologic system behind that behavior. The results of research can be altered depending on the criteria one uses. Even if the addict is off his drug for five years, is he well? It doesn't matter how long he is off if he hasn't resolved the driving forces. He is in a holding pattern, waiting for his next fall. He will fall, perhaps, because his need has never changed and has never been experienced; the need that drives him to seek painkillers. It is people in pain who need painkillers, as obvious as that may seem. It is hard to believe that something that happened at birth can drive the impulse to drink at age 30, but it is so. It is the best-kept secret in the 12-step approaches. It is a mutually unconscious pact; none of us will attest to the effects of birth; therefore, it is a non-event. If we acknowledge the imprint, we know that experience is lodged throughout our systems, and that results in any therapy must also be couched in systemic terms. Yes, it is very important to stop drugs, but that leaves the person filled with pain; that need must be addressed.

Cognitive therapy is massive distraction. The patient sometimes feels better, even oft times feels better, but self-deception is not therapy; it is brainwashing. Denial is a nice, temporary expedient; it makes life tolerable, but the price can be heavy later on—possibly premature death or early disease and a return to symptoms. Still, it works for some when the pain is not too much. There are levels of pain; those on the deepest levels of the nervous system register the highest valence. For instance, we may see a fever of 103 degrees (F) just before entering a feeling. The system treats the imprint as a foreign invader just like a virus. All systems are engaged in the battle against feeling. The battle is against it entering conscious-awareness, believe it or not. One way we know is the radical drop in body temperature right after the connected feeling.

The *Los Angeles Times* ran a report in its Health section on cognitive psychologist Martin Seligman.[5] Seligman purports to provide a blueprint to "make ourselves happier." To do this, he believes, we need to know "how to mind our thoughts, moment to moment. And how to forget ourselves altogether." He suggests that we counter catastrophic thoughts, first by recognizing the despairing idea and then by checking it against real evidence. The despair is taken as a given (from where, no one knows), and then the cognitivists offer techniques to counter those thoughts. "By arguing with yourself, you can separate beliefs from facts, defusing many pessimistic assumptions by editing them according to logic and evidence." I believe that the hallmark of neurosis is "forgetting ourselves altogether." Seligman then cites studies showing that depressed people who learn to recognize and disarm this kind of reflexive pessimism can free themselves from feelings of worthlessness, fatigue, and other symptoms. They are no longer depressed, he claims. They have pulled themselves out of their depths. The idea, basically, is that we argue ourselves out of the pessimism by looking at evidence. But we look at internal evidence and are necessarily pessimistic in terms of our history.

Modern-day cognitivists have seemingly taken over from the church; their admonitions are the same. The only difference is that it is called therapy, not religion. But it is religion in the name of therapy. In fact, the real therapy is not to pull individuals out of the depths but to plunge into them, where the basis for depression lies. They will never know how good life can be once they rid themselves of their deep pain.

Today's therapy essentially says: "Look on the bright side of things," or, "Just get over it." It is what our parents told us as kids: "Stop complaining and get on with it. Don't always look on the gloomy side. There is a positive side to everything. Getting mired in pessimism will make you sick. Let sleeping dogs lie." Cognitivism/insight is a popular therapy because it isn't therapy; it is an agglomeration of homilies tied together in sophisticated language. It fits the zeitgeist perfectly.

The problem with psychotherapy to date has been that it was the psychology of behavior and not feelings. If a therapist saw someone who had been in a concentration camp who was adapting very well, that was good enough; a sign of doing well. If we now change psychotherapy to a true neurobiological science, which it must be, then we will not make that kind of mistake and miscalculation again. We will look to see the level of cortisol, oxytocin, dopamine, noradrenaline, and so on; in other words, we will look at the whole person, not just at a disembodied mind that acts and thinks.

The key phrase here, as in all insight therapies, is to become "aware of feelings." Then they supposedly change. We have seen that they don't and shouldn't. "Aware" and feelings lie on different cerebral planets. But the leitmotif of every intellectual therapy is that awareness helps us make progress. I'll grant that awareness helps; but being consciously aware cures.

It is no accident that in our various brain research studies there was a shift in laterality in the brains of our patients; the brain was more harmonious, sharing the burden of feeling equally on both sides of the brain. Cognitive therapy produces a lopsided, left-dominant brain. We are after a balanced one.

The ideal in cognitive therapy is to control thoughts in order to achieve that elusive "wholesome state."

Another cognitive technique is to help the patient understand and forgive his parents. "After all, your parents did the best they could. They had a pretty tough childhood too." "Oh yes, I understand. They did have it tough and I do forgive" comes forth from the left side. Still, of course, the right side is crying out its needs and its pain, and will go on with its silent scream for the rest of our lives. There is no way around need. "Forgiveness" is an idea that has no place in therapy. We are not here to pardon parents; we are here to address the needs of patients, and what the lack of fulfillment did to them.

I regret to say that much of current therapy and particularly cognitive therapy is about a moral position; well hidden, couched in psychological jargon, but, at bottom, moralizing. The therapist becomes the arbiter of correct behavior. After all, the therapist is trying to change the patient's behavior toward some preconceived goal. That goal has a sequestered moral position: you shouldn't take drugs, yell at your wife, eat too much, hold a grudge against your parents, and so on. We'll help you change that. Cognitive therapy means, in essence, thought control. This may seem like an exaggeration, but consider that our thoughts cannot be trusted. Others tell us how to think. "They" know better. I think the same applies to the human state. Thought control (or whatever euphemism we attach to it is a totalitarian notion) is suppressive of basic need in deference to an idea or ideal. The ideal in cognitive therapy is to control thoughts in order to achieve that elusive "wholesome state." Whenever need is left out of the theoretical scheme, whether of the State or the individual, the answer must be reactionary. The person is forced into compensatory behaviors, just as society must build new hospitals and prisons to control those whose needs get out of control. Both therapy and the fascist state must seek to control the outburst of needs rather than fulfilling it. It is always dangerous to tell people what to think. And it is useless to tell them how to feel.

Thought control works in subtle ways in the family. A young boy misses and needs his daddy. He is told that daddy has to work and be gone most of the time. The boy understands, and gets a bit of "love," or at least approval for understanding. He gets what passes for love, an idea, but no real love. The boy no longer "misses and needs" his daddy. He has been told how to think, albeit quite subtly. Later, when he is asked as a grown-up if he was loved, he will say, "Yes. They did the best they could. My father had to feed his kids." Need is lost, and with it part of one's humanity. The crime is doubled when the now adult goes to therapy and is again given the rationale, "They did the best they could." Or worse, in the case of Albert Ellis, "Who says you need love, anyway?" This is in effect saying, "Give up on love. You don't need it." How could anyone deprived for years by parents do that? We cannot give up on need. It is hard-wired and a matter of survival. Yes, the need is back then in childhood, but let us never forget the imprint. Need that is not fulfilled during the critical period endures.

> *Whenever need is left out of the theoretical scheme, whether of the State or the individual, the answer must be reactionary.*

Thought control is a way of forcing the patient to lead the life of the therapist. For example, telling a patient he doesn't need drugs when his whole body cries out for it, driven by pains sequestered far below recognition. Or to try to dissuade someone from shoplifting as a bad habit when she has always had to work for love and approval from parents and now wants something for nothing. "Love me no matter what. Don't make me fight for every scrap of love." Of course, it is not to be approved of, but we need to know the dynamics behind it. Why won't ideas and dissuasion work against shoplifting when the person risks jail every time? Because knowing about risk and being aware of the danger, are never a match for old needs.

Therapists cannot bestow truths on other human beings. There are precise truths for each of us. Each truth can only be discovered by the patient. The idea that any symbol, as in dream analysis, has a universal meaning is untrue. Patients may have very similar dreams with quite disparate meanings, depending on their life experiences. Patients must communicate with their pasts, not with the therapist, or at least secondarily with the therapist. They must first confront themselves.

Let me give an example. A magazine story recalls someone who had a "conversion experience." He reported that during the night he woke up with a great pressure on his chest, a little man was sitting on his chest strangling him and he could not get his breath. He pinned his arms in front of him and tied his legs together. He knew at that moment that he was visited by an alien force. Let's put all that in its proper context; during birth there was a lack of oxygen and sense of strangling with the accompanying pressure on the chest. The arms were pinned in the fetal position and the legs were locked as they are in a birth Primal. The sense was alien, so it was then projected as an alien force—aliens. No therapist can interpret that experience. We would not even know where to begin.

I must hasten to add a caveat here. Nearly every cognitive/insight talk therapy fills the needs of the patient symbolically. The patient is acting neurotically in the hope of getting well. She is being a good, smart, helpful patient. The therapist is focusing only on her. How long has it been since someone paid exclusive attention to her? And for an hour! Is it any wonder that her therapy is addicting; the insights are a small adjunct to it all. The attention is preponderant. I point out elsewhere that the choice of the therapy is often another act-out. The patient is going back for love, caring, and approval. She gets it and it is another symbolic act, and therefore her neurosis is reinforced. The therapist gives us exactly what we needed from our parents; it is, unfortunately, 20 or 30 years too late. It is a bottomless pit that no one can fill.

Insight therapies are an outgrowth of old-time religion, with the preacher telling us about our lurking evil and how we must avoid it. We learn from therapists how to think in trying to understand ourselves. We become obedient novitiates. It is the parent again, a benevolent one, telling us kids what is wrong with us and how we should behave. And we listen because we are "good" children and want to be loved. And they are the authority, the kind, gentle authority, but they carry the power. They really want us to be good children, thinking good thoughts.

Misery is a state of being. The job of therapy ought not to be finding the right words to make us feel comfortable, but finding the right feelings that make us feel our misery—so that we can be done with it. Anytime the power of therapy resides outside ourselves, it cannot succeed. Guidance yes. Counseling yes. But not deep therapy. The price we pay for relinquishing inner power to others is more smoking, drinking, and tranquilizers, because the body knows it should be leading its own life and not someone else's. So, yes, we may get off drugs for a time, or even permanently, because our doctors insist on it, but our needs haven't changed.

Leaving Biology Behind: Escaping Into the Psychological Wilderness

From a neuroscience viewpoint, the problem with cognitive therapies is that they move the patients so far into the left frontal area that they are effectively sealed away from their truths and their feelings. The whole thrust is to move the patient away from her history, enlarge the split, and disrupt harmony in the brain. No wonder they report feeling better; no wonder the client in eye movement desensitization response (EMDR) reports feeling good.

EMDR is a therapy that combines a bit of voodoo with some insight, and a very elaborate explanatory system. Basically, it involves alternating input from one side of the brain to the other. One rationale is that it stimulates both feeling and ideational hemispheres and produces a neurologic balance. Patients say that after a session, the pain is but a distant memory, something they feel alienated from. That means, implicitly, that they are alienated from themselves, the selves where feelings lie. EMDR reinforces repression. That is not mental health; it is deception in the name of mental health, the left hemisphere turning mental handsprings to convince itself that the right/limbic forces do not exist. If one ignores history, every approach is an illusion.

Directed daydreaming or imagining therapy is another approach that relies on words, suggestions, and images. You can imagine you are relaxed, floating on a cloud all day long, and still have anxiety churning down below. But we are not on a cloud and not relaxed, except in our frontal cortex. It is not reality. How can we get well based on unreality? Our body is saying we are in hell, and our mind is saying we are floating on a cloud. It is a consciously willful, deceitful (self-deceptive) act under the direction of someone else under the guise of therapy. Instead, our head should be where our feelings are.

There was a study some time ago by Nicholas Hall of the George Washington University Medical Center on directed daydreaming. He used positive images to change the patients' immune systems and the symptoms of asthma. Sometimes the image suggested to the patient was "little men with hammers pounding on the cancer cells." The lymphocytes were elevated for a short time, but then returned to their previous level. Words were helpful for a time, but the system fought back and returned to its neurosis again with a decline in the number of circulating lymphocytes. The problem usually is that when the imaging stops, the white cell count (and the hormone thymosin, in this case) plummets.

I sometimes describe cancer as a betrayal—our body becomes our enemy. I can't help thinking that when feelings are alienated they can become the enemy. They then do us harm—by inadvertence. While not exactly on the subject, allow one more pure speculation. I have lost several friends over the past years, and in most of the cases of cerebral stroke, it has been my observation that it is those repressed individuals who fled to their heads who succumbed to stroke. It seems as though the left brain was shouldering too much of the burden of holding back feelings. At a certain point, the brain was overwhelmed and crumbled. After all, if the right brain is sending leftward great pressure it is likely that the left will falter. How much pressure? If one could see my patients, who are not especially sicker than the average population, cry for months and months in the deepest fashion possible, week after week, we can just begin to get an idea of the tremendous pressure that lies inside so many of us.

Imagining therapy, whatever the name, is a mind game directed curiously away from internal reality. It is EMDR under another name: distraction. Directed daydreaming using the frontal cortex and limbic images may temporarily override a symptom such as obsessions and anxiety, but it is neither going to last nor get us down to the brainstem where birth trauma and the origins of anxiety lie. The story we make up in a dream or in a sexual ritual is but a cover for real feelings; that is why we get patients to act out in group, using their ritual to reach their feelings. The meaning of the dream and/or ritual lies in the feeling, as it does in life. A dream of being stuck in a confined space may be a direct image out of a feeling of being stuck at birth; a feeling compounded by a family life where the child feels trapped and "stuck." Individuals can act out feeling stuck (in a marriage, relationship, or job) by trying to cut free. But no matter what happens, how many times one leaves a relationship, there will never be the feeling of being free.

Constantly being on the move is a good example of this act-out; a mad flight from the feeling, just as others who feel as if they are failures are in a desperate search to try to feel like a winner. As I have noted, the definition of an act-out is behaving out of unfulfilled needs. Unfulfilled needs start the accelerator going. Even in depression, which looks like total lethargy and passivity, there is a highly active system.

Remember, the later developing cortical neurons are designed not to tell us the truth of our inner life, a truth buried with our history. I don't doubt it is possible to imagine that the elevator is not a fearful space but a place of calm and peace, of floating on a lake. But meanwhile the brainstem is saying about the elevator, "That is a terrifying space because it provokes the old fear in the incubator." We have therefore widened the gap between thinking and feeling, which is an act that can never be curative.

Freud ascribed to the id some kind of deep, immutable, perhaps genetic force because he never saw what could happen to us early on. He thought "early" meant infancy, and most current-day therapists think the same. So the Freudians, myself included decades ago, thought that the patient could remember his childhood, cry about it, be given insights by us omniscient souls, and all would be well. The danger really was from what the patient could not recall.

In Primal Therapy, she would remember, however. The difference is that while there is no verbal recall of early trauma and deprivation, the body will remember in its posture, facial set, chronic cough, and constant fears. We need to match memory with the whole organic state. It cannot be done when the patient is sitting up in a well-lit room discussing matters objectively. There are many memory systems, not the least of which is our immune system, which "remembers" a vaccination for decades.

We can see, therefore, that anything that calls itself cognitive therapy is confining, to say the least. Make no mistake, I consider psychoanalysis a cognitive approach, sprinkled with a few tears to differentiate it from other approaches. It is still about insight and ideas. *Discussing* a patient's past is using a level of the brain of the patient that was not present at the time to discern what was going on. That brain is a stranger. It can only guess about what is inside in the unconscious, and anybody's guess is equally valid. A guess by a therapist made out of some ancient theory is, at best, invalid. But it may have the sound, the authenticity, of a well-constructed theory and therefore can be believable.

I spent a long time in my psychoanalytic days analyzing dreams. It was a nice intellectual game, but I never saw any progress from it. The analysis of dreams turns evolution on its head. It is using a late-developing frontal neocortex to figure out what feelings are hidden in the limbic system—the system that fabricates the images in a dream. In the case of Eva, there was a very early terror imprinted that intruded into her life and into her dreams. Eva's dreams were often filled with images of pain. In her dreams she felt hurt, lonely, isolated, and without help. That stratum of hurt lay just below the thought level. Finding and feeling the source of the terror gave meaning to the dream. To follow evolution we need to speak the limbic language, sink into the feelings of the dream, which are always exact, and the meaning will arrive all by itself out of those feelings. Verbal and feeling languages are universes apart. The meanings of dream images are direct offshoots from the feeling itself, which may reside very deep in the brain. Dreams have no universal meanings, only personal ones. The only person who knows what a dream means is that person.

I practiced Freudian insight therapy for my first 17 years in practice and always had to guess what was in the patient's brain. The guess was always based on received knowledge—received from theories that are now more than 100 years old. That is no longer necessary.

Helping Patients Get Where They Need to Go

Phobia of an elevator offers a good example of how memory works—and how memory ultimately is the key to healing. We enter into an enclosed space. We feel anxious. We have no thoughts or memories about why but we are very nervous. But the lower brain "remembers" when, for instance, we were placed in an incubator right after birth. Otherwise why would we suddenly be nervous? It is clear here because the fear is specific, confined, and well circumscribed. Generally, in anxiety we are not so lucky. The fear is widespread and is not focused on any one thing. But a circumstance alone, such as an elevator or a cave, can set off a memory and terror with no recall whatsoever. It is a body memory. If, rather than try to argue the phobia away with reasoning, or to condition it away through a behavioral approach, the patient submits and is immersed in that fear, we can track it down to its origins. It is a process of total immersion. Or, in general anxiety, using specific techniques, we help the patient down into the physiologic terror and then to its imprint. It means giving in to the sensation.

We try hard in our therapy to make the patient the font of knowledge. It is the job of a Primal therapist to search out historical reality, wherever it may lead. The therapist is a catalyst who follows the patient and helps lead him where he needs to go. It means not having preconceived ideas of what feelings the patient must feel, nor preconceived insights.

I perhaps minimize the role of the therapist in Primal Therapy because, after all, it takes six years of training to learn the techniques we use. Even advanced Primal therapists attend training sessions every week. And our training is based on an inalterable equation: the amount of access and empathy we have with others is a direct result of the amount of internal access we have. The closer we are to ourselves, the closer we can be to others and feel for them. The more we feel, the more we can sense the feelings inside our patients. But in our therapy, the power rightly belongs to the patient, not to some omniscient, paternal therapist. We do not want to rob the patient of her curiosity and discoveries. Everything she has to discover is already inside waiting to be liberated.

The left prefrontal cortex can reflect on what happened to us early in childhood, but it hasn't the power to dredge up feelings. Moreover, insight must always come from the patient, not the doctor, and must follow the development of the patient's brain: first line first, second line second, and third line connection and insight last. Insights must come out of the right brain, and one of the ways we see it is the effortless flow of ideas after a patient has a feeling. This is not apparent in cognitive therapy. We can see in the cognitive/analytic patient's face his cogitation as he tries to develop a certain insight out of the left brain. By contrast, there doesn't seem to be any thought processes going on in patients who have just come out of a feeling in a Primal session. Their insights have such a ring of truth about them, and then the patient will say, "That's why I did this." Once feelings are retrieved, the thinking cortex can add its bit of brilliance to the feeling and can look back to see how that unconscious feeling produced which neurotic behavior and what symptoms. Her lifetime behavior is explained. I think it may be another one of those biologic laws: if we have to think about an insight, it is not a true insight. If we don't, it is. The insight has to hit us from below, an "Aha!" experience. I think that the essential difference between our approach and cognitive is that they want to get the patient's "head on straight," and we want to give them back their lives. That means feelings, which is the essence of life.

> *Insight must always come from the patient, not the doctor, and must follow the development of her brain: first line first, second line second, and third line connection and insight last.*

One of our patients felt her mother's screams at her, day after day, and what it did to her. She came out of the feeling with, "No one who screams like that could love you." She then plunged again into the feeling of being unloved and how she desperately tried to please everyone to keep them from screaming at her. She even forgot about trying to get love. She spent her life avoiding screams and anger. She gave in during any confrontation. She was so beaten down she gave up trying even in school. Simple yet profound. Her behavior was timid, hesitant, and meek. All to avoid parental screams, yet that behavior and those fears continued into adulthood.

In cognitive therapy she could have been encouraged to have more positive thoughts, to try in school, and to assert herself, but all that would have been a vain battle against powerful forces in her history. She was trying desperately to keep those screams away; those screams were inside her. During a Primal, the patient hears those angry tones or screams again with all of their intensity and shrillness. This is partly because the rationalizing, filtering frontal cortex is temporarily out of commission. The truth is that the patient actually is responding to those screams all of the time in her timidity, her lack of aggression, and her diffidence. The limbic system is hearing them all of the time. She is anticipating a response that is already alive inside of her—those screams.

Earlier I mentioned the importance of tears in therapy. When terrible things have happened to us, we need to cry to start the healing process in motion. We need to think about this because tears, copious amounts of tears, manage to raise the human growth hormone levels, as shown in the research of neurobiologists David Goodman and Morton Sobel. Growth hormone plays an important role in the healing process. Goodman and Sobel did research some 25 years ago on our therapy and found correlations of improvement with the depth of crying. Children are fast healers because they weep as soon as they are hurt. The problem is that too often that crying is stopped, either because there is no one to cry to or because it aggravates the parent. This may also happen in adulthood, such as when we block a patient's weeping reflex with tranquilizers.

We know that it is not we, the therapists, who decide the depth of crying. It is the memory that dictates; we just let it happen. We produce the silent, padded room and the techniques where it can take place. We do help make it as soft a landing as possible. I want to reiterate that the crying that occurs in insight therapy and the deep sobbing and weeping we see in Primal Therapy are moons apart. Crying in insight therapy seems to be prefrontal left cortex with a touch of the right, while what occurs in Primal Therapy is a total immersion process in the right.

The tears released from the lower levels of the brain are very different from and far more powerful than tears when a patient "cries about"—that is, cries from the cortex down, as an adult observing his childhood. It's as if some stranger saw some tragedy and cried about it. That stranger is the left prefrontal cortex. Once disconnected it could belong to anyone. It is that neocortex observing the hurt child and empathizing with him but not fully feeling his pain. The left frontal cortex cannot fully comprehend what that child is feeling inside until the right side feels what that child was feeling at the time. It then must inform the left with its passion, a passion that eludes the left side. It is one of many ways we know that the lower level imprints are still intact. I have experimented over many years with trying to get patients to duplicate their cries of 15 minutes earlier in a session. They never can. It is like waking up out of a dream and trying to get back into the dream. Not easily done because the experiences are on different levels of the brain.

Is There a Place for Cognitive and Other Insight Therapies?

I do believe in help for those with transient problems. There are many people who are lost, who don't know what direction to take for a profession, for example, and they can certainly benefit from discussion and guidance. Certainly, both marital and child counseling can be most helpful. There are those with transient depressions who just need to talk to someone. But we must not mistake a profound problem as something that would be amenable to counseling. The confusion comes when we think that those ideas exist in some isolated, insular world. When cognitive therapists treat depression as something about wrong ideas, they do not see the long fibers from the depths of the brain reaching up from the brainstem to shape current attitudes and moods. They do not see the memory of early lack of love and traumas stored in pristine, crystal form, cloistered together behind a barrier of neuroinhibitors, terrified of leaving the cloister and venturing into a world of awareness, unchanged despite all of our later experience. They do not see desperate need pleading for fulfillment and the agony of the lack of that fulfillment. What a strange thing the imprint is. It is impervious to experience. Even shock therapy cannot erase it. It is not strange that someone has a heart attack while living comfortably in the mountains. His experience is not one of calm. It is the internal anxiety that won't let him rest. The imprint is the central experience he responds to continuously.

Not everyone needs heavy surgery, but for those who do, they must be careful not to use small bandages when serious therapy is necessary.

Case Study: Daryl—Three Non-Feeling Therapies

In cognitive behavioral therapy, the therapist focused almost exclusively on asking me to "change my negative thoughts" to more positive thoughts. For example, I was feeling very negative toward myself at the time this therapy occurred, and I would find this kind of self-talk happening within myself: "I'm a failure in my career." The therapist would ask me to "re-word" this statement to myself to say, "I'm not succeeding in my career at the present time." Well, this did not help at all. In fact, I simply got all jumbled in a lot of mechanistic ways of trying to handle internal problems that only ended in frustration and discouragement.

Another key approach of this cognitive behavioral therapist was to present me with a list of 12 "should" statements that people tend to use. Then, she would ask me to repeat the statement without using the word "should." For example, one of the original statements might have been, "I should be more competent." She would ask me to re-phrase this to say, "I am competent." Of course, this did not help at all because I did not, in fact, become any more competent by simply saying, "I am competent." Much of her approach revolved around convincing me of the irrationality of my behavior in using "should" statements. To a great extent, she provided me with a list of rules and asked me to obey those rules. This approach completely ignored the feelings below the surface that were driving me to feel what I felt and, therefore, to say what I would say. Her approach did not take into account the principle of repression.

This therapist became very frustrated working with me. In fact, she discounted and denied the role of feelings in the therapeutic process. I reacted to her approach by being frustrated, discouraged, and disillusioned because her approach did not work for me.

In Jungian therapy, the therapist introduced me to the classical concepts within Jungian psychology: archetypes, anima, animus, collective unconscious, persona, shadow, active imagination, guided imagery, the Self, and interpretation of dreams. He also tried to stay within the classical Jungian psychological model in his therapeutic approach with me. He was a very intellectual person himself, and my gaining an understanding of these primary concepts was important to him. Therefore, he spent a lot of time with me in simply helping me to understand all of these Jungian terms and concepts. He did acknowledge and recognize the principle of repression, and he said that those things that have been repressed are now in "your shadow." His whole approach resulted in one prerequisite to healing on the part of the patient: the patient must have an understanding of these terms, concepts, and principles. His premise was simple: once the patient gains an understanding of her/his problem and these Jungian concepts, healing will naturally occur. So, understanding automatically brings healing.

But, in my case, understanding did not bring healing. Understanding brought mental gymnastics. The process of gaining an intellectual understanding brought a false illusion of healing. I frequently said to myself, "Now that I have an intellectual (intelligent) understanding of what the problems are within me, I will be cured. I had this belief over and over, but it never did bring about true healing. Instead, it brought about a temporary false sense of confidence that "now I've got the problem nailed down, I will be okay."

The Jungian approach helped only temporarily and then, only slightly. However, each time I came to understand the problem, I truly thought that I would be cured. It never happened. As a result I became discouraged and disillusioned. In fact, the process of intellectualizing actually slowed down the healing process in that it covered over the real feelings that needed to be felt.

In Gestalt therapy, the therapist gave an initial impression that feelings would play a primary role in my therapy. In fact, they never did. Gestalt therapy, for me, ended up somewhere in between cognitive behavioral and Jungian therapy. My Gestalt therapist made use of role playing as a way of trying to help me gain insights into my behavior. At times, she would say, "I want you to play your father and use this scenario." At other times, she would ask me to play the role of the boss with whom I was having difficulty at that particular time. In all cases, the role-playing scenarios did nothing to bring about healing. The therapist was very impressed with her approach and what she thought was happening, but I was not experiencing anything significant in terms of real progress. Therefore, over a period of six months to a year, I became discouraged and disillusioned with the process. In fact, I lost confidence in this particular approach as well as in the therapist. She sensed my frustration and this caused friction in our relationship. Eventually, I discontinued my therapy with this therapist.

In conclusion, let me comment on what I see as the need for patients to evaluate and provide feedback to the therapist. It would be so simple for therapists of all psychological approaches to develop an evaluation/feedback form in order to seek feedback on how the therapeutic process is going. What the therapist thinks is occurring might not be the case at all.

7

The Prototype: What Makes Us Who We Are

If we understand how the brain formed during its evolution, we know that the sympathetic, alerting system was first to develop. It accounts for the rapid development of the nervous system, which warns of danger and must function at optimum levels early on. The parasympathetic inhibitory system, which helps control evolution of the brain and our feelings, developed later. The parasympathetic is a slower-acting system. The sympathetic-parasympathetic (*sympath* and *parasympath*, as I have noted) are compensating systems for each other; they are in balance when we are well connected to our feelings. They are governed by the hypothalamus, in large part by the right hypothalamus. The parasympathetic system, more lethargic and slower to arouse, takes more input to get it going. It helps uncouple sympathetic activation so that our breathing returns to normal, as does blood pressure, body temperature, bladder function, and digestion.

Parasympaths and Sympaths

The importance of this balance is that when we are skewed heavily to one side or the other, we can almost be sure that later on there will be some serious affliction. There are some kinds of cancer that are more sympathetically dominant that rise out of sympathetically dominant systems. Others take a certain form as a result of parasympathetic dominance. It is my experience that migraine sufferers are often parasympaths. A loss of oxygen during birth can affect the blood circulation system, resulting in migraines later on. The anoxia is accompanied by helplessness in the primal imprint so that in a current situation that is fairly helpless, the person will develop a migraine; that is, the current helplessness will resonate with that of birth so that the blood circulation system will again be affected (massive dilation and then vasoconstriction). All this happens on an unconscious level, making the symptom and its appearance a mystery.

To save itself, the baby's system slows down and goes lifeless. The physiologic necessity becomes hardwired. The result is that the person becomes resigned to his fate. The prototypic personality—passivity—becomes a personality characteristic that remains in place throughout our lives. It is literally "in our bones," our blood system, and our muscles.

The imprint can determine how we function sexually as adults. The parasympathetic individual doesn't have the biochemical equipment to be sexually erect, tenacious, aggressive, assertive, optimistic, or future oriented. This is because the nervous system mode has a global effect on his entire physiological system. His whole system may veer toward less testosterone, dopamine, glutamate, and noradrenaline (hence, less assertiveness); lower serotonin; and higher cortisol. Almost as an underline of this point there is a report by Rudolf Wu, director of the Center for Coastal Pollution and Conservation at the City University of Hong Kong found that newborn male zebra fish outnumber females by three to one when oxygen levels are reduced in their water. The few females that do get born tend to have inordinate levels of testosterone in their bodies. Wu notes that hypoxia (diminished oxygen) may affect sex determination and development.[1]

This can also happen if the mother takes painkillers during her pregnancy. The drug enters the baby's body and has a lifelong repressive effect. The mother's pain can also influence the baby when she does not take medication but has a less profound effect than pills. Likewise, the mother who smokes during pregnancy is stamping in a passive, down-regulated system in her offspring, as tobacco contains a number of painkillers. The same is true of a mother on heavy drugs or tranquilizers, or calming pills such as Haldol. The newborn will have a parasympathetic dominance—he will cry less often and less strongly and his responses will be weaker. The mother's drug has removed the activating neurohormones the fetus/baby needs to be alert and aggressive. He is born passive and lacking in energy. He will be unresponsive and nonreactive. He is such a good boy that we rarely comprehend that something is wrong until months or years later.

The birth experience of inadequate oxygen may already reinforce an existing tendency in the fetus not to use up energy due to a mother's smoking. At birth, the parasympathetic prototype is impressed all the stronger; the result is an individual who does not try too hard at anything. He is now stuck in an inflexible crucible that directs his life choices and interests. He is not going to be a salesman or a paramedic. Perhaps he will choose a reflective profession such as being a writer or poet. His focus is "inward" not "outward."

When a carrying mother suffers deep repression due to a major trauma (for example, her husband has left the home), this can be downloaded into the fetus, who may be plunged into this mode and have a lifelong tendency for passivity. At age 30 he may be impotent and cannot maintain an erection. His body is speaking the language of the parasympathetic prototype: "I am helpless and weak. There is nothing I can do to help myself." The loss of an erection is speaking a language, and we need to understand what it means. To understand, we need to eschew words and speak the language of emotions and sensations in Primal Therapy. We need to "speak" the same language as the patient's through his symptoms. It should be clear that the body does speak. After all, we attach electrodes to a suspected criminal's arms (galvanic skin response) to see if his body is telling the truth.

There is a good deal of research to indicate that the mother's stress levels during gestation can affect the offspring's sex hormone output for life. This is a time when the sex hormone system is coming online in the fetus and developing its set-point. A prolonged trauma in the mother can imprint a different set-point—a hypo- or under-secretion—as the system accommodates itself to mother's feeling of defeat and resignation. Hence, the male adult suffers from impotence decades later. Not surprisingly, in a noncontrolled study of our male patients we found lower starting levels of testosterone in men who were parasympaths. We are planning a more up-to-date, controlled replication of this study in which we shall include women. There was study in the June 2005 issue of *Biology Letters*, indicating that 34 percent of the difficulty women had in reaching orgasm was genetic. Here, again, they may have overlooked nine months of gestation.

Converse to the parasympath's defeated and passive imprint, "giving everything you've got" is something that runs through the personality of many other individuals. There is the fighting to get out at birth when the going is tough, struggling desperately and using every bit of energy in order to live. This sympathetic dominance, with all systems full speed ahead, becomes the prototype—struggle means life or death. The person will then go on to push too hard in other situations throughout life and not know when to give up trying. Friends will say to the sympath, "Let it go. Stop driving yourself!" But the person can't. For the parasympath, giving up is truly a matter of life at the bottom end of the neuronal chain. However, giving up equals death for the sympath; driving on, being driven, means life. This is a good trait for success, but is not so good for longevity.

> *From day to day, over and over, based on the predominant prototype, we react either striving to fulfill needs (sympath) or giving up easily without hardly trying (parasympath).*

For example, a man with a sympathetic-dominant personality is doing a project that is just too much for him to handle. He cannot back off. Nor can he ask for help because part of the original imprint is, "There is no help; I have to do this alone." He may learn in cognitive therapy that he needs to let go and not try so hard, but down low in his brain remains the imprinted memory of the necessity for trying hard and never giving up. He is living out the initial patterning—the nervous system mode—the prototype, and he may drive himself to an early death.

It is logical to seek out and do what worked before. That is why, in a life-threatening situation, our entire life will pass before our eyes as the brain scans the history of a lifetime for a survival response. Some of us spring to action; others freeze. Day to day, over and over, based on the predominant prototype, we react either striving to fulfill needs (sympath) or giving up easily without hardly trying (parasympath). The needle is stuck for a lifetime on one record or the other. And it is literally a record that plays ad infinitum. It is the record of our lives; the background music we dance to, even when we can't hear the beat. We may dance fast because the music is fast, forcing a rapid metabolism, pressured thoughts, and impulsive behavior. We move to a slow waltz if we are parasympaths, and more "up" music if we are not. Even if we can't actually *hear* the music, the body still dances to it. The heart is doing rocking and rolling while we may want to waltz. Or the music drags on in the parasympathetic beat, and we barely have enough energy to dance at all. In Primal Therapy, all we are trying to do is tune in and make the music conscious so we can dance to our own individual beats.

If there is a lack of touching in the first weeks of life, baby Jane may learn emotional alienation as characteristic behavior. This imprint would reinforce the tendency already stamped in earlier. There is now a compounding going on. It is not necessarily a new imprint, but a compounding of an earlier one. So here is the dilemma: A high level function, such as thought and concentration, may be driven by a primitive, reptilian brain, something we generally have no access to and cannot even imagine is possible. It is the brainstem that maintains the tone and rigor of the frontal cortex. The neocortex needs an optimum amount of input and energy to keep it functioning properly, but when the input is inordinate, the frontal cortex breaks down, and it no longer functions properly. There is confusion and lack of concentration, as well as easy distractibility. That breakdown is the result of an input from pre-birth and birth history. As long as we neglect that history, we cannot understand the breakdown.

A Vietnam combat veteran remembered looking over a field of wounded and screaming, "I can't save you." In therapy he was allowed to go deeper to when his mother overdosed on drugs when he was very young; he felt, but did not articulate, "I can't save you, Momma!" It was the compounding from the past that caused the adult breakdown. If we only observed the battle situation, we might conclude that it was the sole condition for his breakdown. It certainly seemed obvious. But there were complicating factors requiring a wider perspective.

> *Primal pain is a wound that doesn't hurt; repression sees to that. We cannot experience it precisely because it hurts so much.*

If the parasympathetic system is the prototype imprinted at birth, it may result in the need for removal and dissociation of the self from the pain. That is, there was no other behavioral options at the origin other than complete repression. This happens if disengagement is the principal and only possible defense at birth, against strangling on the umbilical cord, for example. If this experience is compounded by a lack of closeness to the mother right after birth, we can become detached from ourselves, and become emotionally aloof, even before we see the light of day. The impulse to extract ourselves from experience becomes a prototype. We become abstracted, and first distant from ourselves, then from others.

Conversely, if we are to become more social, we first need to come closer to ourselves. This helps us get closer to others. The parasympath is more likely to act shy and timid and hang back. He will be more reflective and less impulsive than the sympath, whose mode is "all-out." As an adult, when someone gets too close, the parasympath will shy away because it can bring up the pain of never having had the closeness he needed. His shyness is protection against primal pain, a pain he cannot even recall but is registered in every part of him: his posture, facial expression, gait, cadence of speech (slow and methodical). All of those are aspects of memory. He has lost access to these memories, but the prototype remains as a memory of a past long gone. Who we are is memory incarnate.

The sympath focuses externally (one key function of the left prefrontal brain, while the parasympath looks inside, is more introspective and philosophical. The sympath is action oriented, as he has been since birth, because, in her mind, action equals survival. By contrast, the parasympath cannot react spontaneously, and constantly ruminates about her life. She is in the down-regulation mode biologically. Her vital signs are uniformly low. She is the depressive, feeling hopeless and helpless. But it is difficult sometimes for her to cry, as repression prevents it. She is slow to arousal, in sex and in general emotions.

The sympath is rarely, if ever, depressed. His physiology doesn't lean that way. He is ambitious and constantly looking ahead, as this was stamped in at birth. Everything about him is in a rush—he feels the need to hurry, is impatient, and wants to get it over and done with. He has to keep going all of the time—plans, projects, and trips. The parasympath is rarely as manic as the sympath. She has been slowed down at the beginning of life, it is stamped in, and she continues on that way. She is wary and nonexpansive, less curious and adventurous; she does not seek out the new and is comfortable in her old routine.

The sympath is tenacious. He forces issues that he shouldn't, because tenacity meant survival at birth. The unconscious formula for him from birth is that a lack of struggle, lack of push, means death. One patient had a prototype at birth of struggling to live, and this continued through childhood with his mother, who made life difficult for him. He told me he was always looking for a reason to live, some sign of encouragement that would allow him to go on. He gave "everything he had," but to no avail. He was too aggressive in his search for a reason, impelled by the need to live at birth. He tried too hard with women, which turned them off. He was always seeking out compliments, hoping to find a reason to live. He told me, "I can be bought by one little compliment."

Even the voice accommodates the imbalance. The sympath may have a high, squeaky voice, and the parasympath has the low, slow, mellifluous one. Does birth trauma determine the way we speak? Often, yes. It determines the cadence, as well. The parasympath is in no rush to explain herself. She may have a speech pattern that takes up very little space; her words do not fill up a room; rather, and because of her low energy level, they barely escape from her mouth. By contrast, the words of the sympath just tumble out, one word on top of the other.

In left/right brain terms, the parasympath is awash in his right-brain feelings. The sympath can rise out of that, plunge into his left brain and become almost solely externally focused. He cannot look inside and, not surprisingly, is less apt to engage in feeling therapy. We see more parasympaths than sympaths in Primal Therapy.

The Prototype and Our Physiologic Processes

The prototype "bends" our physiologic processes globally, across all systems. For the sympath prototype, there seems to be an excess of secretions, while the parasympath remains in the "hypo" mode, in which many of his essential hormones are below normal output. Where we have found low testosterone levels in parasympaths, the opposite was the case for the sympaths. As a result of these prototypes and their systemic effects, the parasympath may tend toward impotence and the sympath may have a problem with premature ejaculation, a more externally aggressive response.

Trauma to the fetus and infant causes the sympathetic system to gear up, producing more adrenaline, dopamine, cortisol, and noradrenaline. The danger is a lack of fulfillment. And that danger is accompanied by an inordinate secretion of stress hormones. The whole system is on alert and hyperactive, and stays hyperactive as long as the imprint is fixed in the system and needs are not met. Once a need remains unfulfilled, we are activated. Our reactions to unfulfilled needs become imprinted pain after a time, which keeps the sympathetic system constantly active. When the stimulating stress hormones become overactive, as they do with chronic pain, they can affect brain cells and produce cell death, perhaps not immediately, but over time.

We don't react piecemeal; the system reacts as an organic whole. For the parasympath, migraine is an example of the reaction. Lack of effort at birth was life-saving because of the relative lack of oxygen, but now any stress can activate the symptom. The person remains in the energy-conserving mode due to the imprint of lack of oxygen. Remember, the prototype is the first major life-saving maneuver of our lives. Any current adversity can set off the old memory of reduced oxygen and the migraine just as any situation where we are alone can set off a primal loneliness from infancy or early childhood.

A lack of oxygen at birth may lead to the constriction of the blood vessel system and consequently strictly reduces the need to breathe deeply. All a newborn could do while being deprived of oxygen was shut down and not use any energy. Total repression was necessary originally where there were no behavioral options possible. This becomes a personality tendency upon which later traumas are laminated. The person becomes an energy-conserver, a passive person who is often depressed, a person who sees no alternative solutions to his problems because at the start there were none. We call it depression until we arrive at the depths of the imprint. Then it is what it was. Why a migraine? Because each new level of consciousness elaborates what already exists. A terrible adversity in the present can have enough impact that the blow travels down through nerve circuits set up at birth. A migraine can occur because the emotional blow has descended to the brainstem/limbic area that registered and processed the vasoconstriction (narrowing of blood vessels, a precursor of a migraine), in the first place. The minute the feeling touches the first line, there will be a headache. In brief, the first line contains a tendency to headaches just waiting to be triggered.

On Halloween, everyone at the Primal Therapy Center comes as their secret selves to get to feelings. They come in diapers, in armor, in clown costumes, even as cash registers. One came totally wrapped because he was the "invisible man." His parents never "saw" him. These costumes represent, in succinct form, the act-out. For example, the man who came as a cash register was a money-making machine, pleasing his parents, who always spoke about money. He wanted their love. The way he thought to get it was through making money. It was his act-out.

In group, patients act out in a safe atmosphere. Someone who is obsessed with looking at ecstatic females in pornographic magazines will be encouraged to bring the magazine to group. The need one patient arrived at was, "Be happy to see me, Momma." In this case, the boy had a chronically depressed mother. She was not happy to see anyone, but he felt something was very wrong with him that she showed no sign of joy when he was present. He saw great joy in the faces of the porno stars in magazines. No child is objective enough to see that it is the parents' problem. When we are young, parents are the whole world to us. Their moods become our feelings; their caprice—our life.

Fetal Life and Drugs

All psychiatric drugs cross the placenta and enter into the fetal blood system. Once the drug has entered the fetal bloodstream, it has easy access to the brain. Drugs can also pass to the infant through the mother's milk. Nonetheless, the infant is less able than an adult to metabolize whatever amount of drug has entered its body. Some drugs ingested by a nursing mother, such as lithium, can make the infant low in energy, phlegmatic, and passive. Other tranquilizers can make the infant excitable. What happens during womb-life can help set the stage for addiction two decades later. The critical period occurs when the key brain synapses are being built, which, in humans, starts from the sixth month of pregnancy and goes on after birth to age 2 or 3. The drugs, if ingested by the mother, can create an imprint that resets the set-point of hormones and physiologic chemicals (for example, later we lack serotonin or thyroid).

A study by Finnish scientists M. Huttunen and P. Niskanen investigated children whose fathers died either while the mother was carrying or during the first year of the child's life. The offspring were examined over a 35-year period using documentary evidence. Only those who lost their fathers while the child was in the womb were at increased risk of mental diseases, alcoholism/addiction, or criminal behavior.[2] Clearly, the emotional state of the mother was affected, and that possibly had lifelong deleterious effects on the child. The results of this study suggest that the emotional state of the pregnant mother has more long-term effects on the child than the emotional state of the mother during the years following birth. And when we are investigating addiction, we must pay attention to womb-life.

We know from animal experiments that those deprived of touch and love right after birth tend to consume alcohol later on when offered, versus those loved animals who refuse it. There is a good study of monkeys that demonstrates this point. Those more stressed early on were more likely to drink alcohol. Eighty rhesus monkeys were investigated; half were separated from their mothers at birth. This group responded to any later stress with 25 percent more stress hormone release. Later both groups were offered drinks with alcohol in it. One fifth drank nothing. Among those who did consume alcohol, those with the higher levels of cortisol before the experiment were the heavy drinkers. Those monkeys weren't saying any irrational things to themselves, as the cognitivists might have it. They reacted in terms of their history. We may ascribe some alcoholism to genetics, but this study makes clear that those who were unloved early in life took to alcohol.

We know from animal experiments that those deprived of touch and love right after birth tend to consume alcohol later on when offered, versus those loved animals who refuse it.

We are still those primates, but with a cortex added on; we've put on a thinking cap—permanently. If monkeys can be neurotic without words, so can we. If they can be addicted, so can we. Because these monkeys were deprived of love early on, they later felt the need to comfort their pain and did so with alcohol. The basic pain and physiology of two primates, humans and monkeys, are pretty much the same. We hurt in the same way with basically the same physiological equipment. It is clear from so many similar animal experiments, and there are literally thousands of them, dating from the early work of Harry Harlow to the present, that words do not matter and cannot permanently ease the pain.

Recent research by A.R. Hollenbeck, another specialist in fetal life, documents how any drug given to a carrying mother will alter the neurotransmitter systems of the offspring, especially during the critical period when these neurotransmitter systems are forming in the womb. He states that administration of local anesthetics, such as lidocaine (to aid the birth process), during sensitive (critical) periods in gestation is capable of producing enduring changes in the offspring's behavior.[3] Brain chemicals such as serotonin and dopamine can be changed permanently when an animal undergoes birth even with a local anesthetic. This again affects the gating system.

The more painkillers a woman takes during labor, the more likely her child will be to abuse drugs or alcohol later on. Karin Nyberg of the University of Gothenburg, Sweden, looked at medication given to the mothers of 69 adult drug users and 33 of their siblings who did not take drugs. Twenty-three percent of the drug abusers were exposed to multiple doses of barbiturates or opiates in the hours just before birth. Only 3 percent of their siblings were exposed to the same levels of drugs in utero. If the mothers received three or more doses of drugs, their child was five times more likely to abuse drugs later on.[4] Enough animal studies have been done to confirm the finding that exposure to drugs in the womb changes the individual's propensity for drugs later on.

There is some evidence that a mother taking downers during pregnancy will have an offspring who later will be addicted to amphetamines, known as "uppers" (speed); while a mother taking uppers during pregnancy—coffee, cocaine, caffeinated colas—will produce an offspring later addicted to downers—Quaaludes, for example. And the reason that the person can take inordinate doses, such as drinking two cups of coffee before bedtime and still be able to sleep easily and well, is that there exists a major deficiency of stimulating hormones—the catecholamines. In short, the original set-points for activation or repression have been altered during womb-life and persist for a lifetime.

I have treated patients who have taken enormous doses of speed and have shown very little mania as a result. While other patients have taken lethal doses of painkillers in previous suicide attempts, enough to kill anyone else, and still lie awake hours later, only feeling slightly drugged. The severe brain activation by imprinted pain resists any attempts to quell the system.

The more painkillers a woman takes during labor, the more likely her child will be to abuse drugs or alcohol later on.

Psychotherapists must ask the question, "Why does a tranquilizer or painkiller that works on lower centers of the brain calm the patient and change his or her ideas?" We know that it often does. We know that someone suffering an acute heart attack can feel terrible, yet when given a shot of a painkiller, it changes his ideas and attitudes about the experience. This alone should inform us that feelings drive ideas, and not vice versa.

When there has been compounded neglect and emotional pain in early childhood, the amygdale and hippocampus of the limbic system carry a heavy burden. They sense threat and warn us of danger. It is a warning in the only language it has—agitation and mobilization. What is the danger? A lack of love or a near-death experience at birth. In a diabolic, dialectic fashion, the very traumas and early lack of love that weaken the structure of the frontal cortex, reducing its synapses, add weight to the limbic forces, which now threaten the integrity of the cortex. Joseph LeDoux, the acknowledged acolyte in the study of the amygdala, believes that a person becomes anxious and depressed when "emotional memory" is reactivated through the amygdala system. His research pinpoints the neural structures involved in the reactivation of emotional memory.

What does a cognitive therapist do, essentially? Bolster left hemisphere control in the patient by immersing him in ideas. In Primal Therapy, we work on the bottom end of the brain's evolution, reducing the power of deep imprinted forces so that they no longer challenge the prefrontal cortex to drive ideas. One study reported in *Science News* (2004) tested subjects who were asked to suppress unwanted memories and then had their brains scanned. The prefrontal cortex dampened activity in the hippocampus of these subjects, thus interfering with memory retrieval. In brief, repression and gating lessened access to oneself and one's history.[5]

Tranquilizers are indeed painkillers, and some tranquilizers can be given in higher doses to produce a surgical anesthesia. Here again we see an interchange between emotional and physical pain. For instance, when someone has a bad back and takes painkillers for months, and then continues to take them after his back is healed, he's considered addicted. But the same pill that calms his back pain also calms his history—his imprint—hence the continued need for the drug. The original "antipsychotic" drug, Thorazine, was first used by a French surgeon, who noticed that it made surgical patients indifferent or apathetic toward the pain they were undergoing. One author noted that scientific evidence supports a theory that most psychiatric drugs "work" by producing a kind of anesthesia of the mind, spirit, or feelings.

Work by R. Gaunt put rats under stress (tied to a board), then gave them tranquilizers. They seemed indifferent to their problem, but their bodies weren't. There were high readings in stress hormones. We need to keep this in mind when we take tranquilizers; for the wear and tear on the body goes on even if we are unaware of it.

Nearly all of us are prisoners of our prototype—our dominant mode of functioning. Cognitive therapy assumes we have an ample amount of free will. I am not so sure. We can make choices within the prototype, but it tends to offer a narrow range. What we are free to do is go back and find out how all that got started. That is what ultimately will widen our range of choices in life. It will free the parasympath to widen her vision and take more chances. It will allow the sympath to ease off the incessant struggle that never lets him relax. Finally, it puts our system back in balance so that our system can find equilibrium so that we are no longer prisoners of medication after medication, drug after drug. A balanced system means the parasympathetic male's chronically low level of testosterone is normalized—something we have found after one year of therapy. It means he is now more assertive and less depressed. A balanced system means not having to drink five cups of coffee a day or being hooked on caffeinated cola. It means not having to smoke, which ultimately will shorten our lives. It is the true meaning of being free.

Case Study: Katherina—Anorexia, Bulimia, and Sexual Trauma

(Note: PC is the Primal Center counselor. K is Katherina, a patient.)

PC: *And why did you come to us?*

K: *I came because I briefly suffered from anorexia when I was 11 and 12, and when I was 14, I was suffering from bulimia. Nobody knew about it, and it got to the point where I was feeling like I was destroying myself and I needed help and I didn't know what to do and where to go and I needed to tell somebody, and I knew what it related to. I needed help.*

PC: *Describe exactly what anorexia is for you.*

K: *Anorexia? When I was 11 I stopped eating. I was in public school, my mom had remarried, a lot of difficult things going on in my life, and I needed my mother to see that I was dying, that I was not able to cope with all these things that were happening to me. I needed her to see that I was in pain and I needed help. Being unable to ask her for that help and being unable to make it known, not even knowing that I needed help; I wanted to be as thin as a skeleton. I wanted to show her that I was dying. I wanted to show everybody that I was in pain. It was a cry for help. I didn't know it; I thought it had only to do with being thin and my girlfriends were thinner or that it had to do with food.*

I wanted my mom to see that I was not happy in her new marriage, and that I had all these problems. I shut down my natural urges to eat. I was so shut away from myself that I was not hungry. You'd think that if you weren't eating you'd be hungry; I was not hungry. I couldn't eat; it was impossible. I just wanted to die. It was so strong and I felt so hopeless. That was my only hope of reaching her.

PC: *You also had bulimia?*

K: *Later, I would go through periods where I would not eat and then I'd be so hungry, I'd eat a lot and I'd freak out so I'd throw up—I'd get rid of it. It just became so easy. It was so much easier than starving or exercising. If I had a test or something going on that was really stressful, I would eat and throw up and then I would eat and throw up again. It was like masturbation. It was a tension reliever. It was where all my tension and anxiety was going. I didn't really have anybody to talk to, so it was my way of releasing all this tension and dealing with it. Sort of dealing with it, putting it aside so I could go on with my day, and be functional in school. I got straight A's in school. Everyone thought I was little Miss Perfect; I had this perfect facade going. Nobody really ever knew that behind that I was killing myself. And that's why it was possible for me to look so perfect because I had all this acting-out so outrageously behind the scenes.*

PC: *What part of the bulimia was the tension reliever?*

K: *Throwing up. Eating relieves tension too, but it also causes tension. Because then you're worried "And then if I get fat, then everyone's going to think I'm okay and Mom's not going to see that there's problems with me, so I have to get rid of this food." While eating could be very satisfying, it kind of makes you feel more loved, like you're full, you have something. If it was sitting there too long, then I'd have to get rid of this or it would cause more tension. So the actual throwing up would...I got rid of it so I don't have to worry about getting fat. It was just the best tension reliever above all until the feeling was pushing again. I had to do it again. And it became every day, all the time.*

PC: *What feeling?*

K: *The general feelings during that time of being unsupported, unloved, not listened to; I was the only one who knew what was going on with me. I was in a teenager phase where I felt really unsafe talking to anybody. Those were the present-day feelings that I was going through. I was molested when I was 5 1/2 years old until I was 8. What actually brought me to therapy was that I found out. I'd always remembered being molested, it was not something implanted in my head, it was always there, but I had blocked out that my friend was molested by the same man with me later during that three-year span. She had a memory of it, but when I was 15 and she told me about it, my whole world crumbled; I couldn't keep it together anymore. I was throwing up so much I was losing it, and then my best friend, who was like my sister, I found out this happened to her, and I got a slew of memories and I needed help. That's what brought me here; I had a breakdown. Being molested, the way I was molested, I had very specific memories. Do you want me to go over the specific memories?*

PC: *What do you mean you had a breakdown?*

K: *I remembered that I'd been molested. I always knew. I always remembered the first time. When it was just me, I thought I could handle it. You know, I can be strong; there's nobody who understands, I'm not going to make a big deal out of it. She was younger than me, and when I found out what he did to her, it just tore my world apart. Not only was I having all this input from her, what happened, which made all my lost memories come flooding back, but this person in my life who was so dear to me, like my sister, this horrible thing happened to her that I would not wish on anybody. I hated myself because I couldn't protect her. I was older and I couldn't do anything. I would do anything if I could have kept that from happening to her, if I could have protected her. I was bingeing one night after that, and I woke up my mom, and I just felt like if I threw up one more time, I would somehow just never stop. I just hit some point and I was crying and I woke up my mom. I said, "Mom, I need you to keep me from throwing up; I can't." And she had no idea what I was talking about. I was crying and I said, "Mom, stay with me, don't let me throw up."*

I was going on a self-destructive rampage; I was killing myself. She stayed with me, and I cried and cried. I had been seeing a psychotherapist at that time for my problems, dealing with these memories coming from my friends. I hated it. I really liked my therapist, she was a really nice person, but I would come in there and I would start crying. I would be on the verge of a memory or just having a feeling and she would say, "Let's make a list." She'd stop me. "And this is because," she would say, and she'd start telling me all this stuff. It just wasn't working; I knew I had to do more. I knew that as soon as she stopped me from crying, I would just feel horrible and I'd feel horrible for the rest of the day. There was no relief. It had to go further.

I said, "I need help, Mom, I don't know what to do. I can't. The therapy's not working. I need to see somebody." I had always sort of known about Primal Therapy, and I asked if she still had the books, and I read a book and it was exactly what I needed. I knew I had to go back to those memories, and I knew I needed to deal with them for myself, not just for my friends so that I could stop hurting myself and start living my life again. My life was on hold for so long.

PC: *What caused the anorexia and bulimia?*

K: *First of all, anyone who's been molested knows that it takes all your power. You have no power. You don't understand what's going on; you feel dirty, you feel fat, you feel ugly, you feel worthless, you feel stupid. It destroys you. And at such a young age, you have no rationalization for what's going on. Your rationalization is, "I must be bad or this wouldn't happen to me. I can change. I must be able to change this." Throughout my life, I was Miss Straight A's; I was the perfect little girl, I was doing well in school, and it was this constant need to be a better person. If I was not perfect, then I got hurt. And if it was not my fault what was happening, then it was my mom's fault, or it was his fault, and I can't change that. If I can change me, there's hope. The rationalization for a 5-year-old is, "The problem has to lie in me. The fault has to lie in me because if it doesn't, then it's hopeless; I can't change it. If the fault lies in me, I can be better, I can do better in school, I can change and be thinner, I can be prettier, I can be this, I can be that," etc. So when something that crazy and terrible and terrifying is happening to you, you strive to be better.*

I was molested every morning before I was taken to school. My mom was living with this person; it was her boyfriend. We were living with him. She would go to college. She had to go earlier than me; my school didn't start till 9 a.m. I'd wake up and he'd be molesting me. That was very confusing. I have serious problems with morning time in general; I hate the morning. I mean, I don't anymore. Now I kind of enjoy sunlight in the morning, but I would wake up, and for hours I would feel horrible and depressed.

If you look at the situation, I was going from being totally abused, to school, where I had to be happy and do stuff and be with these people, and I was going through this hell at home. So he'd get me and molest me, and I'd be awake, and then let's get dressed and let's eat breakfast. I remember my mom didn't let me have sugar. Once, we got this sugar cereal. Normally, a kid is like, "Sugar!" and they're happy. I remember sitting over this bowl of smushberry or something, and just wanting to throw up. I was supposed to carry on with this daily routine after what had just happened, and I'm sitting over this food and part of my feeling was wanting to throw up, part of it was, "What's the use of eating?" It was hopeless. "What's the point of living? What's the point of me going on?"

After what just happened, I had no desire to eat and I was so sick, and it was like, "eek!" while I was eating; it was like sandpaper. It's like I can't taste the food anymore. I get like that when I'm bingeing. I'm not tasting what I'm eating. I'm eating anything in the fridge, lots of it. It's this way of reliving that feeling, being forced to eat when you have no desire to. You're not tasting the food. I'd be shoving it down my throat and then I'd be sick. And I would eat so much I'd make myself sick. And at that point, one bite of food was too much 'cause I wasn't hungry and I was sick. That's definitely a really strong memory I had to go through. I had to go through the devastation of what just happened and I would never be the same, and I also had the sadness, the loss there, the confusion and the wanting to run out of the house and scream and call my mom and cry and throw the food.

The biggest of all things was the bulimia, like forced oral copulation, which would make anybody throw up. That was a memory that I got later. I came to a session, and I had just eaten. I was sitting in my session and I had been throwing up a lot during the time period, and I had just eaten and I could feel the food in my stomach, and I was telling my therapist, "I have to throw up. I'm going to die. I have to get this out of me. I'm going to die. I have to. I'm sorry." I was stopping the session; I have to go get rid of this, it's going to drive me crazy. "I can't handle it. I need to throw up. That's how much of a compulsion it is." He told me, "Go with it, stay there." And I just started gagging and retching, and all of a sudden I felt this hand on my neck. It had nothing to do with food. I was being forced to swallow something terrible. It was making me throw up.

When I keep food in me, all these feelings come up, all these memories and all the sensations, needing to get rid of that food so I don't have to deal with it. That is the way I don't have to remember it. I don't have to deal with the memory. The memory doesn't even come up. I'm recreating the situation, only this time I can get rid of it. I am throwing up. By keeping that food in me on one day, I had this memory that was so big a scene; it changed my life. All the therapist had to say was, "Go with it." My body was right there; it was already experiencing, was reacting to this food and the feeling of eating as though I was 5.

My body was still trapped in this time period where all these emotions have been unfelt; they were in desperate need of release. That's my body's reaction and that's why it was such a compulsion. Because when I eat, if I'd eat too much or if I was in a certain state and I'd eat, I was right back there. I've had people tell me, "How can you do that to yourself? It's disgusting; you're hurting yourself." You're not thinking like that when you're doing it. You're not thinking about your body, you're not thinking about your teeth, you're thinking, "I'm going to die if I don't do this. I'm saving my life." It kept the pain from coming up.

My thinking wasn't rational; it was thinking like that 5-year-old. So your emotions take over and you're not saying, "This is bad for my teeth." That's what a compulsion is. There's no room for rationalization, unless it's in the direction of, "I can throw up because I eat a bunch of cheese and it wasn't good for me anyway." You can rationalize that way. Now I've reexperienced some of my childhood pain, and I am more in touch with my body. I can tell when I'm hungry and when I'm not hungry, and I'll catch myself eating and I'll be like, "K, you're not hungry, you don't have to eat right now; you're upset because you just got in a fight with your dad," or whatever. But before I couldn't be in touch with that. I couldn't have been in touch with that because I wasn't thinking clearly; I was not using my knowledge. I was a victim of my feelings.

PC: *How does reliving it help you?*

K: *By going through these things in my life, these events that were not completed, and really reexperiencing them in a safe environment and reacting in the ways that I never could have. It was not safe. It was impossible. By doing that I have been able to realize that it's not my fault, I had no control over the situation; those are two important things that I've realized. As a child I thought it was my fault and was all confused. By reliving it, I've been able to understand my behavior for myself because after reliving things in a session, I'll sit up and I'll be like, "That's why I did this, that's why," it was because of this incident where I'm sitting over this cereal and I'm 5 1/2 and I'm terrified, and I have this feeling. That's why I eat when I'm not hungry; that's why I feel devastation. Before it was an unconscious behavior; now it's a conscious behavior.*

PC: *What were the causes of those feelings?*

K: *Feeling hopeless, feeling hated, being abused, not having anyone to talk to, not being able to react, having to deal with all that was going on my own. All that stuff going on and having to take it all and deal with it, and you don't even have the mental capacity to conceive what's happening at that age; you have no idea. And having to deal with that made me never ask for help throughout my life 'cause I never could. I never asked for help with a test, never asked for help with anything. So throughout my life I've had this secret side of me that's destroying myself, and it's been this unconscious behavior driven by all those times when I needed help and there was no one there and I couldn't ask for it, and I couldn't even know I needed help. I didn't know what was happening. I didn't know what was wrong.*

I was bulimic, thinking it was because I wanted to be thin. And now it only comes up when I've seen some rape scene in a movie, or I'm in a sexual situation and I get uncomfortable and I don't do anything about it; I don't stop it. I have to relive the forced oral sex, then the urge goes away. Anything that triggers that old memory makes me want to eat and throw up; it's not that I'm thinking, "I want to be thin." I know that I'm doing this because of this or that memory which is coming up; knowing there's more memory in there.

I had so many repressed memories that my brain would just rationalize a way to release that pain. It was always through my food and starving and bingeing behaviors. So reliving that has connected me to what the problems really are. If somebody is disrespecting me now, I know. I can tell they're doing it, and I can say, "I really don't like this, this is not fair to me, I'm really uncomfortable with this, I need it to stop." I can get angry.

Connecting the past with the present through reliving those memories has empowered me, has given me my power back, and it has enabled me to know what I'm feeling and why I'm doing the things, and why I have the urges to do the things that I do and what they relate to and why I had them in the past and how I can stop them now. It helps me communicate and know how I feel, being in tune with my body, knowing when I'm hungry, knowing when I'm not. Just overall I know more about myself, and my body. That's really important.

8

Disconnection and Dissociation: The Brain's Gating System at Work

People often refer to someone who is well adjusted as "grounded" or "centered," or they say that he or she has "got it together." Perhaps a more accurate description would be that such a person is "connected," because a fully connected brain is what someone really has when they've "got it together," which is absolutely necessary if one is to experience true conscious-awareness. *Connection* means there exists a completely operative flow between lower levels of the brain on up to the top, and from the right prefrontal cortex to the left.

Neurosis, on the other hand, is a state of disconnection; systems that should connect simply don't. This is doubly true of psychosis, where the pain levels are so much earlier and deeper than neurosis. There are radical alterations of nerve cell placements in psychosis so that some neurons are upside down in limbic structures. Trauma disrupts connection much in the same way that static interferes with a clear telephone call: the more static there is, the harder it is to hear. With the brain, the greater the trauma, the greater the noise. The brain will cut off and put aside the pain of any trauma that is too great for it to bear, creating an imprint that gives rise to myriad physical and mental health problems.

Once the brain has suffered trauma during the critical period of development, the more difficult—and painful—it will be for the individual to reestablish a connection; they will have to relive and feel that pain of the trauma in all of its original intensity. I did not say "re-feel" because that portion of memory was not been fully experienced originally. Recall at the beginning of this work I stated that only a small piece of very early traumas can be experienced (felt). The rest is put in storage until we can feel again, given a conducive therapeutic environment. What has not been felt is the suffering component locked away with the memory of the trauma. Suffering is part of the memory, the feeling part that has been repressed through the gating system.

It is not possible to truly get well by way of some easy, feel-good process, which is what the selling point is behind meditation, hypnosis, acupuncture, and all cognitive therapies. What they offer is a temporary palliative to the patient's suffering, and for a period of time, at least, the patient will feel better. But after decades of work in the field of clinical psychology, I can tell you that if the patient isn't suffering in therapy, there is no improvement. No pain, no gain. It has been described by our patients as a pain that doesn't hurt; the minute it is felt, it turns into a feeling. Feelings are natural.

To be dissociated from a strong feeling is what I call disconnection: literally, a severing of ties from lower level structures to the prefrontal cortex, and from the right hemisphere to the left. This disconnection results from *gating*, a system within the brain that prevents pain from getting through. We see this every day in Primal Therapy, because patients who come close to connection do feel intense pain, a joining of low-level imprints with conscious-awareness. When imprinted memory starts to lock onto conscious-awareness, the person experiences suffering, the exact amount of suffering that occurred with the original experience—the same vital sign patterns, for example. The patient's response is exact; neither more nor less. When it is about almost dying at birth from lack of oxygen, the suffering is indescribable. We see immediately the role of gating and disconnection. We see it in very high blood pressure, heart rate, and body temperature.

When patients reach a state of *almost* feeling, they hurt; actual feeling puts an end to hurt, even though the experience to be felt involves pain. Almost feeling means that the suffering component is entering conscious-awareness but has not yet created the connection. Connected pain is no longer pain; it is feeling and it is need. (Thus, in a dialectic process, feeling the original pain makes it turn into its opposite. Not feeling it keeps pain intact.) As the feeling wends its way from the brainstem up through the right side of the brain to the orbital-frontal area, it gathers force, resulting in a "break free" from left-side control. Once that happens, it then rushes toward its counterpart on the left for connection. The gathering force is due to the compounding—the prototypic event layered on by post-birth, infancy, and childhood traumas. As neurobiologist Dr. David

Goodman puts it: "Primal Therapy pulls from its hands the reins of the pain from the past that steers us." There is a new unified command. There is no longer the hippocampal/amygdala turbulence below the surface to make us miserable.

Feelings are meant to follow evolution, moving toward prefrontal cortical connection and integration. Feelings seem to always try to escape the trap of unconsciousness, as though the system recognizes that unconsciousness is ultimately a danger and not a natural state. Feelings are a system of adaptation; they help us select out of a maze of input what is important and needs tending. They tell us what is pertinent and relevant and what should be neglected. The obsessive cannot "neglect." He has to attend to things he should not be attending to, and when he arrives at deep feeling, the obsessiveness stops. Joseph LeDoux believes that emotional systems have been preserved in evolution for adaptation. Good and bad feelings help direct us either away or toward stimuli. Often, we choose a therapy that makes us feel good and avoid one that evokes pain. Our therapy is chosen by those who are already in pain and feel it all of the time.

> *It is not possible to truly get well by way of some easy, feel-good process, which is what the selling point is behind meditation, hypnosis, acupuncture, and all cognitive therapies.*

Every system strives to be conscious because consciousness means survival. There are two dynamics at work. One is a tendency toward consciousness, and the second is a tendency toward disconnection/unconsciousness when consciousness of pain threatens to become overwhelming. We need to be conscious but not so conscious that the system, particularly the thinking/navigating system, is in danger. We have to be aware of danger that is internal as well as external.

The Evolution of Feelings

The limbic system is fairly well developed by the age of 3 years when the orbitofrontal cortex comes online to represent feelings on a higher level. It is the time when we begin to use language to describe our feelings. We have a whole lifetime of emotional experiences sealed into our systems by this age. Here we begin to set the stage for living in our heads instead of our feelings; we lose touch with our instincts and our bodies. Our physical bodies are not well coordinated and we become awkward. We are not good in sports but better in intellectual abstract pursuits. Not good in fine eye-hand coordination but better in philosophy. It is an inchoate beginning of the flight from our internal world toward the external one. It is clear why so many intellectuals are not coordinated in sports. And as I quote elsewhere from the study by the London Institute of Psychiatry, the basic traits we develop at age 3 follow us throughout life.

The traumatized brain has different cognitive capacities. It is not so much that one trauma compromises the brain; rather, it is an accumulated lack of love that does it. When we consider that the right emotional/limbic brain is in a growth spurt in the first years when touch and love are absolutely crucial, it is clear that a lack of it will have lifelong consequences on our emotions. This is particularly true as the right brain relates to, and informs, the left intellectual side. Toward the end of the second year of life, there is a leap in growth on the left side of the frontal area of the brain.

> *The level of repression is commensurate with the level of the trauma, and keeps the system under high-level pressure at all times.*

When low-level imprints cannot send information to higher levels, communication is poor and connection becomes difficult. In a rather figurative and often literal way, the neurons that should be reaching out and up for contact do not do so. There is less synaptic connectivity and fewer dendrites, resulting in a retraction or shrinkage of neurons due to trauma. The brain, "knowing" that connection is overwhelming, seems to retrench, pulling back its nerve fibers from locking in. The distance between experience and its awareness becomes more distant, and we have a wider "Janovian Gap."

Lack of connection and/or integration ultimately means a disintegration of mental and physical systems. If the energy of early trauma is powerful enough, its spread is broad, and the symptoms more serious. When the pain is early and catastrophic, chances are it will lead to symptoms that are equally catastrophic. The reason is, the level of repression is commensurate with the level of the trauma, and keeps the system under high-level pressure at all times. Thus, if the trauma was life-threatening, it may lead to afflictions that will be life-threatening. To put an end to this we need connection.

We understand that any inordinate input hurts, whether of cold, wind, or heat. When a feeling is felt, it is shorn of its agony, and it becomes simply a memory. That is because what was lived for the first time in therapy was the agony portion of the feeling. It is now integrated into the system. The most severe agony lies on the first line. We understand that when we do not experience the hurt in full flower, we must adapt compensating measures (known as act-outs) to hold it back, perhaps with medication. It is the price we pay for not feeling. In some cases, we paradoxically use medication as a means to get to the pain, not to avoid it—to reduce the power of the suffering component into small, bite-sized bits of feeling. That is why there can be no hurry in Primal Therapy; the system will only allow so much integration at a time. Medication is used to permit access, not to prevent it. To be clear: when a feeling is overwhelming, such as a feeling of total abandonment or a feeling of terror due to living a childhood with a violent, drunken father, only a small bit of the feeling can be experienced. We use tranquilizers such as Prozac and Zoloft (the serotonin elevators) to soften the pain so that some of it can be felt. The problem is that any current situation, such as a tyrannical boss, can reawaken all of the early terror resulting in terrible anxiety. The anxiety is pure terror so catastrophic that it can only be felt globally—system wide—as anxiety rather than a specific terror from early in life, as, for example, the birth trauma.

One patient had to give a speech in class. She was overwhelmingly anxious, and she stammered and stuttered. She "knew" she was going to do it wrong. We took the speech situation and the feelings within it and helped her into her past where she was constantly criticized by her mother. Her mother made her feel wrong even if it was her sister who disobeyed. From there she went back to breech birth, where everything seemed to have gone wrong. What was engraved was a sensation or presentiment of everything going wrong. It took on a meaning later in life, "Things are going to go wrong."

Nothing in the human system is capricious; pruning of neurons exists because it has a biologic function. When there is early trauma, there is also a pruning of the neurons (a radical elimination) in the amygdala and the orbitofrontal cortex so that the connections between them are less robust, which is part of the defense system. What pruning really means in our schema is that pain from lack of love and/or trauma causes the brain to amass its forces where needed, and prune where it is less needed. The brain structure changes! As a result, we have a brain that is out of balance, with less cortical control over impulses and less information being delivered from down low to the top. Trauma also tends to thin out the right-left circuits in the corpus callosum so that connection is literally much more difficult. It is very much like reducing a four-lane highway to a single lane—a diminished flow of information traffic getting through.

Connection normalizes every aspect of our being. The system is in harmony. In cognitive therapy there may be a great disharmony between what we feel and what we think. Too often the attempt is to rearrange one's thoughts about feelings resulting in a lack of harmony, especially when no one knows what those feelings are. Connection means a flow between feelings that originate in the lower brain and the higher-level frontal cortex, where thoughts occur; more specifically, from the right frontal area to the left. I have not seen the notion of connection discussed in the cognitive or insight therapies, yet it is the essential element of a cure. As our patients begin to approach deep feelings in sessions, the heart rates mount to dangerously high levels. Those levels drop precipitously after connection. The question that any psychotherapist must answer is, "Why does this happen?" This points again to the fact that imprinted feelings can be dangerous and will mobilize the brain system to meet the threat, just as if it were a virus.

The Right OBFC: Keeper of Connection to Our History

So where's the bull's-eye, the target that lower-level centers of the brain need to reach in order for real connection to occur? It's the right *orbitofrontal cortex* (OBFC), a key structure that enables a person to experience conscious-awareness (that is, to have conscious-awareness of feelings of pain that were too great in force to feel). The OBFC, which is the part of the neocortex that sits just behind the eye sockets, reaches maturity between 18 to 24 months of age. The right OBFC receives feeling information on the right side of the brain and helps code it; it helps control feelings, and, above all, is involved in retrieving feeling information and integrating it with the left OBFC. This is a big job. Thanks to the right

OBFC, we can know what we feel and feel what we know—if only it will inform the left prefrontal cortex about what it knows and feels. The left prefrontal area filters and regulates sensory input both from outside and inside. Often it will not permit emigration from the right, which can be treated like an unwanted alien.

If we want to regain conscious-awareness—full consciousness—we need to use the orbitofrontal cortex map to scan the nonverbal brain, the right limbic area and brainstem to retrieve the most remote, ancient memories.

The orbitofrontal cortex provides a map of our internal-historic life and registers information from below, from preverbal memories, and then provides a high-level coding system that labels the feeling. It is like a GPS (global positioning system) that constantly informs us of who we are, where we are, and where we're going. That map will be in a neuro-biochemical language. Its frequency signature will also be noted. One key way we store information is by certain frequencies that then resonate with higher centers to help produce the connection. It may be that the imprinted feelings "know" they have friends in higher circles and need to make their acquaintance. What is important about the OBFC is that it contains representations from the depths of the brain. In this way we are aware of our internal life, a life that has nothing to do with words. When I say we are aware, what that means is that the information in the right OBFC is channeled to the left, and it is there that we become aware.

Because the right OBFC provides a map of our internal environment, most early abuse and lack of love can be found coded there. Because the right side develops before the left, many of our life-and-death experiences in the womb and at birth are registered there. It makes retrieval by a left-hemisphere–oriented therapy (cognitive) almost impossible. If we want to regain conscious-awareness—full consciousness—we need to use the orbitofrontal cortex map to scan the nonverbal brain, the right limbic area and brainstem to retrieve the most remote, ancient memories. What repression and gating do is inhibit retrieval; that repressive process uses up energy continuously. We see this in depression when there is a kind of heavy heart; labored breathing; and labored, ponderous movements. It is one way we know that depression involves heavy repression; the energy is being expended in the service of holding down feeling memories.

By and large, "awareness" is left brain, but that does not necessarily mean language. Conscious-awareness is right-left brain working in harmony. Incidentally, a 2002 study out by two psychologists at UCLA, Eisenberger and Liberman, found that people who experienced less discomfort had more prefrontal cortex activity.[1] Again, higher centers are able to suppress and calm the lower ones. They also found both physical pain and emotional pain use the same pathways in the brain. In brief, pain is pain no matter what the source; emotional pain is physical. It is not just in our minds, it is not just psychological, and cannot be treated on the psychological level alone.

We know this occurs when there is awareness without connection during a session—known as "abreaction." The vital signs rise and fall in sporadic fashion, rarely below baseline. This is what often happens in the pseudo-Primal therapies where patients are told what and how to feel. Here the vital signs do not move at all. It is why we measure vital signs before and after each session. We measured a new patient who had mock Primal Therapy. He went through early feelings that looked real. His vital signs never changed, indicating an energy release but no connection. So long as there is no connection, nor a shift in brain processing from right to left, there will be no commensurate change in physiology.

This is not to be confused with appropriate emotions where a person is expressing anger over an injustice or grief due to the loss of a loved one. Those are appropriate feelings, not neurotic.

The right limbic brain/brainstem is responsible for a great part of our arousal, while the left brain is the calming agent. When there is hyperarousal due to brainstem/limbic unfulfilled needs and memories, the left orbitofrontal cortex can help dampen that arousal and produce a false sense of calm. This is one key element in cognitive therapy. Indeed, as I pointed out, one reason for the development of the left brain was to help in the repressive process; keeping enough pain at bay to allow us to function in everyday life.

The orbitofrontal cortex can also inhibit or dampen the arousal that leads to hyper-secretion of stress hormones ordered by the hypothalamus. The OBFC, when properly developed and connected, can block impulses for aggression and control terror. It has been shown that murderers have less prefrontal activation of the OBFC when presented with certain tasks, and therefore have less control. It is also true with those who suffer from attention deficit disorder (ADD). The ADD syndrome generally indicates left-right prefrontal impairment. All those buried feeling imprints are like the hordes trying to get over the moat (the corpus callosum) to reach home, but overnight someone worked on the highway and narrowed the lanes considerably. There is now a jam-up, and it becomes difficult to pay attention to a homework assignment when all that "noise" is going on; all that early pain scrambling for attention. All the feelings are bunched up, trying to get through. As long as there is no connection, there will always be this noise, because the noise is those feelings, disconnected.

I have likened the orbitofrontal cortex to a dredge, dipping down to bring up the detritus from below. What is brought up is often not pretty, a forgotten incest, for example, or the hopelessness of ever getting love from one's parents; an enormous trauma that we see every day in our patients. When we retrieve old memories beginning with the right OBFC, the whole right side trailing down to the amygdala/brainstem "lights up" and is activated.

With connection, feelings have found a home, and the system can rest. The person no longer has to engage in compulsive hand-washing because she unconsciously feels "dirty." Remember, the higher prefrontal regulatory systems have connections with the brainstem/limbic areas with information going in both directions. We can feel our feelings, and we can block those feelings when they are too hurtful. With a weaker prefrontal cortex to handle input, we have amygdala-driven feelings that impact our higher centers directly, possibly driving us into unceasing mental activity. If there were ever a universal affliction, it is that unceasing activity. People cannot sit still and relax. Movement as an imprint may have been the road to life at birth, and it does so now as a memory.

It is my experience that the wider the gap is between deep feeling and awareness, the greater the unreality of the belief system; the more remote the feeling, the more far-out the belief system, and the more tenacious its hold on us. We had one patient at the Primal Therapy Center who was fixated on aliens coming from another planet to attack her. After many lesser-strength feelings, she finally felt what those aliens actually were—her alienated feelings; unknown terrors that she converted into attacking aliens. She needed to justify or rationalize her fears. Because they were so monumental, her beliefs soared into the bizarre area.

Dislocation of the Mind

Once feelings are blocked from conscious-awareness, any belief system can fill the bill. No matter how outlandish the belief, it will be adopted if it serves to symbolically fulfill old needs. The trajectory of the belief system begins deep in the brainstem and in ancient parts of the limbic system where devastating imprints are stored. The pressure/energy moves upward to cortical centers and forward to the orbitofrontal cortex.

The right OBFC is doing its best to contain the pressure, but some of it escapes and travels to its ultimate destiny: the left prefrontal area. But because the need/feeling is partially blocked, the actual context of the pain cannot be connected. The result is a vague pressure from the feelings on the left side. It then concocts ideas about those needs/pains: "God will watch over and protect me." These ideas are the wrappings for the pain that provide symbolic fulfillment. That is why the exact nature of the need/pain is not known. But if we strip away the covering, the pain mounts to the surface immediately. The symbolism slips in before the pain can become conscious. Its function is defense, and that is why it can be "far out." It is dealing with a mysterious internal reality without even knowing what that internal reality is. The deeper and more powerful the pain/need, the more abstract and abstruse the ideation and belief. The ideas may be crazy, but the feelings are not. If the ideas are challenged, the person will continue to defend them with one rationale after another—all to keep reality at bay.

A study reported in *Science* by researchers at UCLA, Princeton, and University College, London, found that faith in a placebo changed the brain's circuitry, specifically those circuits that process pain and diminish its intensity.[2] A study reported in *Science News* (2005) found that just thinking you are receiving treatment is enough to make you feel better. When subjects were given pills that were neutral, but told they were painkillers, there were changes in the brain exactly as though they had received real painkillers. There was a significant increase in the secretion of endorphins—the pain-killing chemical in our brains.[3] That is why patients in conventional insight therapy feel better and imagine they have made improvement. The fact is they do feel better, and that is why almost any therapy is addicting. It is identical to going to a doctor for a shot of morphine (endorphin is an analogue of morphine). The wonderful thing about this is that the injection is painless and done without benefit of a needle. A kind, attentive look by a therapist, and there are squirts of morphine secreted in the brain. Implicit is that the doctor is going to make you feel better, and of course you do. You think the therapy did it but, in fact, *the thought* of what the therapy can do is what accomplished it. In contrast, what we offer in our therapy is pain, not as an end in itself, but as a necessity for getting well.

Science News (2005) discussed what positive thinking does. What they found is that many of the same areas of the brain that respond to pain also respond to mere expectations of pain.[4] What was found in the study was that expectations of less pain (how the therapy is going to help you) yielded as much relief as less pain. In other words, how we respond to pain depends in great part on what we believe about it. Placebos work on the same areas that process pain. So, in a cognitive therapy that alters how one perceives pain, there is bound to be a lessened response to it. Thus one can quell the pain of childhood by adopting a different perspective.

Placebo reactions are a good example of denial. Through someone else's ideas, we can be so removed from ourselves that we completely deny an agonizing experience. That is not only the case with cognitive therapy; it mirrors how some of us grew up, in a kind of cognitive milieu. We were denying pain and getting on with life. Denying agony is not the same as being out of it. There is believing—believing in healing—and then there is real healing.

What we see again and again, particularly in new studies, is how beliefs can diminish the experience of pain. When someone gives up drugs or alcohol and adopts new beliefs, his brain accommodates just as if he were still on drugs.

According to a 1990 Gallup survey of 1,200 American adults, one in four believed in ghosts. One in six had communicated with someone deceased, and one in four said they could communicate telepathically (through the mind). One in 10 claimed to have seen a ghost or been in the presence of one. One in seven said they had seen a UFO. One in four believed in astrology, and 50 percent believed in extrasensory perception.[5] In another Harris poll only 22 percent of Americans believed that we evolved from earlier species. Fifty-four percent thought that we did not evolve from earlier species. Forty-eight percent believed that Darwin's theory of evolution was not correct. Two-thirds of the population polled believed that human beings were created by God.[6]

The number and type of belief systems is limitless. As long as beliefs are not anchored in oneself and in one's feelings, they can take off and encompass all sorts of delusional notions. When separated from other aspects of memory (the disconnection), the prefrontal cortex can soar into the delusional stratosphere without boundary. This applies to the most intelligent of us, including scientists who, disciplined in their own fields, once disconnected from their feelings, can believe in the most irrational of philosophies and psychotherapies, approaches that have not one ounce of proof about them. Once unhinged from feelings, anything is possible, and intelligence has nothing to do with it.

Dr. Martin Teicher confirms a strong connection between trauma and brain impairment: "Harsh punishment, belittling and neglect are thought to release a cascade of chemicals, which produce an enduring effect on the signals that brain cells send to each other." When there are fewer dendrites, due to deprivation of love early in life, there is weakened communication between lower centers of the brain and higher control areas. Later we will discuss in detail this disconnection between deep feelings on the one hand, and one's "conscious" reality of thoughts and beliefs and behavior on the other, which may be shaped by the former without the person ever knowing what "drives" her.

It is easy to become entangled in a mesh of thoughts that bind us, the more labyrinthine the better—hence the attraction of insight therapy. One is now a captive of those beliefs, and he enters into his slavery willingly, because this slavery is also an important defense. If fascism were ever to come to America, it would no doubt come by popular vote not by autocratic edict. We would slip into unquestioning obedience to the leader gladly, for it would relieve us of having to think for ourselves. He would protect us from the evil "out there." I am reminded of those who dive for sharks in steel cages. They have no freedom of movement but it is a fact that the sharks cannot get to them. Their steel cage is their defense and their prison. Chemical prisons are just as strong as those steel ones. They allow for few alternatives in behavior. Beliefs are the psychic equivalent of repression. We can rechannel the flow but we will not change the volcanic activity. We can cap the explosion with ideas, but there is always a danger of another eruption; sometimes it is in the form of a seizure, other times it is found in being seized by a sudden realization—finding God and being born again.

The pateint I discussed previously who was about to enter the terrible pain of incest saw the hand of God reaching down to protect him (and take him out of the feeling). He was saved from himself. His experience and feelings. He was saved by the *idea* of God, unless we really believe that someone up there was listening and really did reach down. The idea intruded itself into his awareness in order to stop the agony. He became aware to avoid full consciousness. The idea took the place of the pain. He had to go no further into his archives of suffering. He came out of the feeling with a jolt. He came out of his past and into his present; that present defended him against his history. There was a sudden, abrupt shift from his right brain to his left, from internal focus to the external. And the pain did it all by itself; no willpower was involved. Instead of saying, "There is an automatic governor in my system that won't let me feel too much pain," he believed that there was divine intervention that stopped him from suffering. God became interchangeable with serotonin.

We get a good idea about evolution from all this, both personal and the species. First there are sensations, such as choking, gagging, suffocation; then feelings, such as unhappy, sad, fearful; then ideas. One flowed into the other as the species developed, as well as in our own personal development. Ideas are the court of last resort. We stretch them into absurd lengths until we reach psychosis, where there is no longer any real grounding in external reality. If we can contain the pain with our migraines and high blood pressure, so be it. If we cannot, then we adopt belief systems. If we can block it out with drink and drugs, so be it. If we cannot, we again seek out beliefs. It is all evolutionary. We obey the obdurate commands of the brain's evolution.

> *The trajectory of feeling is circumscribed and follows evolution from deep brainstem to right limbic to right prefrontal cortex, finally to the left prefrontal cortex.*

Even young children can take drugs to calm themselves long before they are capable or organizing a belief system. Once they are in their late teens they can exchange anxiety for beliefs, let go of drugs and alcohol, and flee into the realm of ideas. Once we view beliefs as part of evolutionary brain processes, it all begins to make sense. It is why obsessive thoughts are way stations to more bizarre problems of psychosis. It is all part of a continuum of using ideas to quell pain. Psychosis is the last station on this journey. It is difficult to tell the difference sometimes: "If I hang this amulet around my neck, no harm can come to me." Is that an obsession or psychotic ideation?

The trajectory of feeling is circumscribed and follows evolution from deep brainstem to right limbic to right prefrontal cortex, finally to the left prefrontal cortex. It all depends on the valence of the pain; the stronger it is, the more pressure on the ideational cortex to manufacture notions and beliefs. If an obsessive belief can stem the tide toward psychosis, so much the better; in my Freudian days, we thought that psychosis was the result of decompensating obsessional beliefs. Obsessional beliefs involve a fairly intact frontal cortex. In psychosis the first and second lines replace the third so that history becomes one current life. The past fully occupies the present and one can no longer distinguish between the two.

The body must find a way to translate the trauma's overwhelming charge into something else, so it mobilizes primitive defenses, which will repress the pain. Each pain is answered with repression, the brain's manner of covering up emotion. Later in life, equipped with the cortical ability to substitute ideation for feeling, the traumatized baby will call upon a God to save him from his inner pain, even when he doesn't know where the pain originated, or even that there is pain. He just calls upon a God to watch over him, see that he gets justice, be someone who won't let him down, and, above all, be someone who will help him make it into life, both literally originally, and currently in a figurative sense. Faith, ideas, mysticism, and magic are ways we channel the high voltage imprints left by traumatic events that are often preverbal. Remember, because imprints often involve life and death events, they make death a constant in the mind of the person. Therefore, the belief must entail some management of death.

Reconnecting the Brain

There is more and more evidence that brain tissue at the extreme anterior (front) part of the prefrontal cortex is responsible for integration of emotional states. The recent work of a Yale team, Patricia Goldman-Rakic and Pasco Rakic, focused on the corpus callosum (the bridge between right and left brains) in which they developed a model of symmetry in the brain. What they state is that cells in the corpus callosum are marked so as to attach to mirror-image cells on both sides of the brain. There may be either a certain resonating frequency that helps each side recognize each other or there may be a chemical affinity that allows cells on one side to join up, connect, with cells on the other side. As I mentioned, connected memory may exist when lower-level imprints resonate with the same frequencies higher up in the brain. When the prefrontal cortex and sub-cortex meet, there seems to be a pattern of recognition; it's kind of like finding a soul mate. More possibly, the lower-level imprints rise to seek out their other halves higher in the nervous system. Once joined, they form an integrated, unified circuit.

In an excellent book by David Darling called *Equations of Eternity*, the author discusses how nerve cells, and more specifically axons, behave. "Different groups of axons must be able to recognize different signposts, or else most axons in the nervous system would grow in the same place. Evolution has sited many different receptor molecules on the surface of nerve cell, each of which will stick to only one specific molecule."[7] The result is that nerve cells have a guide that directs them toward connection with other cells. All that is required for connection is that other nerve cells have matching receptor molecules. The cells are able to ignore all other nonmatching nerve cells.

Darling goes on to point out that these cells establish a "skeletal nervous system upon which all subsequent fibers can build." This is one way that each new level of consciousness elaborates on previous levels. Thus axons grow from the lower level brain tissue to its proper target. Darling states that these cells "know" when they have arrived at connection because the receptors on axons are found only on the correct target nerve cell. He goes on: "By unfolding stages, the brain organizes and interconnects itself."[8] Even in the womb, he believes, the brain is preparing itself for when "it comes into daylight." I will quote further because what he states in a neuro-philosophic way dovetails precisely with our clinical observations: "Already, the individual has recapitulated, while in the womb, the physical evolution of all life on earth. Now it is racing through the stages by which life evolved mentally."[9] The stages are "from mindlessness to shadowy awareness to consciousness of the world, to consciousness of self."[10] Each new level is an elaboration of the previous lower level until we arrive at full consciousness. Critical here is the concept of connection; the merging together of related neural networks.

Without lower level connection to higher levels, we are only considering the late-developing cortical brain and not the brain as a whole. He points out that in our personal evolution, the brain is racing through the stages of all of human history. In Primal Therapy, we race through the stages in reverse. Only it is not a race; it is more like a crawl. No one can make a connection (insight) for us; it must come out of a feeling, and it must do so in slow, orderly fashion. When the patient has the connection, we know it is time. When the insight is forced by a therapist, it usually is not the time. It must come organically, it defies evolution—ideas after feelings, not before. What Darling points out is that truth is an "unbroken reality." Neurosis manages to fragment that reality (disconnection). Feeling therapy reestablishes that total reality. There is a unity of nature that happens only with connection. Neuropsychologic laws do exist. It is up to us to find them.

> *There is no way to go deep without first going shallow—no visiting the past without first dealing with the present.*

Some of us may also lose our coordination as internal cues (from proprioceptors) do not make it all the way up to the top for integration. Thus there is an awkwardness, a maladroitness, and a lack of coordination because there is a disconnect between body, muscle function, and higher brain control centers. The person is not all together.

Early trauma impairs the proper evolution of the right brain, so we later misperceive, cannot sense nuance, and over- or underreact. We cannot sense nuance because that is right brain, and we are disconnected from it. Thus there is a tendency to be literal and not see the implications in certain situations. Right-brain impairment may also cause us to lose our ability to empathize because that too is right side. Anything that involves feeling, in short, is missing with disconnection. It is critical for a therapist to have right-brain access, and, even more importantly, to be right-left brain integrated. She must see beyond the words of the patient.

In the example of waiting in the previous case, it is clear that unless we go all the way down the chain, we will not have complete resolution and change. If we relive the waiting in childhood (the need to go home after being in boarding school), we would resolve only a part of the trauma. There will still be an urgency about waiting but not so desperate as before. What gives waiting its life-and-death urgency is the birth trauma, which indeed was a case of life and death. This is a general rule about any problem or act-out. The compulsive-obsessive aspect of it is largely driven by preverbal traumas, which are usually pure impulses. It is what makes sexual act-outs so difficult to treat. And unless a therapy arrives at the prototype, the act-outs will not be eradicated fully. The difficulty here is that first-line trauma underlying the act-out already has an urgency about it. The devilish aspect of this is that there is no way to go deep without first going shallow—no visiting the past without first dealing with the present. We must obey evolution, albeit evolution in reverse.

In rebirthing or LSD therapy, the patient is plunged into early remote pains; too often the result is incipient or transient psychosis. One of our patients went to a weekend meditation group that practiced deep breathing. (This was without our knowledge. It is forbidden in our therapy, for obvious reasons.) He came back to us in pieces, totally symbolic, speaking of cosmic forces and past lives. That deep breathing weakened his defenses and opened the gates artificially. The overload threw him into symbolism as the frontal cortex struggled to make sense out of liberated pains that were not ready to be felt and integrated.

In psychotherapy we must trust evolution and devolution; not skip steps. If, in therapy, we go immediately to birth traumas, we are defying evolution. But if we lock into a present situation, such as waiting in a doctor's office, the feeling will be there (as per our patient who could not wait). We have only to keep the patient in the current feeling, and it by itself will take her down where she needs to go. But we will only descend in orderly steps so as not to be overwhelmed. Feeling is a vehicle that transports us down nerve tracks to origins. If we do not interfere with the patient and force her beyond her capacity, there will be a shutoff when the pain is too much. When the pain becomes excessive, we all have an automatic governor that shuts us down again. That fact should tell us that defenses come into being automatically by pain. Being defensive is not something bad that we do. It is a necessary survival step.

One wonders that if human evolution makes so much sense, why doesn't it provide for access to ourselves naturally as we grow? Well, evolution got as far as repression and stopped. From fleeing external enemies, we developed the ability to flee the internal danger—feelings. But unfortunately, we need help to gain access. Meanwhile, we walk around each day in the survival mode—repressed.

> *No therapist who is left-brain contained, who is circumscribed by ideas and insights, can be trusted.*

It should be clear that dissociation restricts consciousness, not awareness, and we need consciousness, not awareness, for control. I can make this same impatient individual aware (left frontal area) in therapy that he is terribly impulsive and cannot stand waiting, but that does not produce the bottom-to-top connection that allows for control—the connection between deep right brain and left prefrontal brain. Even with full awareness, the right lower brain sends impulses throughout the body that gnaws away at various organs. The result may be colitis (often first-line originated) or bleeding ulcers, which cannot be stopped without first-line access. The aware person can be totally unconscious of all of this. The unconscious has no way to become conscious in the neurotic. Neurosis means an altered state of consciousness. That includes defective or impaired bottom-to-top brain circuitry. In brief, the brain is rewired. In the adult, instead of feeling the need for love and caress, one may feel immediate sexual impulses or the drive to eat. The more that those circuits are deviated and continue to fire in a specific way, the more the rewiring becomes reinforced.

We need to go back and relive the times of first deviation if we are to make headway to resolving it. We go back to reset the set-points toward normal. That is why, in Primal Therapy, the naturally produced inhibitor or repressor, serotonin, is enhanced after one year of sessions. Its set-points have been reestablished. It is sometimes possible to get relief by delving only into later childhood traumas, leaving the prototype in place. If the threshold for symptoms is raised by this approach, all the better. There will be no overt symptoms but the tendency is still there. Thus, an alcoholic may not be forced to drink when some of the pain is relived, but he will always be in danger thereafter. If we are looking for total personality change, it will not be possible without addressing the imprint. If one is happy with having no symptoms, then so be it. It is the patient's life, not ours.

Early trauma, birth, and pre-birth will generally interfere with the proper evolution of the right brain and its connections to the left. It remains so excited that even neutral events can set it off. Do we need a therapist to help us see outside reality? No. We need a therapist to help us find the internal one; the rest takes care of itself. We need to access the right brain because that brain (specifically the orbitofrontal cortex) contains a map of our emotional history and our internal state. With access we don't have to figure out what happened to us at age 2, we can reexperience and *know* it. That is why recall is so different from reliving. Recall is processed by frontal cerebral cortex. It recounts but cannot relive. Thus, there can be a recounting of an abuse by an adult when we were 4, which may not be true—a confabulation. Contrarily, reliving is systemic and all encompassing. In reliving there can be bruises from birth that reappear (such as the doctor's finger marks on the newborn's skin), or one begins to gag and choke as one relives oxygen deprivation at birth. That is a sure event not to be confused with a recounting. Reliving includes how the lungs reacted, how much mucous was secreted during birth—because during a reliving of birth it is again secreted. Recounting has nothing to do with it.

> *In reliving there can be bruises from birth that reappear (the doctor's finger marks on the skin), or one begins to gag and choke as one relives oxygen deprivation at birth.*

When I discuss right-brain control, it is the orbitofrontal right cortex that has direct connections to the amygdala of the limbic system. With a well-functioning right brain there will be the ability to modulate emotional output. But we also need right/left connections, largely through the corpus callosum. There must be right bottom to right top connection, and right top to left top connection, and right bottom to left top for total integration. This may sound complicated, but for the healthy brain it is a "no brainer."

The encoded imprint is registered throughout the system. Recall treats an encapsulated left-frontal brain as an entity in itself—confusing that brain with the whole individual, so when the person understands we believe he is getting well. Only her left brain is getting well. The rest remains sick. The left brain, expert in strange concoctions, can really believe all is well while the dissociated aspect of memory, the suffering component, is writhing with its silent scream. It is the right that gives us an overview of our lives and how we manage in it. The left dissects and is analytical, but it cannot see the grand picture. It can criticize but not create. Now we know how critics operate. And those in conventional insight therapy are talking to a brain that has no words and wondering why therapy cannot cure anyone. It is a dialogue of the deaf from those who cannot see.

Third liners seek out other third liners to relate to, and they choose third-line cognitive therapies to reinforce their intellectuality to keep feelings away. They stay in the realm of ideas when it is the opposite they really need. Our therapy is chosen by those who hurt, who often have too much access and not enough control. The therapist needs right-brain access so that she can empathize with the patient, sense what she is feeling, and know when pain should be avoided for the moment. A therapist will earn the patient's trust when the patient senses that the therapist knows what is going on inside of her, does not make inappropriate moves, and allows for the free flow of feelings. A therapist who interrupts feelings, who cannot sense the readiness of a patient to feel certain levels of pain, cannot be trusted. That distrust is inherent in the situation. No therapist who is left-brain contained, who is circumscribed by ideas and insights, can be trusted. None of that sensitivity can be taught. We cannot "teach" feeling. We cannot teach connection to the right brain; we can only allow it.

Because brainstem and limbic structures on the right largely make up the unconscious, the task is to bring the right brain into symmetry with the left. Remember, events are unconscious because early trauma impacts the right brain far more than the left, and that brain loses touch with conscious-awareness.

How Memory Is Formed

The notion of frequency signaling is discussed in a unique way in *The Field: The Quest For the Secret Force of The Universe* by Lynne McTaggart.[11] Amidst a long discussion on the communication among molecules, McTaggart states: "According to Benveniste's theory, two molecules are then tuned into each other, even at long distance, and resonate to the same frequency." It seems that all molecules have their own specific frequency.

Famed neuroscientist Karl H. Pribram found that when we first notice something, certain frequencies resonate among neurons in the brain even below our conscious-awareness. These neurons send information to other concerned parts of the brain to form memory. What is important in this rather esoteric discussion is that the brain processes information "in the shorthand of wave-frequency patterns and scatter these throughout the brain in a distributed network." It is in this manner that memory is stored and recuperated. Essentially, the brain is a frequency analyzer. But when the resonating information spells intolerable pain, contact is severed/disconnected. The left brain says, "I don't want to have anything to do with someone who hurts me." The right is pleading, "Hey, doctor left, I've got a hell of a load here; I'm just asking if you can help out a little." But no, inhibitory neurotransmitters are called into action to prevent direct communication from the right. This all takes place on the subcortical, rather than cortical-cognitive level. Even when we have words, there are still those underlying biochemical processes and those all-important frequencies. Why do we call him "doctor"? Because he fled to the left intellect and studied and studied to avoid feelings.

> *We cannot be healthy and mentally strong so long as there is disconnection; so long as there is a war going on between the two halves of the brain, mental health is not possible.*

Various key neurons may have a chemical attraction to their counterparts and lock in when they meet. For now, this is supposition, but the fact is that once there is a locked-in feeling or need, the system immediately shifts to the compensating nervous system to achieve balance. That is the test of connection; an equilibrium of the nervous system with vital signs falling below baseline.

We have done four separate brainwave studies of Primal Therapy patients. The beginning patients have greater power (hemispheric amplitude) on the right side of the brain, but after one year of therapy, there is a shift of power to the left. This implies a more balanced brain. There was a strong correlation between the patient's feeling of well-being and the shift in the brain. We have completed a two-year follow-up study of 14 of our patients. Over time the power of the brain moves not only from right to left, but also from the back of the brain to the front (higher alpha frequencies), where there is more control. There are higher frequencies in the frontal area, which may mean better integration and control of feelings. An anxious patient, not well repressed, may come in with a higher brain voltage of 50–150 microvolts at 10–13 cycles per second. Just before a reliving (a primal), the alpha amplitudes can reach double or triple the normal resting rate (300 microvolts). This tells us how close to conscious-awareness the memory/feeling is. It gives us a diagnostic tool to measure access in the patient.

Left/Right Brain Connection

Connection means the liberation of the right feeling prefrontal cortex from control by the left. The left can now perform its important function of integration instead of suppression. And, of course, the relaxation of the patient and her sense of ease is another key piece of evidence. Most important, once there is a lock-in of feelings, the insights become a geyser. After a feeling, one patient discovered why he could never dine in an indoor restaurant; he wanted nothing over his head (which turned out, in a birth Primal, to be smashing into the pubic arch). He could never have anything above him, even symbolically, like a boss. Of course, his father was a tyrant; he avoided authority like the plague. Thus, the first- and second-line components of the feeling were discovered.

We cannot be healthy and emotionally strong so long as there is disconnection; so long as there is a war going on between the two halves of the brain, mental health is not possible. Neurosis means there is a disconnection. It is not possible to get well through more of it, which is what happens in hypnosis and all cognitive therapies, where the left is driven further from its right counterpart.

Connection has neurologic roots. The Swedish neuroscientist, David Ingvar, using a CAT scan of the brain, found that a perception of pain involved both sides of the prefrontal area working in tandem. When emotional pain is repressed, I would assume the right side is more involved; the right amygdala picks up volume. As I pointed out earlier, the right amygdala tends to swell when there is feeling. Thus, disconnected pain is more active on the right side than the left.

It is as though there is a secret underground in the brain where messages are passed back and forth, but on the side that should be aware, there is no recognition of them. So the right side "tells" the left side, sotto voce, "Look, I can't take any more criticism. It means I am not loved." And the left side says, "Okay. I'll defend you against having to feel so bad.

Just don't tell me too much. Anyway, I'll twist the criticism by the other person, and make them wrong." And the left side jumps in immediately and automatically as soon as there is a hint of criticism. "Don't worry, my right-wing friend, I'll keep those feelings of feeling unloved and criticized under control even though you haven't told me what they are." So the left side acts out the feeling; the act-out is unconscious because the right side feeling is not connected. The left is not yet consciously aware.

We see this clearly in split-brain surgery (the surgical split of the left and right brains), where the surgeon will feed input into the right brain, but because of the lack of inter-hemispheric connection, the left is forced to rationalize a feeling it doesn't even recognize. The doctor will feed something funny to the right side while the left laughs and concocts a strange explanation for his laughter: "That white coat you are wearing is very funny." The fact that the left frontal area doesn't recognize the feeling doesn't stop it from manufacturing all sorts of rationales. In brief, the right side input is forcing it to create rationales, as it does in both meditation and neurosis where the disconnection is enhanced.

There is a study in *New Scientist* (2005) indicating that in practiced meditators there is a thickening of the nerve tissue in the prefrontal cortex.[12] Meditation may well enlist the thinking, intellectual area to help in repression. The jury is still out on this, but to think that any gimmick or trick, no matter how seemingly sophisticated, can work when it ignores history is pure self-deception. In other words, meditation is a defensive operation to keep feelings down. That is why taking a patient's word is not always the best way to measure progress in psychotherapy.

Rationale

When someone says, "You are wrong about this," or, "You made a mistake there," the left brain quickly says, "Yes, but the reason I did that was...." The feeling is, "If I'm wrong, I won't be loved by my parents. I must defend." It is defending against the feelings on the right. "If I'm wrong I will feel useless, like a nothing, not deserving of anything. Not worth being loved." That feeling of being unloved, I must underline, is already there! The trigger in the present lights it up and swirls the feelings again. One rationalizes because one cannot stand one more bit of criticism and the terrible feeling that it sets off. The left accommodates and does the defending without even knowing why.

Neurosis, in many respects, is a split-brain state. The essence of neurosis seems to be to concoct rationales for one's behavior, which is driven by unrecognized forces. That is why one cannot penetrate elaborate rationales and explanations for other's behavior. "Why should I give up drink when it always makes me feel warm and cozy?" said an acquaintance. He had no recognition of the constant tension he suffered. So long as feelings are hidden and repressed, the defenses must remain intact. When the insight/cognitive therapist attacks this defense, trying to dissuade the person from her ideas, it is a vain cause; he has neglected the split-brain effect, which tends to be literal.

Rush Limbaugh, the radio commentator, has admitted to taking strong painkillers over many years. His ideational brain and strong-minded philosophies are anchored to feelings of which he is not aware. There's no more use in talking him out of those feelings than it would be to try to change his whole history. It isn't just that he has "unreal ideas," it's that his disconnected system forces him to both quell his pain on the physical level with drugs and to dampen his pain with a philosophy that may be at odds with his feelings.

Effective Connection

In any effective therapy, it is the connection between the deep right limbic to orbitofrontal areas that will resolve so many of our problems, from anxiety, which is pain leaking through a faulty gating system, to depression, which is pain butting up against rigid, unyielding gates. Why? Because many of our later problems derive from experiences in the lower right areas that never make it to higher level connections. Rather, they continually do their damage on lower levels (for example, chronic high blood pressure or the inability to get close to others). A report in *Science News* states that feelings of hopelessness in depression "markedly raise a person's likelihood of suffering a stroke."[13] It is reported that depression is equivalent to suffering from high blood pressure, in terms of risk of stroke. I have found that depression is often accompanied by deviations in blood pressure. They form an ensemble.

Preverbal pains are sequestered like an unwanted guest that we keep in the garage where we store undesirable items we'd rather not look at. What does get through is a vague sense of discomfort and malaise—the suffering part. The undesirable is knocking at the gates (almost literally) saying, "Can't I come in from the cold and join you?" The system, however, keeps the gates high, implying, "Sorry, but I can't tolerate all you've got to say. Let's wait for a better day."

That better day is when we are older, when the critical period is long gone, and we are able to tolerate the previously unacceptable. As adults we have a stable environment, are no longer dependent on neurotic parents, and perhaps have love in the present, which are elements that allow us now to face our childhood. Meanwhile, the brain has done its best to block the feeling, providing detours from the right-limbic information highway heading upwards and leftwards. The blockage is not complete, however, because the feeling drives act-outs. "No one wants me" becomes trying to get everyone to want her—being helpful, kind, and unobtrusive. The feeling becomes transmuted into physical behavior. The energy, which needs connection, has gone to our stomach and created colitis; to our cardiac and vascular system with palpitations or migraines; and to our muscles, making us tense. It may make us act meek and diffident, as if no one wants us around. It causes an inability for males to become erect. What we try to do in our therapy is to allow feelings to go straight up the feeling highway to the right OBFC and then to make a left turn to reach their destination.

Connection is always the brain's prime destination. If we only turn left and never go right, we will never make the connection. I believe the system is always trying for connection, but it gets blocked by gating. Because of the constant push to connect, feelings tend to intrude and disrupt our thinking; hence, the inability to concentrate or focus. Once connected, those diversions will no longer be necessary to drain the energy. The energy always spreads to the weakest link. "Weakest" means a vulnerable area or organ either due to heredity or to damage done earlier in life. Forexample, a blow to the head in infancy may end up as epilepsy, or a history of allergies in the family may result in asthma later on.

Here is what Stan, a patient, wrote about his seizures. I make no claims about a cure for seizures. I do say that there are proclivities, a brain vulnerability, for example, that given other later trauma and lack of love (which I remind the reader is a trauma), compound and manifest into something like seizures (or higher blood pressure, migraine, etc). This is the same as with those who have genetic tendencies to migraine or high blood pressure. It may take added compounded trauma to make the symptom appear.

Case Study: Stan—Grand Mal Seizures

I had grand mal seizures, about one a year, before therapy. I would have smaller seizures all of the time and also while sleeping. I would bite through my tongue. When I would wake up from a seizure my muscles would be sore to the point that I couldn't stand up and my stomach would burn. My whole body would ache and I was completely exhausted and hurt. The recovery period was typically about a week. I couldn't talk because of a swollen tongue due to the biting. I would have this feeling in my head that I can't even describe. It was like my head was underwater and I couldn't think clearly, so I usually slept for the first few days after the seizure. I would feel suicidal for about a week afterwards. Although my inclination was to kill myself because I was in so much pain, the thing that kept me going and the reason I didn't kill myself was that I would repeat over and over to myself, "I didn't feel this bad yesterday and if I wait long enough this will go away."

Details are hard to remember because everything was a blur, and it was difficult to think clearly. Immediately after a seizure it would take me about 20 minutes to remember what day of the week it was, but I would remember my name and I would know where I was. Typically, I would lose two to three days of work. After a seizure my eyes couldn't take in light. It was like I was in a really dark room and the only light I could see was any light that was directly in front of me, as if being in a dark tunnel with a train coming at you. I had other occurrences, like standing in line at the supermarket where I would not know where I was. The doctor told me that it was probably a type of a seizure, but on a small scale.

I have no idea how many feelings I have had. I didn't cry for about the first year and a half of Primal Therapy. I could tell that feelings were coming up because I was feeling bad, whereas before therapy I was feeling nothing. The single most important event in my therapy was going on Klonipin. My very early pain, some from birth, was pushing up, while my mind was pushing down. My feeling level seems to have been getting smashed. Klonipin allowed me enough access to start feeling; otherwise I was overloaded (and vulnerable to seizures).

In a session, I would start to cry briefly and then I would start coughing and shaking and I couldn't go back to the feeling. The Klonipin relaxed my body enough so that I could cry for a longer period of time and I could descend from things that bothered me in the present to the same things that bothered me in the past. I cried for one to two hours, twice a week, for three years. The biggest feeling was that everything is hopeless. The hopelessness was that mother was never going to love me, my father would never love me, and that I was in a world of shit; that nothing would ever get better. I had this feeling that my life was a prison sentence that I had to endure. I thought about suicide constantly because it seemed that it was the only way out of the prison. For example, I was in a scene in therapy in the house I grew up in, at the bottom of the stairs, looking up to my mother who was standing at the top of the stairs, and I was crying because I wanted her to come down and talk with me. She never talked with me. I would cry about wanting my mother to pick me up and to hold me and to talk with me.

During this period there was very little birth feelings. I had one previously [where I] had feelings where I felt stuck and my mother wasn't helping me to be born. Although I don't know for sure, I suspect that a seizure is an explosion designed to get me unstuck and born.

Eventually I got to feelings of "please love me, please talk to me, and stop ignoring me." These are the feelings that changed my epilepsy. The key to it all is that I have all this stuff I have had to keep inside. I was never allowed to show any emotion and I had to act like everything was fine. So, after 20 years of having to hold everything in, it was like a pressure cooker and my body couldn't hold it in anymore, and I started to have seizures. Every feeling I have in Primal Therapy reduces that pressure a little bit more.

As a result of years of feeling, that pressure has been reduced enough that I no longer have seizures. Today, I am off all medication, and I feel good more often than I feel bad. I used to feel bad 24 hours a day, seven days a week, but now I might feel bad only a few days out of the month.

Here is another patient who is epileptic. I think it is quite instructive to see how feelings tend to diminish seizures.

Case Study: Sonny—Epilepsy

During the last two weeks I have just had a new breakthrough in my fight against epilepsy. Since my seizures gradually have decreased from grand mal to petit mal as a result of feeling, I now and then have had a mini petit mal, which starts with an aura (according to the neurologists' nomenclature) followed by a weak scream-crying-shivering coming from deep down [in] my stomach. The phenomenon has usually been triggered by emotional circumstances that I haven't been able to handle. I'm almost conscious and can describe and talk about it afterwards. It lasts for 10–20 seconds. The other day when it happened I could suddenly go on from the start of this petit mal into a growing sound of very strong crying. What a relief!! I have been waiting for/expecting this during months, yes years.

I've had grand mal for over 40 years without any help. By throwing away medicine, going straight into my seizures, converting it directly to the [P]rimal feeling, I have gradually discovered the roots of my epilepsy, which now only are a fraction of what it originally was. I now know what it means to have full access to one's feelings with a tremendous spontaneity and capacity to absorb and to enjoy life.

What I have seen in group therapy is an epileptic patient begin to have a seizure and, with our help, turn it into the feeling, usually first-line, behind it. The patient then has the primal instead of the seizure. Again, this is by no means in every case, but it does happen. I used to say that psychogenic seizures were the result of faulty gating, but I now believe they are due to complete repression so that the brain has no other outlets for behavior. This often happens in a highly disciplined household where the child is kept under tight control. Even the child's sexuality is controlled by religious parents; warning about masturbation, even though new research indicates that frequent masturbation can avoid all sorts of problems. Clearly, release is important, and seizures are, in one respect, a release factor. Painkillers and tranquilizers can slow the transmission of the pain message and thereby soften or avoid the seizure altogether. It is not surprising that new research has found that the same drug used to control epilepsy can also control and reduce migraines. It would seem that, in one sense, migraines are a seizure of the blood vessels that constrict and then give way to dilation. In any case, more and more research is finding pain underlying so many disparate symptoms. In some types of epilepsy there is a "release" phenomenon where repression falters for a brief time and there is a massive random discharge of neural energy. It is logical, therefore, that tranquilizers that aid the gating system would help epilepsy and migraines.

The Limbic System and Its Connections

It is the right amygdala that forms a sensory gateway from feelings and sensations in the lower realm of the brain all the way up to the OBFC. The amygdala also provides emotional information to the OBFC, which takes over some of the memory and codes it. The amygdala not only regulates memory formation but also the level of emotional power. When the amount of information is overwhelming, the message does not travel all the way to the OBFC for connection. It can be blocked at the level of the thalamus and sent back down, retaining the disconnection. We then have a headless monster rummaging around the lower depths of the nervous system without guidance.

People who feel uncomfortable in their own skin sense that rummaging monster but don't know what it is. They just feel that they want to jump out of their bodies. It is not difficult to understand someone who has an "out-of-body" experience. Those with terrible first-line pain do sometimes have "out-of-body" experiences where they leave their corpus behind and travel to another dimension. It is another way the defense system works; it is the flight from the pain on the right to the left brain with its imaginary powers. The person has made the leap out of himself—out of the feeling self—to an imagined state. We see intrusion of this "monster" literally, in our sessions when a patient will be reliving something from early childhood and suddenly be seized by a coughing jag, her feet and arms changing to fetal position. Here we have tapped into a childhood pain that has roots deeper in the brain. Sometimes the intrusion continues, such as a loss of breath, and interferes with a full reliving of a childhood event. If the patient is ready for the first-line experience, we may go there. This is rarely done in the first months of therapy. The rule is gentleness: going for the most recent and hence lesser pains first; opening up the system in sequential order a small bit at a time so that each pain can be integrated.

In some cases when the amygdala is carrying too much pain, the hippocampus can modulate its force. But when there is early trauma, the hippocampus cannot do its job. Unfortunately, this structure (the hippocampus) is very sensitive to long-term output of stress hormones. Stress, even before birth, which raises stress hormone set-points, can begin to affect the still developing hippocampus. We may not see these effects for 50 years when memory starts to falter and serious memory loss begins. Here we note how important the altered set-points are. It means that the imprint produces a higher than normal secretion of cortisol throughout our lives; this has all sorts of physiologic ramifications. Over time there may be some brain damage because some structures, such as the hippocampus, are very sensitive to high cortisol levels. Later in life, this can spell serious afflictions, not the least of which may be Alzheimer's or Parkinson's disease.

There is new evidence for my position: A report in *Science News* (2005) that very early stress in animals can be "brain-altering and memory sapping."[14] The implication is that early trauma can lead to serious memory loss later in life, and implicates the hippocampus in the problem. Based on our clinical experience with humans, it is not a stretch to apply these findings to our fellow human beings. What the researchers point out is that inadequate care and loving to young animals "delivers a delayed hit to the brain." Another study published in *Scientific American* (2005) found that one way tranquilizers work in the brain is to dampen the pain-processing structures (hippocampus and amygdala).[15] In other words, while adrenaline soups us up and makes control of feelings difficult, the drugs that quiet adrenaline (tranquilizers) makes recall of old traumas more difficult. The more old traumas (lack of love) are closer to consciousness, the more we suffer.

It is the right feeling brain that is responsible for a good deal of the secretion of the endorphins and serotonin. Early imprints may change these set-points for a lifetime.

The Delusion of "Adjustment"

The weakness of the OBFC is often seen in our disturbed patients who relive first-line events in the first days of therapy. We know from this that there was very likely pre-birth and birth trauma. Institutional children placed at birth relive these traumas very soon in therapy. The direct impact from the amygdala to the prefrontal area can alter how we perceive reality because another more importuning inner reality is affecting our perceptions. The cognitivists may try to deal with those perceptions, but when they neglect the deeper forces, they ignore what's orchestrating them.

The inhibitory neurotransmitters also work to prevent information from traveling over the corpus callosum to the left prefrontal area. So we may have an awareness of an early trauma such as, "My mother gave my dolls away," or "She sent me to boarding school," but the part that hurts is repressed: "I need my mommy!" It is the suffering component that remains unconscious on the right brain; it is that part that wants to inform the left frontal area, but to no avail. We have a paradoxical need: to feel the hurt, and not to feel the hurt; to be protected from shattering pain, and at the same time, to connect to it and get it over with.

"Mental illness" means the representation of lower forces on our mental, rational, and logical processes. The brain is so good at disguising its pain that most of us don't even know we have it; even if we do, we don't know what it is or where it comes from. Worse, we don't know how to get rid of it. It is diabolic because we may seem to be making a very good adjustment—we smile, our job goes well, we have a happy marriage, and so on. Yet, the primal hell is bubbling below, waiting for its chance to make us sick and ruin our lives. Until that happens we have no clue about our primal pain. Does it matter if we claim to feel well adjusted? Only if we know the consequences; then it is a matter of choice. It may be true that we have had a bleeding ulcer, but it has been controlled by medication, so we assume there is no need to worry further. That ulcer may be the result of the pain energy making a pit stop in the guts, just as "mental illness" is a sign of it landing higher up. Medication for the ulcer may quiet the pain, but because the generating source of the pain may be hiding inside the symptom—the ulcer—painkillers may be suppressing both pains at once. It is not exactly killing the pain; it is masking it. And it is the same medication that helps mental illness and psychosomatic symptoms. Why? Because they may have the same origin. They are just different ways we manifest the same pain. Cognitive and insight therapists are at a disadvantage because they don't recognize that they are dealing with an impaired brain that will not respond to ordinary reason. The traumatized brain has different cognitive capacities.

The true meaning of optimum mental health is harmony and balance. It is also the meaning of emotional-intelligence, which allows our feelings to guide us toward a sane, intelligent life, and not one filled with broken loves, drugs, tobacco, alcohol, and esoteric intellectual pursuits. Harmony and balance enable us to lead not only an intellectual life, but a healthy and intelligent one as well, one not driven by compulsions and the inability to relax.

The Tango of the Two Hemispheres

It takes two to tango: we need both the feeling aspect of an experience and also its comprehension. That is the mark of an integrated feeling. Once there is a locked-in feeling, the system immediately shifts to the compensating nervous system to achieve balance. That is the test of connection—the balance of the nervous system with vital signs falling below baseline. It means the liberation of the right feeling prefrontal cortex from control by the left. The left can now perform its important function of integration instead of suppression. And, of course, the relaxation of the patient and her sense of ease is another key piece of evidence. It is not just a balanced brain; it is a balanced human being. That balance will be reflected in the state of health and ultimately will affect longevity. Without a real connection, a proper hook-up, there is no significant change in the sympathetic-parasympathetic, right and left brain systems.

There is a way to measure connection of feelings; for it is only connection that allows for qualitative improvement in a patient. What all this means is to connect history with the present, deep right-brain processes with higher left brain ones, and to be liberated from one's unconscious. It is, in effect, to find the meaning of life, for meaning resides in feeling. "Getting something out of life," first means to feel the life inside of us. Joy isn't "out there" ; it is "in here."

Rutgers University neuroscientists Leonid Goldstein and Erik Hoffman found in a study of Primal Center patients that after connection there was less of a left-brain bias. The left was no longer "on its own," ignorant of the right side feelings. It was now integrated—a balance of power on both sides. That means that as the blocks to feeling were removed, the left prefrontal area was ignited to do its proper job. The projection of the lower level nerve fibers from the thalamus, limbic, and brainstem areas could connect up at the prefrontal areas. The message of pain/feeling was then spread to both sides of the brain.

One reason for the evolution of the left frontal cortex was to produce a brain system that could distance itself from the other areas of the nervous system where painful feelings lie—a way of not being overwhelmed by what lay below so that we can get on with life and deal with daily problems. It is a system that can bolster defenses and keep us out of inordinate pain. Another important reason for the evolution of the left hemisphere is that the left frontal cortex evolved with the use of tools. It is the left frontal area that is involved in precise tool use; for example, hammering a nail. Precision has become the domain of the left frontal area. If we are looking for a good surgeon, we should find one that is left-brain dominant. We can be assured that she will be precise. If we want a therapist who can feel and sense things, we may want a right-brain dominant individual; but, of course, someone with a balanced brain is always the ne plus ultra.

The Road to Mental Health

We must not refute the importance of feelings and their connection in psychotherapy. Further, we must not take at face value someone who is apparently well adjusted who claims contentment. Because we are all too often bound by the externally oriented left frontal brain, we tend to focus on the apparent and observable. We must look beyond statistics, facts, and "proofs," and focus on the subtext—feelings that make sense out of all those facts. There are (right brain) truths beyond (left brain) facts that involve a different kind of language. But we need to give credence to the language of the right brain. Otherwise we are bound by the left brain; we see the notes but do not hear the music, and cannot feel the truth of a level that has a language all its own. Too often, research deals with externally quantifiable behavior and tends to neglect feelings; adept on the left brain and inept on the right.

As a patient in our therapy approaches connection, the vital signs mount radically. It is a sign of pain on the rise. The only thing that can stop that rise is connection. Otherwise there is simply a discharge of energy. Discharge feels good momentarily; therefore it can be confused with connection. The pain I am discussing is almost never seen in conventional therapy. Conventional theory won't permit it. Primal pain has been called a "pain that doesn't hurt." As I pointed out, it only hurts when we try to block it. I understand why the profession is slow to accept this. I never saw such pain in all my professional practice until I started Primal Therapy. Intellectuals may doubt and refute the importance of feelings in psychotherapy. One prominent psychologist says that the imprint is unimportant or even nonexistent, because he knows concentration camp internees who have later made a very good adjustment. These people don't speak the right (literally) language. They are bound by a brain that is apparent and observable, which is taken as gospel. The cognitivists want to see statistics to reinforce their case. But when truths are offered beyond the facts, truths that involve a different kind of language, they are abjured as lacking precision and "objectivity." Left-brainers want and relate to statistical truths, when mostly what we offer are biologic ones.

We must not be afraid to go deep into the unconscious with our patients if we know what *deep* means and how to get there. It has to do with getting the self back, the self that is hidden away from conscious-awareness, deep in the lower registers of the brain. It then gives us empathy and sympathy, the ability to feel inside the suffering of others because we have felt our own. It has taken some 30 years to refine the techniques for this subterranean voyage, but I believe we have achieved our goal.

Case Study: Frank—Disconnection and Beliefs

I was born into a fundamentalist family in a small Oklahoma town. So much was considered sinful: movies, television, any sort of profanity, dancing, makeup, jewelry, drinking. I was made to go to church three times a week, with the terrifying threat of growing up a criminal and getting sent to the electric chair if I didn't obey my parents.

I never felt like I fit in anywhere, and I was ridiculed and tormented by other children, including relatives. My memory of childhood is of almost always hurting.

I filled the emptiness of my life with an obsession with science and chemistry. When I was 12 years old, I discovered the theory of evolution and tried to explain it to my parents and other relatives. They were horrified by what I was telling them and denied that it had any validity. I felt confused and shunned. But scientific atheism gave me some comfort from the incomprehensibility of my parents' religion and my painful life.

My obsession with science got me through life until my wife died and my house of cards began to collapse into a nightmarish alcoholic hell. I attempted to escape into the study of psychology. Maintaining my atheism, I became a therapist at 23. By that time I had become addicted to drugs (including eight LSD trips), alcohol, cigarettes, food, and deceitful relationships. I also developed an addiction to a new belief system that seemed to make sense of my agonized life and ease my suffering.

In 1973, a reputed amateur psychic told me that I could be doing something that had never been done before. That I would help a lot of people, but to do so I had to "release the little one and let go of the old one." It was a cryptic message, but my ego was fed. I felt like I would be somebody.

Although I was still essentially a scientific atheist, I succumbed to the idea of taking a small dose of LSD and going with my best friend to see Baba Ram Dass, a former Harvard psychologist who had become a touring yogi and was giving public talks. Since I was a veteran of LSD use, the one-third hit I took did not make me hallucinate. I only noticed that one area of a white wall seemed a bit brighter than the rest. Yet I was pleasantly high. After playing some sonorous music, chanting for a while, and giving a mystical talk, Ram Dass began to tell the story of when he had gone to see a guru in India. The guru had held his hand over Ram Dass's head so that a circular bluish light played on his hand. The light then turned into a plastic manmade medallion with the guru's image on it.

At that moment I thought, "Well, I believe that happened to you, or at least that you believe that happened to you, but nothing like that ever happens to me." Suddenly, under my left hand (with which I had been propping myself up as I sat on the floor) I felt an object. In amazement, I grasped it. It was a pearlescent blue ball, obviously manmade, with no hole in it, so it was not part of a necklace. I thought, "It must have just appeared. No, someone must have just dropped it." I held it up. People around me looked at it and smiled. No one claimed it. I thought, "Maybe Ram Dass dropped it. Maybe he put it on the floor and this is supposed to happen; it's part of the show." Then I realized I didn't really know what had happened and couldn't rationally figure it out.

At the break I showed it to Ram Dass. He said, "It's a blue pearl. Swami Muktananda wrote a book called Guru about the teaching of the blue pearl. Love it but don't be fascinated by it."

After the break, wanting to feel important, I sat next to Ram Dass on stage with others. In addition to working in the counseling clinic, I taught psychology at a university. In the audience I could see some of my students and patients. How crazy this must have looked. Ram Dass made pointing movements over the top of my head, as if to say, "This one here." Later, when I asked Ram Dass a question, we both said the same words at the same time. It seemed like we were the same person.

The next day I felt compelled to go see him at a radio station. I said, "Bless me, Baba." He held me to his chest and autographed his book for me. I felt confused, and I wondered about all that had happened—what had really *happened, and what it meant.*

I read the book Guru, *which Ram Dass had mentioned. It was nothing remarkable. But I had decided to say goodbye to my students and patients and move to Los Angeles. There was one man in the group I could not say goodbye to because I felt I would see him again.*

A few months later, I saw signs along Santa Monica Boulevard advertising, "Be with Swami Muktananda." Although his book had not really done much for me, I was drawn to seeing another guru. I went to see Muktananda and asked him about what had happened to me with the LSD, Ram Dass, and the little blue ball. He said, "Just keep meditating and you will understand." I touched his arm and walked with him and others. I chanted. His picture on a card I had been given seemed to become conscious. I thought he enabled people to trip without LSD.

Some months later I went to visit my family in Oklahoma. After a couple of weeks, it was time for me to leave. But for some reason I could not pull myself away. I thought that saying goodbye to my university would help. I drove to campus and pulled into the only parking space left on a certain block. There in front of me was a poster announcing Swami Muktananda's arrival the next day. I thought, "So this is why I was unable to leave." I had had no conscious knowledge that he was going to be there. When I went to see him, among many others in the audience was the man I had been unable to say goodbye to. We laughed together and exclaimed, "We knew. We knew." I thought it was all very significant, not just a series of coincidences.

Later in the summer, after I had returned to Los Angeles, as always I was seized by deep loneliness. But no longer liking bars, I went to a local yoga meeting. There I told a friend of mind that I would like to see Swami Muktananda again. He said, "Well, he's coming." I thought, "Oh, yes, this is how he works. Wherever I go, he turns up." That's how it seemed to happen.

Again I went to see him, at an American Indian festival he was participating in. Non-Native Americans were invited to join in a large dance around two sacred war lances planted in the ground. We were told not to dance between the lances. I noticed that several people did, which troubled me. I recall crying over something Muktananda said and picking up his Dr. Pepper bottle as a souvenir.

Some days later, I heard that Muktananda was in the hospital, having had a stroke. A few days after that, I ran into a faculty member who had been at the Indian festival. I told her about Muktananda's stroke. Surprised, she told me she had known of some of the American

Indians who wanted to punish Muktananda's followers for dancing between the war lances. She said they had gotten hold of some of his clothing threads and had "done some magic" on it. They didn't want to kill Muktananda, just hurt him to punish his followers for their disrespect. I believed that she and I were the only people who had this information. Something scary and weird was going on. Something horrible might happen. That was how I felt.

Rather than return to L.A., I flew to Oakland and stayed in the ashram where Muktananda was for about 10 days. I felt full of anxiety and pain. Much of the time I felt like I was tripping on LSD, thought I hadn't taken any for almost two years. I felt excruciatingly guilty for having left my son and for being a bad son in abandoning my parents. I felt I needed to return to them. It was almost impossible for me to sleep. I alternately cried and chanted. I feared that if I were to tell anyone what I had been doing and what had happened that something worse than death would happen to me. I didn't want to believe in hell.

I returned to L.A. and asked my son if he wanted to come to Oklahoma with me. He did. We went to Oklahoma, to live near my parents. I worked in a correctional facility. I meditated and tried to feel. I tried to be a vegetarian. I tried to be celibate. Nothing helped. I took Meprobamate because I couldn't sleep. I was alone and freaking out inside.

One evening I took some Robaxin, went to a nude bar, and had a few beers. This next morning, I woke up crying, consumed with the unshakable obsession that I would have to kill myself.

Baba Ram Dass came back to Oklahoma. I threw myself at his feet, hoping desperately to hear some words that would make me feel better. He was the only person I trusted enough to tell the suspicions that only I and the other faculty member possessed. But Ram Dass told me to get my economic scene together and be as loving to my son and parents as possible. I suppose he was trying to give me some sort of practical guidance.

I was deteriorating rapidly. My family doctor sent me to a psychiatrist, who prescribed Sinequan for me. Taking one, I got worse. I felt like I was coming out of my skin. My parents wanted me to talk to their preacher. I tried to get them to see that I really was sick and needed help. The preacher talked me into getting saved that afternoon. That night I took another Sinequan, but was unable to sleep. My head was filled with Daliesque images with Christ in them. I had hardly slept for five days.

I realize now that I felt like I was coming out of my skin because the pill had calmed the onslaught of my feelings just enough to allow it to rise. It was literally coming out of my skin. It was all my needs that were driving me crazy. Instead of feeling them I was running away as fast and far as possible. I decided to feel them, and as I did those nutty beliefs soon dissipated.

The Meaning of Integration

I have used the terms *integration of feeling*, or *resolution of feeling*, throughout my writing. Perhaps it is now time to specify what that means. Usually, when someone has an integrated feeling it means that feeling has become part of her or him. How does that happen? Where was it before it became part of him? One quick answer: it was *apart* from him, deep in the recesses of the brain—in the unconscious. Where are those unresolved, unintegrated feelings? Reverberating in loops below the level of the awareness; still doing their damage, still affecting the heart and vital organs. We know that because beginning patients have aberrant vital signs and high levels of cortisol (stress hormone), which change radically as soon as there is connection and integration. That means to me that the energy portion of the feeling is wreaking havoc below the level of integration. When I say, "energy portion," what does that mean? It means that the actual imprint has a force or valence that is measureable. It contains the agonizing part of the feeling without connection. It is "headless," if you will; like a decorticate animal, lacking direction and purpose. The early need rises in force so long as it remains unfulfilled. The energy is the system mobilized for the fight for survival. It provokes into being its counterpart: repression. One day when it rises to the prefrontal cortex for integration, the agony portion of the feeling is connected and no longer doing its damage to the body, vital organs, and brain processes.

Integration means access to one's deep unconscious, not something alien and alienated. We can see how non-integration works because when someone in primal pain gets close to an old feeling, she runs a fever, often 2–3 degrees higher than normal. That does not happen to a feeling person with good access. That fever is a sign of an alien entity intruding into the system very much like a virus. And the body treats the early feeling, "No one loves me. It is all hopeless," just like a virus. The system in pain is not welcoming and is indeed most wary. The devilish part of this is that the person is rarely aware of the cause of the act-out and the feeling under it.

One structure among many that is involved in feeling memory is the hippocampus. When the feeling/limbic system, particularly the hippocampus, gets active, it provokes the prefrontal cortex to get busy in suppression. The more the prefrontal area is active, the less we see of hippocampal agitation; as though the cortex is busy suppressing excess emotional memory. So long as this takes place, there is no integration. Herein lie the horns of a dilemma: we go to a therapy where words and talk are the main tools, the very tools that help suppress feeling. In this sense, conventional therapy prohibits access to feeling. In brief, we cannot integrate through any mode of therapy where words predominate. Yet we obsessively go to therapies where feeling is not possible. In brief, we go to get our defenses bolstered when we need a treatment modality that weakens defenses.

If we follow evolution and allow feeling before ideas in psychotherapy, then we cannot go wrong. If we defy evolution, and use ideas before feelings, then we must, perforce, go wrong. The same is true for those rebirthers who decide to plunge patients into remote and devastating pains right away in psychotherapy. There is no integration because the valence is so heavy and the pains are thrown up out of sequence. The same is true for those who use drugs and hallucinogens to get to deep early feelings. The system cannot possibly integrate (even though often the patient and therapist are convinced that progress has taken place). Integration means a slow descent from the present and top level prefrontal cortex to lower limbic/feeling areas and finally to the deeply rooted and engraved imprints around birth and infancy. We need to prepare the soil for heavy pains. When they intrude suddenly into the top level, there is of necessity a disintegration taking place. We see this in our vital sign research where signs go up and then down sporadically without any cohesion to them. They tell us there is no integration.

When a feeling from very early in life is imprinted it is also immediately disconnected. Part of the meaning of an imprint is that it is an overwhelming stimulus and cannot be safely connected to higher processing centers. So we have a feeling that is not integrated into full brain processes—it is unconscious: "My parents will never like me, touch me, hold me, or want to spend time with me." The meaning is split from awareness, and involves lower brain processes that are an enclave shut off from the whole brain. The first thing we see is that certain neuronal/brain mechanisms are not connected to other key aspects of brain function. *They no longer interact with those other parts and are not part of the whole circuit.* The lower processes no longer co-vary with higher level centers. They are virtually independent and are unintegrated. When they finally get connected, they form a gestalt—a whole sytem that is solidly interconnected. Now each level can affect and influence the other. It is the neurologic meaning of access. There now should be an integrated pattern of nerve firing; and we know that when neurons fire together they wire together. That means that each area can affect the other. They are mutually dependent. They form an interconnected circuit. This is feeling! When we have access to our emotional centers and their related deep instinctual/sensate connections in the brainstem we are feeling beings. When we are walled off from those centers we have less and less access and are less feeling. Then the unconscious cannot be reached.

Primal feelings may well disrupt our ability to function in life. If they arise abruptly, perhaps as a result of taking a hallucinogen, or plunging into rebirthing therapy (a dangerous procedure), they can distort cognitive function and impair our ability to maintain some kind of mental cohesion in life. That is exactly what happens in psychosis when the defense system is weak and feelings from the depths rush forth to higher levels. This is what is called "a nervous breakdown," a breakdown of defenses against those very feelings, and a rupture of cohesion.

My definition of consciousness is integration; integration means wholeness. It involves the energy portion of a feeling, the emotional aspect and an understanding of what it is and why it is. There is no full consciousness without it. We cannot have our feelings buried down low, living their own lives, disconnected from awareness, and still be conscious/integrated. We cannot subcontract out our feelings to an independent entity and have a cohesive (mental) organization. We do not need cortical control, which is what happens in the ideational/insight therapies that smother feelings, but by a lack of control that allows feelings to rise and take part in higher neuronal processes. Integration is not willful, but rather an automatic process. We cannot perform any ritual to enhance it. In fact, the more we use our willpower, the top-level cortex, to try to integrate, the less successful we will be. Insights are higher level disconnected functions that have no deeper meaning, unless they arise out of feeling. We cannot do evolution in reverse, top-level insights before feelings, and hope to be successful in therapy. Ideas cannot change feelings, but surely feelings change ideas. Remember, we are discussing millions of years of evolution in feelings before we were able to have ideas. We see so clearly that ideas are mostly used to block feelings, not to have access to them.

When insights are used before feelings, they are recruited for suppression. They can be effective for a short time only; then we have to go back to therapy for more insights to keep feelings at bay. While the therapist is analyzing our feelings, we suffer from a compounded error: his higher level processes in conjunction with the patient's higher processes join seamlessly into a solid defensive apparatus. What Nobel Prize neuroscientist Gerald Edelman and Giulio Tononi point out in their book *A Universe of Consciousness* is that integration means that suddenly "many different parts of our brain (are) privy to information that was previously confined to some specialized subsystem."[16]

The problem is to figure out how to join those disparate systems. Mind you, those systems would be naturally integrated were the force of the feelings not so overwhelming. The brain knows better than all therapists who ever lived. It says, "I must shut down to save my sanity." It must go crazy to keep from being psychotic. "I must concoct bizarre ideas to take the place of the real ones that can only spell agony." So consciousness, then, is no more than maximized interaction among neuronal groups and different levels of the brain. What we in Primal Therapy are trying to do is take a group of deviated neuronal circuits that are wired together, liberate and reroute them upward and forward to meet their mates. Ah! Respite at last. Old (neuronal) friends who haven't seen each other in decades immediately recognize each other. Indeed, apart from neuronal aspects, there may well be chemical affinities among circuits between the limbic system and the left prefrontal cortex that make them recognize each other and lock into one another. Now it is no longer the brainstem/limbic circuits that form a closed reverberating loop of neurons; there is now an opening and the circuits rise to meet their counterpart that has been waiting a long time for such an encounter. And the frontal cortex says, "You are now free, my son. Your bondage is undone—that which has kept you sequestered in your chemical prison for so long is over. You can now have a myriad of behavioral options. You no longer have to keep repeating the imprint symbolically ad infinitum. You no longer have to drink alcohol to feel the warmth that mother should have given you." Isn't it easier and more efficient to feel the need for mother's warmth? Particularly, when that sets the system back to normal? Previously, the higher forces were a circumscribed enclosed entity, and the same was true of the lower forces that were tightly contained and isolated. Connection means that they are no longer working in diametrically opposed directions; they are working together toward a common goal: survival. Maximum interaction among brain networks means maximum integration. Maximum interaction means feeling. The better and fuller the interaction among nerve circuits the deeper and fuller the feeling. It isn't just that there is better interaction among brain centers; it is that those centers have their bodily counterparts which enlarge the experience of feeling.

Primal therapy is known as a therapy of feeling because we help patients gain access to their brains and body. When that happens, they feel with all of themselves. Let me put it succinctly: only full reliving with the brain system operative at the time of the trauma is resolving. We cannot recruit the adult brain to do the work that is the domain of the child's brain. If a therapy claims to deal with the patient's history but approaches it from an adult focus, it is bound to fail. If it is the result of any kind of encouragement/insistence, it will fail. It must follow a natural evolutionary course of feeling. Integrated individuals give off an aura—one senses their wholeness, their lack of defensiveness, and their inner harmony. Isn't this what we all want?

9

Awareness Versus Consciousness

The leitmotif of every intellectual therapy is that awareness helps us make progress. I'll grant that awareness helps; but being conscious cures. Unless we are able to achieve consciousness in psychotherapy, the most we can do is tread water, having the illusion of progress without its essence.

When it comes to measuring progress in psychotherapy, it matters whether one measures the whole system or only aspects of brain function. Awareness fits the latter. It has a specific seat in the brain—largely in the left frontal area of the brain. One cannot be aware without an intact prefrontal cortex. By contrast, there is no seat of consciousness. As banal as it may seem, consciousness reflects our whole system—the whole brain as it interacts with the body.

> *What we are after is the awareness of consciousness and the consciousness of awareness.*

Consciousness can be viewed as a vast field of energy linking all parts of the brain and central nervous system, according to neurophysiologists Rudolfo Llineas and E. Roy John. Consciousness has to do with all levels of the brain working in harmony with fluid access among them; the sum total of all systems as reflected in brain processes. It is an enduring organic state; awareness is not. Awareness is a moment-to-moment affair with a specific content. It has an infinite number. Consciousness is singular. There is one consciousness with many awarenesses, but not vice versa. Consciousness has no specific content, yet no content is shut away from it. Consciousness remains even during sleep, while awareness disappears with sleep.

Awareness and consciousness are two different animals. "Aware" and feelings lie on different levels. Awareness is what we often use to hide the unconscious—a defense. Awareness without feeling is the enemy of consciousness. What we are after is the awareness of consciousness—aware of the lower levels of consciousness and their contents. Awareness of awareness is a third-line solipsism; the left prefrontal area talking to itself. When the patient is uncomfortable during a session, therapists typically take the position that "More insights is what we need. She is not aware enough." But it is not the content of those insights that helps; it is the fact of the insight—a belief system that aids the defense mechanisms to do their job. Yet, what lies on low levels of brain function is immune to any idea. We can be anxious and aware but not anxious and conscious.

Consciousness is the end of anxiety. Consciousness means connection to what is driving us. Disconnected feelings are what drive us constantly to keep busy. Their energy is found in the form of ulcers or irritable bowel, in phobias, and the inability to focus and concentrate. They are the ubiquitous danger, shaping a parallel self—a personality of defenses and the avoidance of pain; a self stuck in history forever. In effect, there is a parallel self, the unreal front; and the real self, the one that feels and hurts. Thus, there are parallel universes that make up the human condition—one that feels and suffers, the other that puts on a good front. The latter, the front, is what most psychotherapy deals with: the psychology of appearances versus essences. It is navigating in the wrong universe.

Awareness means dealing with only the last evolutionary neuronal development: the prefrontal cortex. It is the difference between the top level versus the confluence of all three levels, which is consciousness. Once we are conscious, we have words to explain our feelings, but words do not eradicate them, they explain. We are deeply wounded long before words make their appearance in our brains. Words are neither the problem nor the solution. They are the last evolutionary step in processing the feeling or sensation. They are the companions of feelings.

There are types of awareness that are important for our survival. Being aware of a healthy diet is crucial even in the absence of consciousness.

But a therapy of awareness versus one of consciousness has an important difference in terms of global impact. In science we are after the universal so that we can apply our knowledge to other patients. A therapy of needs can apply to many individuals (we all have similar needs); a therapy of ideas usually can only apply to a specific patient. When we try to convince the patient of different ideas (for example, "People actually do like you"), we generate no universal laws. It is all idiosyncratic. But if we address the feelings underneath, we can generate propositions that apply generally; for instance, pain when unleashed can produce paranoid ideas or compulsions. Or the frontal cortex can change simple needs and feelings into complex unrealities, changing them into their opposites.

There are really two awarenesses ("I don't need anyone. I'll make it on my own."). One is left prefrontal—awareness of our external surroundings. The second is right prefrontal—awareness of our inner milieu. When they are put together, the internal awareness becomes part of consciousness. When it joins the left side awareness, we are finally conscious. There is then a qualitative leap from one state to a more comprehensive one. It is the latter that accounts for a radical neurophysiological and psychological change.

> *Consciousness means thinking what we feel and feeling what we think; the end of a split, hypocritical existence.*

A person is suspicious of being hurt by others because he was hurt so badly by insensitive parents; in Dan's case, a cruel mother. He projected this fear onto others who he thought wanted to hurt him. Dan was slightly paranoid at the start of therapy, questioning even the nice things he would hear. "Did you really mean it? I thought you were putting me on." His suspicions went from the personal and idiosyncratic (his mother in the past), to the general (everyone else in the present). "They" are trying to hurt me. When we took Dan back from the universal "they" and transformed it into a personal "me," the paranoid ideas were diminished or eliminated. The general had become the particular, which then produced a general law.

Needs are universal; behavior is idiosyncratic. In our therapy, we place the behavior into a universal context. A patient who feels suffocated or strangled so much of the time may be expressing an imprint from birth. Indeed, one of the hallmarks of that imprint is the sense of suffocation in the present. That sense, though specific, indicates a universal problem: the lack of oxygen during a birth trauma. It can be applied generally.

There are several studies establishing a link between birth trauma and later psychosis.[1] Lack of oxygen and the subsequent birth trauma constitute such a load of pain at the start of life that its overload weakens and stretches the thinking cortex. It forces the person to concoct bizarre ideas in an attempt to cover the pain. This is another way of saying that psychosis is often of first-line origin. The "cortical dam" is weakened and then later, difficult, loveless times with one's parents finish the job. Are psychosis and depression separate diseases? They are only in the sense that very great pain early in life transforms so many physiological processes that it begins to look like a different disease. There are, of course, many factors that play into their development, including genetics, but it is my belief that early trauma is a great part of it.

Psychotherapy has been in the business of awareness for too long. Since the days of Freud, we have apotheosized insights. We are so used to appealing to the almighty frontal cortex, the structure that has made us the advanced human beings that we are, that we forgot our precious ancestors, their instincts and feelings. We may emphasize how our neocortex is so different from other animal forms while we disregard our mutually shared feeling apparatus. We need a therapy of consciousness, not awareness. If we believe that we have an id stewing inside of us, there is no proper treatment because the cause is an apparition—a phantom that doesn't exist. Or worse, it is a genetic force that is immutable and therefore cannot be treated. In any case, we are the losers.

There is no powerlessness like being unconscious; running around in a quandary about what to do about this or that—about sexual problems, low blood pressure, depression, and temper outbursts. It all seems like such a mystery. The aware person or he who seeks awareness has to be told everything. He listens, obeys—and suffers. Awareness doesn't make us sensitive, empathic, or loving. It makes us aware of why we can't be those things. It's like being aware of a virus. It's good to know what the problem is, but nothing changes. The best awareness can do is create ideas that negate need and pain.

Awareness is not healing; consciousness is. True conscious-awareness means feelings, and therefore humanity. The conscious person does not have to be told about his secret motivations. He feels them and they are no longer secret. Consciousness means thinking what we feel and feeling what we think; the end of a split, hypocritical existence. Awareness cannot do that because awareness has to change each and every time there is a new situation. That is why conventional cognitive/insight therapy is so complex. It has to follow each turn in the road. It has to battle the need for drugs and then battle the inability to hold down a job and then try to understand why relationships are falling apart. This also explains why conventional therapy takes so long; each avenue must be traversed independently. Consciousness is global; it applies to all situations, encompasses all those problems at once. The true power of consciousness is to lead a conscious life with all that that means: not being subject to uncontrolled behavior, and being able to concentrate and learn, to sit still and relax, to make choices that are healthy ones, to choose partners that are the healthy ones, and, above all, to love.

The conscious person can be sad but not depressed, for that means repressed.

Awareness can enlarge the Janovian Gap; it will deceive us and alienate us from inner reality until reality cripples us, both mentally and physically. Consciousness narrows the gap and that could mean a longer, healthier life. The conscious person, now in touch with the life inside, has a reverence for all life. There is no liberation like consciousness. This means that finally, having felt the depths of our sadness, there is now the ability to experience joy to its fullest. Feeling those depths means feeling, which is what is liberating.

It is not possible to be conscious and depressed; they are antithetical states. The conscious person can be sad but not depressed, for that means repressed. The aware person can have a false kind of liberation with a fixed smile of joy, but it is hollow. We can be aware and depressed at the same time. In fact, awareness, too often, helps in the job of repression. With awareness we can think we have found nirvana, but alas, we are encircled by a delusion. We have found an idea—an awareness—of nirvana, but it is a state fabricated by the serotonin/endorphin factories that keep pain at bay and allow false ideas to flourish.

We have to look no further than hypnosis to see how easy it is for ideas to block out pain. The hypnotist says a few magic words and you look at your hand being pricked with a needle and will not feel it or even know it is being done. I used to do hypnosis on rare occasions. When I pricked the finger of the subject and asked where it hurt, he was puzzled and then pointed to his knee. I abstracted him from his physical experience. That is what living in a parallel universe, one based on denial, can do: produce a human abstracted from himself, who feels no pain. It means someone who does not feel, nor empathize, nor love.

In hypnosis or suggestion, it is possible to lull critical awareness and replace it with a new set of ideas, to produce a pseudo-consciousness. The person can be a queen in a past life. Or, more importantly, she feels that life is wonderful; all pain has been removed. That is the paradigm for neurosis, a hypnosis writ large. Hypnosis, therefore, can be a mini neurosis. We can't get well with hypnosis because wellness means consciousness. So we imagine we are well, we live in a state of false consciousness—an imaginary state. To be normal and to be unconscious are antithetical notions.

Hypnosis seems to scramble the left side so that it can no longer discern what is real. It blocks integration of feeling, which is a key element of improvement. It helps suppress the feelings in the amygdala, forcing the left frontal area to develop new ideas not in accord with what is engraved below. Then, like any mind game, a person can give up a behavior, such as smoking, but what is the price to pay for this denial of need? Eliminating smoking doesn't change real need. Many of us don't seem to care; all we want is to stop compulsive behavior. What we don't know is that compulsive, importuning need drives compulsive behavior. Again, the need to smoke is a derivative of a real need. Changing behavior does not change need. Stopping behavior leaves all those needs with nowhere to go. Patients often say to me in the latter stages of therapy, "Where was I? I must have been in some kind of coma most of my life." And that is largely what it was.

A rather banal example: One of my patients came into a session on Monday. He said he was feeling bad all day the previous day, Sunday, and didn't know why. From this point on we helped him follow the track all the way down to the following: "Yeah, all of my life I hated Sundays. I dunno why. Every Sunday my mother went out to see her friends and left me in front of the TV. I remember what I was watching. I was watching *Lassie*. I hated that dog! God I hate that dog!" (Patient is angry now and is back in the memory. He is now the child in front of the TV.) "The dog is so good, does everything right, always saving everyone. So smart. So everyone loved her." (pause—tears) "That's just it. She was getting all the love from everyone. (sobbing) I felt like a dog...but no one wanted me." (cries) "Momma, please love me." (child's voice) "I am just as good as Lassie! Don't leave me all alone every Sunday. I need you!" He was becoming conscious. That hatred of Lassie looked totally irrational. But imagine trying to convince him otherwise when all those feelings lay underneath. He hated that dog because he wanted to be loved. It seemed like an irrational hate, but the feeling that drove it was totally rational: love me! Therein lies the paradigm for neurosis; the rerouting of feelings into symbolic channels.

Awareness can be manipulated, as in hypnosis; it can be turned against feelings and against the self, producing a lack of harmony, serving to keep us unconscious, and as such can be harmful. Awareness alone, without conscious-awareness, can be fatal. We can be on the verge of a stroke and it still remains a mystery. In cognitive therapy, the more "aware" we are made through insights, the less conscious we may be; the left frontal area becomes a defense against consciousness. This means that there is a wider Janovian Gap between feelings and thoughts. Any awareness in therapy that arrives before a feeling is suspect. It means that evolution is trumped.

Consciousness cannot be manipulated or turned against the self because it emanates from the self. It is the essence of internal harmony.

Remember that analytic, cognitive, and Freudian insights are left-brain derived. Real insights arise out of feelings in the right brain. It is the right brain insights connected to the left that make for change. They emanate from the unconscious. Left-brain insights do not; they are propelled from awareness. Any feeling that rises into awareness forms consciousness, which is about all parts of the brain working in fluid harmony.

Consciousness means adaptability. It is limitless, a state of being. Awareness may seem psychologically adaptable ("I know what errors to avoid"), but it is not biologically adaptable. History fixes the range of awareness; it doesn't reach beyond left frontal capacities. It is mental adaptation, an imagined state; a state of mind alienated from our deepest being. The conscious person is sexual, which is not necessarily the case for awareness. Awareness does not free the body.

All the awareness in the world learned in prison confrontational groups will never change the urge to rape or to exhibit oneself. Nor will it stop the need for drugs; and a great part of prisoners today are incarcerated because of the use and sale of drugs. Criminals take drugs because the same thing that produces pain in them, growing up unloved, also can cause criminal behavior. Awareness does not put an end to the need for drugs. It can convince one that drugs are no longer needed: a very different affair. Awareness can never change internal reality. It is millions of years of evolution away from that reality. That reality is a reminder of our needs and our survival strategies.

Unconsciousness is not an absence of consciousness; it is an active process of repression and keeping consciousness at bay. It is the key defense underlying all other defenses. Becoming unconscious is a survival mechanism. That is why becoming conscious is not just an act of will. Willpower keeps us from descending into the unconscious. It is part of the left frontal defensive apparatus. We can make someone aware, but we can never make someone conscious.

We can become aware of our impulsive tendencies but remain unconscious of why. That "why" is what we need to discover. "Why" is what liberates us, which is the reason that I say to beware of any therapy that has no "why" in it. If it were easy, we would all be conscious. It is far easier to be aware, far quicker, yet more superficial. Our whole history, our evolution, and the history of psychotherapy, militates toward awareness, confusing that with consciousness.

Consciousness happens when we don't try; when we let feelings come up, when we live on a lower level of consciousness for a time. To be precise, the more we connect with our unconscious, the more conscious we become. In this sense, unconsciousness is the necessary condition for consciousness. To become conscious, the more aware parts of the brain, the prefrontal cortex, must recede. Cognitive therapy does the opposite by stimulating thought and giving it dominance.

The Evolution of Feelings

The notion that thought is first and the brain second, which distinguishes intellectual from feeling therapy, goes back to the old dispute between the logical positivists of the 19th century who saw the mind as primary, and the empiricists, who put experience first. Matter, the brain, obviously preceded mind. There was the existence of billions of years of organic life before there was a thinking brain that could conceive ideas. The cognitivists believe that experience is not experience except in the way we interpret it, that life experience and outside circumstances don't cause us to change. I assume, therefore, that our primitive ancestors didn't change due to their environmental circumstances; it was their interpretation or awareness of it all. Evolution to the cognitivists, implicitly, is a chimera. These therapists have unwittingly joined the Creationists. For both, there are no historical forces nor evolution. It may be that those who have no access to their history, who do not see how life has shaped them, are forced to adopt beliefs that follow suit.

What happens when an animal cannot interpret his experience but changes nevertheless? What happens when animals that were not touched early on have less dendrites and synapses, less serotonin and oxytocin? What happens when they are less curious and they hesitate to explore their surroundings? Is it their interpretation or their experience? Do we not share similar lower brain structures with these animals, and do we not react in similar ways? The intellectual therapies believe we can change experience with our attitudes. Not so. We can change our thoughts about experience, but the experience itself remains unchanged. Insights, ideas, or cognitions can blur, fog, and repress early imprints, and along the way, convince us that we are better, that we have made progress in psychotherapy, that we no longer are in pain, which often is not true. That deception can be done and is being done in every rational, insight, cognitive therapy extant. We call upon the disconnected left frontal cortex to make us aware—and in the name of awareness we become unconscious. It is difficult to convince anyone that they are not better just because they no longer have access to their pain. And I would not try. We are not in the priesthood, trying to convince anyone of original sin or, in this case, original pain. But when people are sick all of the time, it is the moment to take a good look at the unconscious. It is now possible to take a very close look at it.

The Measurement of Stress

What I am proposing is that mental pathology can be measured, not by mental indices, ideas, and perceptions, but by neurophysiology, by the biochemicals involved in consciousness and unconsciousness, and the brainwave activation and amplitude patterns. Witness the high cortisol levels in those who suffer post-traumatic-stress syndrome. In fact, most of us with birth trauma, and we are legion, are all experiencing post-traumatic stress syndrome. That stress is in our bones, muscles, blood, and brains. No part of us is immune, not excluding the immune system. If we later suffer from diseases of any of those systems, it reflects the stress that has been imprinted and where it may have gone. And I propose that we can measure that stress, that perhaps it is possible to develop a grid of pain or of repression, mixing in all of the effects of repression on various systems. Is the stress hormone level high? Is the brainwave amplitude low? Are the vital signs very low? All of these tell us something about consciousness and give a measure of the depth of the unconscious, as do our clinical observations. We need to know this so, for example, we can decide what kind of tranquilizer and what kind of dose we should use with those with too much access; those overwhelmed with rising pain.

I have seen a patient who first came to me after a suicide attempt using massive painkillers. He only slept for 15 hours after taking a dose that would have killed anyone else. The reason: the massive amount of pain activation of the brain that galvanized the system. The drug had met its match and wasn't strong enough to cap the electrical activity and put out his lights. Those who have had very painful cancer, for example, and have been on strong painkillers for a long time, will almost never be able to commit suicide through the use of painkillers. When that pain is unconscious, those who use painkillers may be known as drug addicts only because we cannot see their suffering, nor can they themselves. And the deeper the early deprivation and/or the stronger the birth trauma (and we should not minimize that), the more drugs may be required later on. The drug taker will only feel comfortable when the drug can equal the level of her pain.

The Nature of Addiction

We need to be careful about the term "addicted." If we break an arm and take painkillers for a week, everyone understands where the pain is, how bad it might be, and the necessity for taking painkillers. The person is not called a drug addict. But what if we have a broken heart? What if we have pain that no one is aware of, not even ourselves? A pain that occurred before we had verbal memory? A pain laid down solely in terms of neurochemistry, without words? A pain that came from being abandoned just after birth due to the illness of the mother? Ingrained here is a massive aloneness and terror; a helpless, hopeless feeling that cannot be articulated. If we now take painkillers, we may be known as an addict because we are trying to kill a pain that no one can recognize. And paradoxically, it is those pains, those preverbal pains, that are the most severe and the most likely to cause addiction.

The fact is that feeling pain often eradicates the need for painkillers.

The drugs deal with the pain on its own level in terms of biochemistry. Chemical pain, chemical relief. Addicts are stifling life-and-death pains so it is often a life-and-death matter to obtain them. Of course, one will lie or falsify a doctor's prescription. It is a matter of great urgency. Incidentally, I recently saw a patient who relived the terrible aloneness just after birth, and she realized that she had her child so she would never feel alone. She became far more dependent on her child than the child did on the mother.

In principle, consciousness puts an end to the need for drugs. We don't say that we cure each and every drug addict. There are those who were so deprived that cure is not possible. But the fact is that feeling pain often eradicates the need for painkillers. No awareness in the world can touch that addiction. Consciousness can. Awareness does what it is good at: self-deception. Of course we need to be aware of our environment—what foods we should eat, and what is toxic to our system. But I am writing in a different context: awareness as defense.

We can never fool need—ever. The importance of this is that the conscious person can take himself as object and therefore be objective. The aware person who is not conscious may be totally immersed in unconscious feelings and therefore cannot be objective. We cannot be objective about what we cannot see.

Neurosis, in one sense, is a functional commissurotomy, a splitting of the connecting fibers from right to left brains; we then can be aware and totally unconscious. The integrating mechanism of the two sides is impaired. One reason for that is early trauma that produces that impairment. Unconsciousness represents a breakdown in the integrative capacities of the brain. It results from an overload—too much input to be integrated smoothly. That overload of suffering is what remains in the unconscious. Impulses that normally have specific frontal cortical connections to make us conscious can be overloaded and then rerouted to lower centers to make us unconscious. Indeed, many symptoms come from overload, either from the psychological input or from the physical.

To illustrate the key difference between awareness and consciousness, let's take the example of a well-known experiment in dentistry. A dentist gave his patients an inert, placebo pill and told them that they were receiving a painkiller. They then had a tooth drilled, which should have hurt but didn't. They were responding to the idea of a painkiller rather than the pain of the drill. They were aware of the drill (the event) but unconscious of the pain.

Here we see encapsulated the entire difference between consciousness and awareness. The patient can look in the dentist's mirror and see the drill as it touches the tooth, yet feels nothing; an example of severe pain being shut out of conscious-awareness. The idea or belief of the pill's power had provoked the secretion of internal painkillers, exactly as though they were injected. They can be stronger than a drill against a nerve. Ideas—awareness—can do wonders about making us unconscious, which is the joy of cognitive therapy. It can make us think we are conscious while we remain unconscious. It helps us confuse awareness with consciousness. As I have pointed out, there is no act of will that can make us conscious; but this is not the case with awareness.

> *For a more lasting cure we need to get at the imprint that caused the disequilibrium so that we can normalize the system naturally.*

When someone gives up drugs or alcohol and adopts new beliefs, his brain accommodates just as if he were still on drugs. Healing is a collective force that depends, in some respects, on the memory of wellness: getting back to one's natural state. The devilish aspect of cognitive approaches is that they can feel like healing because the temporary result is feeling better. The usual answer is, "Who cares, so long as I feel better?" And, as I stated earlier, to each one her own life. If you want to feel better for a while, knowing you will pay a price later on, so be it. At least we should be aware of the price and the deception. After that, it is every person's individual choice. It should be an informed choice. Once ideas are involved as the predominant mode of a therapy, our internal drug factory is at work. How could we convince anyone that the therapy is not effective when it actually was? That it made the person feel better? What other criteria does the patient have? We all want to feel better, and that is what we expect of therapy. It is the same with taking tranquilizers, which papers over the real feelings. There is a price to pay, and obviously most individuals are willing to pay it. All I want to emphasize is the cost of awareness versus the reward of consciousness.

It is a complex issue, because early pain may permanently destabilize the production of neuroinhibitors (the endorphins and serotonin). Nonetheless, taking a medicine that ameliorates the deficit can indeed make one feel better. But for a more lasting cure we need to get at the imprint that caused the disequilibrium so that we can normalize the system naturally. Then the system won't have to depend on unnatural, artificial means, and possible tranquilizer use for a lifetime. In our past research, we found that the depth of weeping was related to healing. Because the use of tranquilizers can block weeping, it can also delay the healing process.

To change neurosis we must change consciousness or at least allow it. This is most crucial; for it is not about changing ideas or cognitive concepts, it is about changing the state of being. Ideas are ephemeral and easily changed. Remember: neurosis is an altered state of consciousness, a deformed consciousness, if you will. Reality has been buried deep in the brain and a new false consciousness has taken its place. The false consciousness may be called awareness because the cognitive/insight therapists tend to confuse it with real consciousness. It is a pseudo-consciousness, subject to all kinds of beliefs, irrational thoughts, and false perceptions. For each truth suppressed, a false truth must take its place. This is the origin of pseudo-insights, the ostensible realistic view into ourselves, but is one more invented and shallow rationale.

The reason a rationale may seem realistic is because it is fabricated by the disconnected left brain with no emotional frame of reference. The left side sees it as reasonable because the left side invented it, and no one dislikes his baby. The frontal cortex abhors a vacuum, an empty time and space in its ongoing function. If it stays empty too long, pain might enter. It needs the ideas as defenses. They must be there so long as pain is churning down below. Pseudo-insights fill the bill. In therapy they help kill the pain and therefore deceive the patient into thinking he is getting better.

What is the unconscious, but painful memories? To be conscious means to have access to those memories and to be able to rid ourselves of unconscious driving forces—to become conscious—to make the unconscious conscious. If inside we need desperately and yet we deny that need, we have substituted a false consciousness for a real one. When my patients beg again for love as children, they are becoming conscious, conscious of their need, as simple as that sounds. Consciousness, therefore, is not some mysterious entity that requires the help of intellectual philosophers, it is a matter of experiencing need. In cognitive therapy one can be helped to be aware of need but never conscious; conscious means suffering. There is no way out of that. It is navigating in the world of false consciousness.

I had a patient who continually saw bright lights in the sky and was convinced it was a UFO. Months later he had a birth primal, coming into the delivery room with exceptionally bright lights, which traumatized him. It remained an imprint. He became fixated on UFOs with large flashing searchlights. He saw his history, of which he was completely unconscious.

Our beginning patients have consistently high levels of cortisol, which often accompany the experience of anxiety. When someone is having a severe episode of anxiety, it may be labeled a panic attack; in reality, it is an attack of conscious-awareness. Nearly every pain is this kind of attack. That is what sets the alarm bells ringing. We react with panic because deep feelings are on the way to conscious-awareness. It is saying, "Pay attention. We need to do something here." We want to do something, if we only knew what. But all efforts are usually aimed at relieving the anxiety by driving away the warning signal, instead of trying to find out what it is warning us about. Or we go to an insight therapy to try to "understand" what is causing the anxiety and the panic. Either we connect to the pain or we flee. There is no in-between. When we eradicate the warning, we eliminate the awareness of danger, not the danger itself. This leaves us all the more defenseless.

Appearances and Essences

Another way of looking at the difference between awareness and consciousness is that of appearances versus essences—of phenotype (appearance) versus genotype (generating sources). An approach of appearances is always individual, while that of essences is universal, generating universal laws. Essence is stable while appearances are transient. Essence is historic; appearances are ahistoric. Essences are few; appearances are multitudinous (an endless therapeutic search down the most complex, labyrinthine behaviors). Essences lead to consciousness, the confluence of lower centers with frontal cortical structures. Appearances lead to awareness without consciousness. Essences necessarily mean the understanding of concrete contradictions between the forces of pain and those of repression because that is the essence of the problem of neurosis. Essences mean dealing with quantities of hurt leading to new qualities of being. It means dealing holistically and systemically. Appearances mean fragmentation of the patient, isolation of her symptom from herself—treating the apparent. Progress in psychotherapy is couched in terms of appearances instead of essences; and therein lies the rub.

The reason the Freudians and other insight theorists do not generate universal laws is because they focus on appearances and not essences, on fragments not systems. I should say that sometimes they do posit general hypotheses, but invariably they cannot be tested and verified because they have no scientific base. It is very difficult to compose a universal psychologic law from individual, idiosyncratic behavior that applies to one person only, or from an id or dark forces that no one can see or verify. Cognitive approaches seem to superimpose psychologic laws on humans—on (their) nature. By contrast, we believe that through careful observation we can discover the laws of nature and apply them to humans; after all, they derive from humans. Biologic truths are of the essence.

In Primal Therapy, we make every attempt to meld our observations and our own research and current neurobiologic research. We do this by not having too many preconceived ideas about the patient, and maintaining an empirical attitude. We do not treat each symptom as an isolated entity to be eradicated. Rather, we know that there is an ensemble of symptoms tied together by something that links them. That "something" is what we must get at in therapy; it is of the essence. Thus, we need to see the whole, not fragments of behavior. To see the whole we need to investigate history, which is the context for its understanding. We need to look beyond a phobia of elevators and see historic events (put into an incubator at birth, perhaps) that gave rise to it. The minute we are bereft of history, we are devoid of generating causes, and therefore essences. We remain in the dark.

The Freudians claim to have a deep dynamic therapy, but they stop at plunging the patient into old, infantile brains where solutions lie. They too rely on the here-and-now, on current ideas about the past. Reliving the past and having an idea about the past are not the same thing. One is curative; the other is not. One involves awareness, the other, consciousness. Even tears in psychoanalysis are derivative. There is "crying about" in their therapy: the adult looking back on her life and crying. But it is not the baby crying as that child and needing as that child, something deep that is beyond description that can go on for an hour or more. In "crying about" there is never the infant cries that we hear so often in our patients—a sign of a different brain at work, a different brain system solving its problems in its own way. The patient in the here-and-now, ego-oriented therapies is walking around in his history while the therapist is focusing on the present. He may be physically present, but his emotions are in the past.

What we discover about the cognitive/insight therapists and especially the televangelist psychologists is that they embrace old homilies, morality, and religious ideals that are in the zeitgeist; mix them into some kind of psychological jargon; and deliver them with a folksy air of, "I know what you need." Too often it all amounts to "Get Over It!" And we all shout, "Yeah!" For we too think others should just get down to business and stop whining. That is the George S. Patton syndrome. Develop a positive attitude and you won't feel like such a loser. But it's hard to feel that you are capable and can succeed when you have spent a lifetime with parents who reminded you of what a failure you are.

Every insight therapy has the implicit base that awareness causes improvement. It is founded on the notion that once we are aware, we can make necessary changes in our behavior. Awareness can make us aware, and that is a positive step. But it cannot change personality, which is organic, and it can never make us conscious. We can be aware that we are too critical of our spouse. Maybe with effort we can stop that behavior. But if we understand the concept of the imprint, then we know that anything that doesn't directly attack the imprinted memory cannot make a permanent change. We can be aware that we are working too hard and neglecting our family, but when there is a motor inside driving us relentlessly, that awareness is useless. Ideas are never a match for the strength of the brainstem/limbic forces, which, I remind the reader, have everything to do with survival. There is always a rationale for our behavior: "I have to be gone and work hard to support my family properly." We have applauded this kind of neurosis in our culture, which adores hard work, ambition, and relentless effort. Being driven is about the most widespread of neurotic forms. If only we knew how to finish the equation: being driven by...(Answer: need). Translation: I was not loved in my childhood and I am in pain, which drives me incessantly. And besides, I can't stop because my imprint at birth was that to stop was to die. I have to keep going to keep from feeling helpless, that there is nothing I can do. Those are the truths we find when we feel our imprints—the truths that when felt will stop our drive and allow us finally to relax.

Why is cognitive therapy so widespread today? To a large extent because it is far easier and quicker (and cheaper) to change an idea than a feeling. Insight and cognitive approaches tend to appeal to those in their "head"; this applies to both patient and therapist. Neither the patient nor the therapist is likely to realize the amount of history we are carrying around and how that affects our thinking. How else could we possibly ignore the horrendous things that happen to our patients in their childhood? Nowhere in the cognitive literature have I seen a discussion of basic need as central to personality development, of why the person cannot put the brakes on impulsive behavior. As I have mentioned, the ascending fibers from down below, starting from the brainstem and the associated limbic networks, alert the cortex to danger; they are more numerous and stronger and faster-acting than the descending inhibitory fibers, which, as we know, come later in evolution. Here in purely neurologic terms do we see how feelings are stronger than ideas.

An early lack of love means that there is an even further degradation of these descending inhibitory systems, not only because of cortical weakness, but also because the limbic-amygdala forces holding the imprint are enormously powerful and are importuning the cortex to accept the message. The engorged amygdala is figuratively bursting at the seams to unleash its load of feeling. The dominant direction it can go is determined by evolution—upward and outward, impacting the frontal cortex. There is only one direction that repression can travel—and that is downward, to hold those feelings back. Ideas can help in that job just as tranquilizers can. I suspect that therapists who practice therapies that deny history, and deny imprints and biology, are drawn to such therapies, ironically, as a function of their own history. So long as the connection is poor and access impaired, the therapist is open to any kind of ideas that appeal to him intellectually. And what appeals to him intellectually is what is dictated by his unconscious. And that means that he might choose a therapy that operates on denial, such as the cognitive, because he operates on denial. He makes therapeutic choices that obey this dictum.

If a therapist, unconsciously, has a need for power, he is apt to dictate to the patient; it may be directions for living, relationships, choices, and, above all, insights. He will impose his ideas, his interpretation of the patient's behavior. What he says will become most important in his therapy instead of what the patient feels.

If the therapist has the need to be helpful and get "love" from the patient, he can act this out in therapy. I remember feeling my need to become a therapist and be helpful, trying symbolically to help my mentally ill mother to get well and be a real mother. No one is exempt from symbolic behavior. And it is certainly more comfortable for a patient to act out his needs and get them fulfilled (symbolically) in therapy, and imagine he is getting somewhere, than to feel the pain of lack of fulfillment. It is understandable that the idea of lying on a matted floor crying and screaming doesn't appeal to some. Pain is not always an enticing prospect. Thus, the cognitive/insight therapist can be similarly deceived and entangled in the same delusion as his patient: both getting love for being smart. It is a mutually deceptive unconscious pact.

Any time we are not anchored in our feelings, we are up for grabs—any idea will do. It is good that the left frontal cortex is malleable, but bad because it is too malleable. It is the difference between having an open mind, and a mind that is so open as to be a sieve. The difference is having a left frontal cortex open to the right brain versus a mind too open to others and their suggestions precisely because it is not open to its better half. That is why a scientist can understand a great deal about neurology but practice a therapy that has nothing to do with the brain, which I have seen time and again—the bifurcation of consciousness. What he or she knows scientifically does not translate to the other side of the head because of disconnection or dissociation. He/she may be utterly aware and utterly unconscious.

In appearances, the therapy remains pretty much the same no matter what is wrong. The Freudians have a certain take on development and pathology. They will follow that irrespective of what is wrong with the patient, it all adds up to insights and more insights. Other therapies specialize in dream analysis. They go on doing that without any proof of its efficacy other than patient reports. There are no physiological measurements. They neglect the fact that experience is laid down neurophysiologically, not just as an idea; they neglect essences.

Another example of an essence versus appearance: We can take a tranquilizer to sleep better, avoid sleep problems, hold down acting-out, stop feeling anxious, be less aggressive and less depressed, stop bedwetting and premature ejaculation, and stop using alcohol and taking drugs. One specific pain pill can accomplish this universal task. Why? Because the essence, pain, is behind all of those disparate symptoms.

Pain will always remain pain no matter what label we pin on it or how we choose to deny it. Whether we feel ignored or humiliated or unloved, the pain is the same and processed by the same structures. The frontal cortex gives it different labels and we act out differently, but the centers of hurt treat them the same. Isn't it strange that we use the same tranquilizer to ameliorate depression and children's bedwetting? Maybe it is all one disease with different manifestations, and when we attack the generating source with drugs, all of the manifestations disappear for a short time. We need to learn a most obvious lesson from Prozac: it blocks all manner of symptoms. Therefore, if we, too, in a feeling therapy attack orchestrating forces, we can render unnecessary and eradicate all those different symptoms. Notice also that it is a nonverbal medication that slows down ideational obsessions. It tells us about the relationship of lower centers where there are no ideas to higher level thought processes, which deal with ideas.

In an anti-dialectic approach, which is that of appearances, there is no central motivating force. There is no struggle of opposite forces that move and direct us. It all remains on the surface—static. And because the approach does not contemplate the deep conflicting forces motivating us, there is no reason to delve into the patient's history. It is all non-dynamic. Treatment based on dialectic principles means that there can be no ego or mystical forces that arise out of the blue, containing a mechanical, hereditary "given." When the dynamics are left out, the therapy has no alternative but to be mechanical.

I have seen patients who have spent years smoking marijuana. They often come to us slightly paranoid. They smoke themselves into a partial lobotomy because right-side feelings are activated by marijuana, while the left-side control mechanisms are diminished. This unleashes feelings, which rise to the prefrontal cortex to be twisted into strange, highly suspicious ideas. These ideas are an attempt to deal with surging internal forces. What are those forces? For example, if one feels unloved early on, marijuana will unlock those feelings. They rise, but not directly; rather, they are filtered. The feeling "Not only am I not loved, they even want to hurt me," becomes "The ice cream man is plotting against me. He wants to hurt me." Or, in lesser form, "My friend wasn't very friendly today; maybe he's got something against me." Or, when a friend tries to help, she takes it as a sign that she is weak and helpless.

The permutations are endless, but they filter down to a succinct set of needs and pains. If we cannot see how suspicious ideas arise out of unleashed feelings, we will never understand paranoia—how the frontal cortex can take a simple need, "Love me, Momma! I feel so unloved," and twist it into "They really don't like me. They've got something against me." The "they" in his head really is mother who doesn't like him. It is so painful that it is generalized as "they."

"Well," the cognitive therapist, may say, "They have shown nothing that would indicate that they don't like you, so why not get over it?" Or, "Does everyone have to like you? Can't you get along without the whole world's approval?" Or, "Look, it really isn't true. Didn't he call you yesterday to see how you were feeling?"

"I guess so," says the patient." But the feeling inside the patient is saying, "I still feel unloved."

There is a chapter in a book on ADD (attention deficit disorder) by Ervin, Bankert, and DuPaul. They begin, not unexpectedly, by stating that ADD is related to cognitive deficits including, "a lack awareness of one's own behavior." They advocate teaching children to observe aspects of their behavior and make recordings of them. Not a bad idea, but not as therapy, rather, as a first step in therapy. They admit that ADD is also a problem of poor impulse control and deficient self-regulation. Solution: "To control their own behavior through the reinforcement of socially accepted verbal-nonverbal relationships."[2] What they are suggesting is to bolster the cortical control system from the top down and not the bottom up—to reinforce awareness and work against evolution, not with it. They take it as a given that there are uncontrollable impulses, and set about to teach control. When evolution is neglected, there are no longer what is known as antecedent-consequent relationships. In this sense, they are close to the Freudian position, which is a derivative of the religious notion: we are inhabited by demons (id: negative impulses or shadow forces), and we must control them so that they do not overcome us. The cognitivists would never admit that they are Freudian, but when they take impulses as a given, they are.

Religion puts a moral slant on our hidden "evil" forces, but it amounts to the same thing. Psychology becomes religion by another name. If not, what are those impulses? Where do they come from? Are they immutable forces that cannot be changed? If not, how do we change them? Their leitmotif is that demons live inside of us that shall remain unalterable and nameless, a kind of genetic evil. We are born with it, and that is that. Here is where the cognitivists join the Freudians, who join the Jungians, who join the priests in thinking our main job is to hold down these dark, evil shadow forces. The reason that so many psychologists consider those negative forces immutable is that not having deep access, there is truly no way to change them, hence they are immutable. This is an example of circular logic.

One study found that cognitive treatment was not better than giving cortical stimulants that made the cortex more efficient. In other words, drugs and words accomplish the same thing. However, the impulses, rather than being immutable, are eminently changeable once we understand them. Because of an unloving, traumatic early childhood, the person cannot put the brakes on the amygdala or brainstem structures because he hasn't the neurologic equipment; there is an impaired prefrontal cortex that does that. The cognitivist adds his frontal cortical weight to the patient so that their ideas, welded together, help control underlying forces. "You are strong. You can succeed. I will help you try. You just think you're a loser, but you are not one. You are really a good person, not the evil one you think you are." We see this in an experiment reported in a 2002 volume of *Nature* where electronic stimulation of the prefrontal cortex prevented rats from freezing up after they had been conditioned to do so at the sound of a tone (the one was paired with an electric shock).[3] When the therapist and the patient combine their thoughts in an insight session, it is no different from an electronic stimulation of that area. In short, it blocks the experience of terror and pain.

How is that psychologic notion different from the religious? The difference is that psychologists do not use the word *evil*, they call them *negative forces*. Shrunk to size, they are the same thing. And, of course, the mass of current television psychologists are really televangelists in psychological clothing. They have wide appeal because they combine current religious precepts with psychologese (think Wayne Dyer). It doesn't challenge anyone; it only confirms their prejudices. It offers cachet to them.

Then there are the drug therapies. Patients are given a variety of drugs for almost any condition. Talking to the patient is secondary. Patients are anxious, so they are given one type of drug. They are depressed, and they're given another type of drug. And often the drugs have the same effect on the brain: killing pain. And if the drugs we give to patients do not work, we raise the dose. And if that doesn't work, we change drugs. Meanwhile, there is no attempt to find out and address *why* they are depressed. Though we are trying desperately to find genetic causes, depression is not a necessary part of the human condition.

A recent newspaper article described a woman who is suing her psychiatrist because her husband was suicidal and his doctor kept changing his medication. She said that it made him worse. The doctors were relying on appearances, not essences, and were possibly misled. She claims that no one talked to him. Here is a case where even a little talking and some sympathy would have helped. There is a place for it. Maybe drugs weren't the answer. This approach saves the bother of having to deal with the patient's history and his early life. It saves the troublesome effort of talking to the patient and feeling for his anguish. Just that, feeling something for the patient, can convey empathy and can be therapeutic.

Treatment that primarily involves giving drugs considers the patient as a "case." There is no personal interaction after a few cursory questions. "Tell me about your symptom, but not about your life. Tell me about it, not about you." I have been in that position as a patient, seeing doctors who treat me as a "case." It is not comforting. But then there are the economics. Seeing many patients every hour makes it difficult to empathize or to even know much about the patient. After filling out a long questionnaire, we find the doctor entering the treatment room scanning the file, unable to really take in the essentials about us. History is another victim in current therapy, both medical and psychological. Today, psychiatry has become an arm of the pharmaceutical industry. They tell us what drugs work and we use them. The insurance companies won't pay for us to delve into the patient's history, to take our time to find out about her. They pay for immediate results. The conclusion: we develop new therapeutic theories to accommodate the idolatry of the here-and-now intellectual, drug approach. We have ceded our integrity for pay. We don't do it consciously, but we don't feed our families if we don't accommodate the new reality.

Of course, cognitive approaches are ideal because the therapist can tell the patient, in essence, "Get over it," and "Thank you for coming." In the new zeitgeist, the aim of cognitive therapy is to get the patient over it, not to understand basic dynamics. What is basic in man is his reservoir of pain and how it drives him to behave. Once we neglect basic need, we are thrust into awareness because it is the beginning and end of consciousness. We cannot see the reservoir when we focus solely on awareness.

Therefore, we cannot see the reason so many people are on drugs, both legal and illegal. We try to stamp out the need with words, but we will lose that war because need is stronger than anyone or anything. It will not remain suppressed. No one is stronger or brighter than her need because need is inextricably intermeshed with survival, and survival reigns. If we want to stop the demand for drugs, we must attend to basic childhood needs, starting with the way we perform childbirth.

Riding the Vehicle of Feeling

We need to look at ideas as part of a force-counterforce equilibrium. Ideas and beliefs are often an attempt to counterbalance deeper feelings. A bad feeling down below may force a counterbalancing idea up above. Hopelessness down low may give rise to religious ideas that embody hope, on top. A person's ideas are often an attempt, albeit unconsciously, to find a solution—to normalize. Feeling absolutely hopeless forces one to find some hope somewhere so that one is not plunged into self-destructive thoughts.

Let's see how it may work physiologically: a child feels hopeless about getting his mother's love. He doesn't know it, but his behavior shows it. To block that painful feeling from connection/awareness, there is an increase in serotonin output. This serotonin may also control dopamine release, which can underlie ideas containing hope. So serotonin kicks in to block hopelessness, then dopamine is secreted to help produce beliefs that involve optimism and hope. Incidentally, there is new evidence that addicts have less dopamine receptors than normal. Early trauma may destabilize the dopamine set-points and produce interalia, anhedonia—the inability to enjoy anything. Even a carrying mother's use of tranquilizers can accomplish that.

In the 1940s and 50s we tried to talk patients out of their bizarre ideas because we thought it was mental illness. So we used mental techniques. We were sure that their problem was that they harbored irrational ideas. All patients had to do was become rational. There was no mention of the body that those ideas lived in. Now we know that those ideas make sense when connected to the generating sources that gave them life. Must I say it again? Words won't do it!

Earlier I mentioned a patient named Dan, who because he had been hurt by a cruel mother, imagined others wanted to hurt him as well. In a session early in therapy, Dan related a story about an experience he had at a wedding. He was in the car and a friend was walking to the church. She waved hello and went on in. He got angry because she didn't wait until he parked. He wouldn't talk to her at all during or after the wedding. During a session, as the feelings traveled down his anger-chain, the memory of his mother came into the picture; the anger at her for hurting him all of the time overtook him. Then deep down, amidst a flood of tears and in a child's voice, "Look at me, Momma! Don't hurt me anymore. Please!" Any sign that would trigger that feeling would produce paranoid ideas, such as "they don't like me." His parents sent him to boarding school at age 7 because they really did not like him. He felt no one liked him. He looked for signs to confirm this unconscious feeling, and found them. He could get along fine until there was even a slight indication of indifference, which would set off the old feeling.

> *Primal Therapy is a journey to the archaic strongholds of the mind.*

Suppose we tried to use cognitive/insight therapy on him, and we tell him that the reason he is suspicious and hypersensitive is that his parents didn't love him. "Oh," he would exclaim, "I guess you're right." He knew his parents didn't like him very much, and had sent him away because he was in the way. They were going to get a divorce, for which the child was blamed. To get over this paranoia and to get along with others, in therapy he had to first feel unloved; beg them not to send him away; say how much he is hurt; feel the agony of that hurt, in context; and then, and only then, would he stop having paranoid ideas.

It sounds strange, I know, that a grown man has to beg his parents not to send him away 30 years earlier, but that begging is still engraved there with the hurt. When the patient gets on his knees, hands clasped together, and begs in the child's voice, the sobs stream forward. When patients beg their parents for help, their voices become that of young children, not because they are directed to, but because they are in the grip of that brain that dealt with the emotions at the time. And for all the tears they did not shed back then, they will have to shed them now; the tears go on for a very long time. Left inside, they will eventually make us sick. Tears are a natural process; blocking natural processes makes the system unnatural. Dr. Goodman reminds me that in the Book of Psalms, God saves Hezekia's tears in a bottle and then grants him extended life. Somebody knew that tears were important.

The Patient Has the Power

It is a life sentence to be neurotic, but we can cut that sentence short. Primal Therapy is a journey to the archaic strongholds of the mind. The wonderful thing about exploring the depths of consciousness in our therapy is that we have been able to peer down to the deepest levels of the brain. This means that we no longer have to theorize about the nature of man; we can observe it in its primordial, arcane state. The problem is that we have not known what needs were and how early they started. We now know that basic survival needs start in the womb—when we can see what a mother's depression does to the fetus or what an auto accident does to the baby in utero. We see how terror is imprinted; therefore, we know where anxiety comes from. We found out that the need for oxygen is primary. That is the key early need, for it involves life and death. We see the beginnings of personality and of neurosis, something not possible previously. We know what causes emotional pain. We know how awesomely powerful it is; and this informs us of how it can produce physical disease. To my knowledge, this is the first time we have had such a profound view of the nature of man. It helps us understand what possible contribution nurture can make to the human condition and what is the true nature of man. Is he basically violent? It seems that when his needs are not met, he has the built-in capacity for violence. When they are met, humans seem to be empathic, kind, and loving. What we have found in the depths of consciousness gives us guideposts for the proper rearing of children.

With each unblocking of feeling in Primal Therapy, there is an incremental increase in consciousness as connection to the left prefrontal area takes place. Every aspect of a feeling must be fully experienced to be curative. Even our sensations (for example, the reason we can't catch our breath or we feel suffocated) must eventually become aware and conscious. When we have those sensations in therapy, we help the patient, when appropriate, down into them so that the patient can put them into context. I should emphasize this point: the patient supplies the context. We watch and help. It's not always fun, but it certainly is relieving. And as consciousness widens, there is a more profound awareness and also a greater ability to feel. Consciousness means integration. Integration means balance, something that has physiological counterparts and is measurable in our biochemistry and brainwave patterns. None of this is possible through awareness. It skims along the surface, cozy in its benightedness. Too often, awareness is a theoretical concoction; someone else's theory or notion of what is wrong with us and what is normal.

The patient, not the therapist, is the seat of power in our therapy. He decides when to come, when to leave for the day, and when to leave therapy permanently. If the patient is having trouble, she is invited into the staff meeting to discuss her situation as an equal, not as a case. We listen to what she says because I have found that once patients have access, they are very good judges of what kind of therapy they need. Not always, but often. All this is not for bragging rights but for the good of all patients. It is not difficult to do. It has to do with saving lives. Above all, the patient decides what the insights are. All he has to learn is already inside of him; all he has to do is tap into it. And as it comes out, he discovers what behaviors and ideas were real and what were not real. Ideas joined to feelings place the system in harmony.

There should be predictable changes in behavior and physiology after therapy that can be measured over time; this is a standard that should apply to all modes of therapy.

There should be predictable changes in behavior and physiology after therapy that can be measured over time; this is a standard that should apply to all modes of therapy.

Primal Therapy, born out of numerous research studies and decades of clinical experience, indicates that by having patients go back and relive the overwhelming scene, feeling, or need from childhood, we can, in effect, reverse a traumatic history. In so doing, we can lessen the level of internal pain and, hence, the addiction to painkillers.

We have used EEG (electroencephalograms) in our research, and it can determine the relative strengths and positions of electrical activity in different brain regions. By tracking changes in this activity over the course of a patient's therapy, we can determine brain areas and patterns of activity that mark drug addiction and related phenomena, such as cravings. Primal Therapy alters the biochemicals we carry in our system, as well.

For instance, the activating hormone nor-adrenaline tends toward vigilance and activation, while serotonin puts on the brakes. Nor-adrenaline–containing axons arise mainly from the locus ceruleus, which in some respects is the terror center of the brain. Our research into the activating hormones (neurohormones that accompany the pain) adrenaline and noradrenaline indicate up to a 66 percent decrease after six months of Primal Therapy.[4] At the end of 26 weeks of Primal Therapy there was more than a 200 percent increase in growth hormone level, while there was a 30 percent drop in adrenaline levels. During that same period of time, for those who could not get into deep feelings, there was a significant drop in these same levels.

There should be predictable changes in behavior and physiology after therapy that can measured over time; this is a standard that should apply to all modes of therapy. It is not possible to resolve or eradicate addiction without accounting for changes in neurophysiologic states. There should be characteristic changes in serotonin levels, for example, so that tranquilizers are no longer needed by the individual. And, of course, the level of stress hormone output should be significantly decreased. When we normalize serotonin levels, it clearly obviates the need for tranquilizers whose main purpose it is to supply serotonin to the system.

We are all of one piece, part of an organic whole. Thus, we cannot isolate one factor, such as serotonin, or another factor, such as time off drugs, to make definitive statements about addiction or recovery. The brain can no longer be considered an isolated organ encased in the cranium but must be considered part of an entire physiologic system. Thus, when the body is in distress, that distress can be found not only in the brain, but in hormones and in the blood system, as well. Primal Therapy has established that drug addiction is made up largely of early pain (that is, a lack of love), and that pain sets in motion its countervailing forces, namely repression. When repression is in place but faulty or failing, when the serotonin-endorphin systems are inadequate to the task of managing pain, the individual suffers, and needs outside help in the form of drugs to dampen that suffering. Often the outside drugs mimic the exact biochemicals that should be produced internally. The serious addicts I have treated (including heavy smokers) have been riddled with first-line pain.

The strength of an imprint can often be measured by its opponent—the repressive system. It is my belief that psychotherapy has an obligation to measure pain, its repression, and its effect upon the neurotransmitter and neuro-hormone systems. All of these comprise a grid that forms an index of vulnerability to addiction; it includes, but is not limited to, behavioral factors—such as a patient's ability to stay off drugs and alcohol. Behavior doesn't tell us enough, but the body's chemistry always will.

Case Study: Caryn

It was only two months after having started Primal Therapy that my therapist suggested for me to take a tranquilizer. I raged. I had never in my life taken any drugs before. I always had tried to do without it and rather suffered through enormous physical pain before I even would have taken a simple painkiller.

What I did not know but found later in my therapy was that my phobia against medication was based on, and driven by, exactly the same early painful chain of events that now made it necessary for me to take medication: my drugged birth. But after two months of therapy, I still had no clue.

Two major feelings were driving my phobia against medication. The first was that I am able do it on my own without help, and that I do not need anybody/anything. This is how I always have made it in my life and this is the counter-phobic reaction against the helplessness I experienced when I was about to [be] born. My mother was so drugged that she still has no idea how I actually got out of her, and I was so drugged that I spent my first four weeks in life unable to suckle or even wake up. Pictures of me from that age show me drugged, looking very sick and unable to keep any milk in me. It all ran straight through me, and out again. The other feeling driving my phobia against medication was that I felt utterly convinced that anything that would enter my body would poison me and take me away from myself. Indeed, the nitrous oxide which my mother breathed in during labor and the final shot of an anesthetic when I was about to [be] born did exactly that. They poisoned me, they made me fade away and cut me off from my own body. They left me helpless at the edge of dying. Bad with a capital B.

But six weeks into Primal Therapy, I had no clue about any of that. To me it was totally real and natural that I would do it on my own and that I would never ever let medication enter my body. I continued raging against medication and my therapist continued suggesting it for another six months. Then a traumatic event in my life broke my resistance and I rushed to the emergency room of a hospital for medication. I just needed to rest from the pain; I just wanted to sleep.

I began taking Prozac, 5 mg daily the first days, then increasing to 10 mg daily. The indication was depression (sleeplessness, lack of energy, and that I was unable to experience anything positive). I never made it. After three days on 5 mg Prozac and my first day on 10 mg, I had gotten almost psychotic. I woke up in the night, feeling like a little ball, detached from everything, and I felt I was dying. After that experience, I was so shocked that I stopped taking the medication. I was prescribed two more different SSRIs in the following two months. I did not stay with any of them. They all made me feel like I was getting nuts. Finally I was prescribed 0.6 mg Zyprexa daily—an extremely low dose. I had specifically asked for it because a Primal friend with symptoms like mine had been helped. After the first intake I slept through the entire night, which had not happened for more than 15 months. I continued taking Zyprexa.

Taking Zyprexa continued to help me sleep, something which my doctor didn't want to believe. Zyprexa's indication is not sleepiness, but schizophrenia. What he did not understand was that Zyprexa calmed down my first-line brainstem, which is why I slept through the nights and got the rest I badly needed. I started doing a little better, but still I remained being constantly overwhelmed in my life and not being able to experience anything good.

After another four months I found myself again sleepless most nights and in a constant struggle with my therapist, whom I perceived as doing everything wrong all the time. I was stuck in another depression. Then 4.25 mg Prozac were prescribed to me in addition to 0.6 mg Zyprexa daily. The indication was depression—this combined treatment was a newly discovered approach to treat depression.

And it did wonders. After about a month I began to feel differently, more energetic, less negative. My sessions began to change. I would experience one feeling at a time and not any longer have 10 feelings popping up at once. After a feeling it would take me five, 10, sometimes 30 minutes, and then I felt that I actually was out of the feeling. I had closed down! That had never happened to me before. It made me able to really, on the third line, think about my feeling experiences and to integrate them. I found myself less easily triggered in my life. And I suddenly found myself getting bored in my life because I was not constantly busy struggling with and being in feelings; that is, surviving to my next session. I had stopped constantly suffering and I was surprised because this was, for me, the normal way of being. I thought this is how it is supposed to be. Now I had time [left] over in my life, and at first I was so not used to it that I did not know what to do! But then I actually started to have more of a life! Which gave me strength to drop into bad feelings like never before because now I was able to get out of them, return to a better life, and have a vacation before a next feeling would push.

Because the medication helped me to close down after feelings and to access feelings more clear-cut, I was suddenly also able to realize in my life when I was actually triggered. I could tell the person who triggered me and ask for a time-out to go and feel.

Before taking medication, being constantly triggered into feelings, I was constantly in meaningless, exhausting struggles with people or had to isolate myself to avoid getting triggered.

The most amazing thing though that this combined medical treatment has done to me is that it helped me to separate the lines of memory. Before taking medication I was so overwhelmed that I would start a session with crying without context and then straight drop into first-line reactions; that is, not breathing, feeling crushed, etc. I could hardly feel any separated emotions from happenings in my childhood (second line). Everything turned straight into birth feelings, but they hardly connected to emotions in my childhood or in my present life. Which means that I was not really able to integrate my feelings, or rather sensations, and that I had few insights to base any changes in my life upon. I just stayed suffering in my messy life for months. I literally did not get anywhere, which then triggered me all over again. With help of medication I began to get somewhere in my sessions—I got access to my second line and began to resolve it, and I began to get somewhere in my life with changes based on insights from my sessions.

One example for how medication-supported Primal Therapy has changed my second-line feeling access is my feelings of separation. When my first boyfriend left me, or when I received the phone call that my father had died, I could not feel anything, but was paralyzed. All those were situations when I, back then, without medication, could not react. The experience of separation, of a sudden cut, triggered always and immediately my first line and made me shut down, and I became overwhelmed. The only thing I knew was what I felt in situations of separation from my boyfriend or father: from one moment to the next I could hardly breathe anymore. I got extremely nauseous, my knees got so weak I could hardly stand, and I almost fainted. I felt a "white-out" feeling flashing through me, taking me over for seconds what seemed [like an] eternity to me. After such an attack I would spend hours disoriented, sitting in a corner unable to move. All these described sensations are what I now experience as first-line birth sensations.

Thanks to the drugs, I can now, in Primal Therapy, revisit after-birth, second-line situations of separation without simultaneously having this "white-out" feeling (which actually is the sensation of a sudden cut-off of oxygen supply) overwhelming me. Finally and for the first time, I am able to feel the appropriate second-line feeling: the desperation of the final loss of a person that I still needed to be with me: my boyfriend, my father. This loss and the grief would have been to feel for me when it originally happened—would I not have been so extremely overwhelmed ever since my birth and so easily triggered in my brain stem. Drugs helped me to reestablish what a loving, drug-free and oxygen-saturated birth should have given me in the first place: a good brain chemistry to build a sound brain development upon that would have allowed me to adequately, that is, in a feeling way, react to losses later in my life.

Now in Primal Therapy, with the help of medication, I revisit all those situations of separations. I finally separate from them and from my feelings by expressing them and feeling the utterly aloneness and fear. I finally let go. Also, in my present-day life, I no longer keep accumulating unfelt reactions to separations because now, when I am confronted in my life with a separation, I can actually feel it right away when it happens.

Now, about a year and a half after having drugs help give me structured access to my blocked childhood feelings, I am on my way to slowly and gradually out-phasing the drugs. I have now found my own true life.

Drugs Make Neurosis Work

Neurosis is a disease of unconsciousness. If we are fully conscious, we are not neurotic. Again, consciousness means that all three levels of brain function work in fluid harmony. Most current therapies work to reduce consciousness and thereby enhance neurosis, even unwittingly. A neurosis that works makes us feel comfortable. It doesn't mean we are normal or happy or even content, despite what we think. Drugs make neurosis work, so does cognitive therapy—it reduces consciousness; the former through chemical repression, the latter through insights, new ideas, and mental-verbal gymnastics, which ultimately become chemical repression. We either build defenses or lessen the need for them. Either we give someone a shot of morphine and soothe the pain or we offer insights and a new way of looking at things, which is tantamount to and eventually becomes, a shot of morphine (endorphin) injected from the inside. In the latter case of adopting new so-called more "wholesome" ideas, the frontal cortex through these thoughts and rationales is putting in an order for more painkillers. We think it is the ideas that make us feel better, but more likely it is the internal drugs that the ideas cause to be secreted. Ideas/insights are the vehicle for the secretion of internally produced drugs, especially the morphine we manufacture.

In Primal Therapy, the frontal lobes are freed up so that we can optimize our performance in life. It accomplishes this by aiding the person to gain access to his or her feeling circuits, and thereby live a long and happy life, free of tension, anxiety, and drugs. It means a loving life, a genuinely deeply felt and meaningful one. *Primal Therapy provides the royal road to the unconscious.* It vastly enhances self-awareness and the ability to reveal secrets of the mind formerly locked away deep within ourselves. When that happens, we do not need drugs to feel and/or relax. The access we have in reaching the deepest levels of the brain fully enhances our mental health and imbues us with a sense of total well-being.

We are hoping to study the hormones of love—oxytocin and vasopressin—to see how they change as a result of our therapy. We know that those who feel pain can feel again, and that means they can love again. We must now ask the question: "To what degree will post-Primal people be able to love?"

10

Why We Have to Relive in Order to Get Well

In a reliving, as part of Primal Therapy, we start the session in the present and move from left brain to right—from current perceptions to past context, from an unpleasantness, such as "my girlfriend left me," then down the chain of pain to the deepest reaches of the brain, providing a channel of access to our childhood, where we feel, "My mother left me to start another family." We are moving through history just as if we were in a time machine, thus allowing feelings to finally move upward to connect with the left frontal cortex.

In fact, the brain and its structure are a time machine, reflecting eons of evolutionary history. Here, each pain is coded and labeled as to the date and strength of the pain. The system travels back naturally; first to later and less intense pain, and then deeper to the more agonizing, earlier pain. These stops have been programmed by the brain. We do not have to be guided there; the system is an accurate guide.

In Primal Therapy we make it safe not to block pain, because feelings are preserved with their early scenes intact. Because each higher brain level elaborates the same sensation/feeling differently, we can ride the top level down and it will eventually take us to the bottom—to origins. Once down there, the system, on its own, will move upward toward connection automatically, following the paths of evolution for connection. We then move again up toward the right frontal cortex (OBFC) and then to the left prefrontal cortex for final connection. How do we verify this? We note that in almost every reliving there is a mounting of vital signs to inordinate levels; these levels drop with connection to normal, healthy measures. In a feeling without context—which is an *abreaction*—there is never this kind of organized, coordinated vital function movement.

> *In our therapy, few words are said by the therapist, because words are used to block the patient's defenses.*

No one can command anyone to feel. Feelings have their own intelligence. The minute the focus stays on the therapist, all is lost. It means there is less inner focus. All of our techniques have been aimed at enhancing the inner focus. If a therapist has to be the center of attention and needs to talk a lot and explain things, it is all the more terrible for the patient because the focus is now outside of her, and her own feelings are long gone. For Albert Ellis, the father of rational-emotive behavior therapy, we have seen in films that he talks much more than the patient during sessions. His ideas are the central focus. The patient's feelings recede into a dim penumbra.

In our therapy, few words are said by the therapist, because words are used to block the patient's defenses. Here, the left prefrontal cortex recedes in favor of feelings. Our job is to put the patient on track; after that, she is on her own. Her system knows that better than us. It takes a good scientific knowledge and a bit of faith in the patient to allow her lower brain to take over. The feeling chain is literally a neuronal track, inching its way down to the remote past. In intellectual therapies the therapist wants the thinking cortex to gain control. Neurology militates against it because connections coming down from the cortex to the feeling centers are weaker and fewer than the circuits traveling to that cortex. This is far easier for feelings to gain cortical access than for ideas to gain access to change feelings. It is why rage control is so difficult. It is easier to let it out and then connect it to its origins. The fact is that feelings can change ideas, but ideas cannot change feelings. Evolution doesn't move backwards; it is, after all, evolution.

What we have in a reliving is evolution in reverse, which is why I call our therapy "neurosis in reverse." To recapitulate: the circuit runs from the left frontal cortex to the right OBFC, down to the hippocampus, which scans history to find similar feelings and provides guidance for how to react to those feelings, it does this in conjunction with the amygdala, which contributes the emotional sense of the feeling. Together with other limbic structures, it then assembles disparate parts of the memory, and travels to brainstem structures where the breathing and heart rate and blood pressure are heavily affected. Finally, a connection is made back up to the right side OBFC, then to its left counterpart. It is now connected. The left frontal cortex takes over with its insights. It reflects on what behaviors were driven by feelings. It puts the pieces together. It ties inner reality with outer behavior, and explains what feelings are behind particular behaviors and act-outs. This should be the linchpin for all psychotherapies.

Once the prefrontal cortex is no longer busy in the process of repression, once it is finally connected fully to the right frontal area, it is free to unblock the insights. A study reported in the *Monitor* that the hippocampus is more active in the retrieval of memories, and is less active when trying to suppress them. On the other hand, the prefrontal cortex was more active in suppression.[1] This suggests that people may be using the prefrontal cortex to overcome (emotional) memory processes in the hippocampus.[2] And that is exactly our leitmotiv "that intellectual processes, especially in a psychotherapy, can damage access to feelings," the very access we need to get well. In the name of mental health we are making patients worse. Even when the insights in therapy are right on, it is still a defensive maneuver. Too often when that maneuver has done its job, the person claims to feel better; a testimony to the efficacy of intellectual defenses. Too often, "I feel better" means that my defenses are working well.

The feeling, when it reaches the bottom level of the imprint, turns the person into a historical entity with the exact vital signs and physical attributes as those that occurred in the early traumatic event. It takes high energy and the release of the activating catecholamines (function as hormones or neurotransmitters) to seal in the original trauma, and an equally high energy to relive and resolve it. It is very much like an amusement park where one takes a hammer to pound on a base to send a ball upward to make the bell ring. When that force is too weak, the bell never rings. That is also true of therapy. We cannot cheat our biology. If the energy level in a session is not adequate, deeper levels in the patient's brain will not be triggered off and we will never hit the primal bell; there will not be a resolution and integration of the feeling.

This is why in conventional, or cognitive/insight, therapy we do not see these pains, particularly of the birth trauma, because of the low-level energy involved. They cannot achieve a cure because the energy level in a sit-up-and-talk approach is not enough to activate deep, brainstem traumas. It therefore remains below the threshold of healing. Again: feeling is healing.

In the reliving, the whole system will be engaged as it was when the memory was registered. This is why, in our Primal Therapy research, we found an average 24-point drop in systolic readings in our high blood pressure (hypertensive) patients. It is also why we see such enormous drops in blood pressure during a session, as the sympathetic nervous system, which is responsible for the hypertension, gives way to the parasympathetic, lowering the pressure. It is why a parasympathetic-dominant patient (a depressive) who enters a session with a radically lowered body temperature, will see rises of two or three degrees after the session, as feelings normalize the system. Normalizing blood pressure is very important if we want to avoid cerebral strokes later on. We can "normalize" with medication, but the force is still inside doing its damage elsewhere.

As I have pointed out, there is a major difference between normalizing the symptom and normalizing the system. The latter has great import for longevity. If we normalize one aspect of the system, the rest of the body must compensate, and that is the danger with medication. It achieves apparent results, but not profound effects. As long as the generating source of the problem stays active, it is forever a threat, and a stroke is not the least of the consequences. Again, if we try to "cure" high blood pressure with pills, we are depriving the patient of one aspect of the memory, and she needs the totality of response to the memory in order to fully relive and get better. That is, if we suppress part of the memory, there can never be a full reliving because the whole memory is not completed.

The Role of Insights in Psychotherapy

In any therapy where insight is important, and it nearly always is, the insight must come last, as it did in evolution. In a session it must come after the feeling, never before. Any insight we have before feeling will be isolated and detached, not organic. We must not defy evolution. The insights, as I have mentioned, have an easy flow about them that tells us it is not just the left brain that is involved. Both sides join to make us consciously aware. If we put the evolutionary cart before the horse and give insights before a feeling, there will be no cure. To underscore: cure for us means tying current behavior and symptom to the generating source. Cure in cognitivist/insight therapy is dependent on what the patient thinks about his treatment. What is the cure for cognitive therapy? Feeling. This is not meant facetiously. What is missing in the cognitive approach is feeling, not what the patient describes as her feeling, but the feeling of feeling.

Cure for us always means a process, not a point in time, not only single behavior. There is no single dominating fact; again, we seek the truths of feeling beyond fact. "The reason I did this and that, talked so fast, ate so fast, could not concentrate, had to keep moving, was because...." The start of neurosis is not necessarily a point in time; rather, it is an end result of many experiences. To undo neurosis means revisiting those many experiences. Luckily, we don't visit them one by one. We visit the feelings, which encapsulate and resonate as a single entity underlying them all. They then fall into place. To be clear, it would seem that a single feeling subsumes a whole host of experiences with similar resonating frequencies.

As I pointed out earlier, memory is impressed into the brain when the system is stimulated at a high energy state because it is usually a life-and-death matter. This makes sense because the imprints are guideposts or templates to direct us in life. It is yet another reason why we cannot get rid of emotional memories, and why when we evoke the memory again, the same activation must take place. To dislodge a feeling from storage we need a high valence activation that can only come about when we reproduce those exact early conditions as they were originally. There seems to be a certain frequency of activation that resonates with the imprint and unhinges it. Thus the patient must be in the grips of that early brain when and where the charge had been registered; he must cry and scream with that same force.

An adult thinking back on his childhood cannot arrive at that energy level. The memory is sealed concretely in the amygdala/hippocampus and other related structures with the help of the inhibitory neuro-hormones. In fact, outside of therapy, there are few situations that can unhinge memory. Sex, for example, with its high excitement level, can set off the old memory with its elevated energy level. It is why sex can reawaken so many latent problems and needs in us; why we may get so kinky in sex. All of our earlier pains mount to the fore, and force us into strange behaviors. Let's be clear: The feelings rise just as they do in a Primal, but in the Primal we feel the pain. In sex, it gets deviated or dislocated into symbolic channels. We need to be whipped or spanked, for example, to find relief and orgasm. In a Primal the person may feel the humiliation by his mother and the pain; he is not acting out this humiliation in sex. "Be nice to me, Mommy. I didn't do anything wrong." That is the ultimate, permanent relief. Another Faustian bargain in sexual act-outs: "You can beat me and humiliate me first, and then maybe I can enjoy myself." First he pays the price in sex, which is what his mother expected (she wants him to suffer).

Sex and therapy act as grappling hooks, lifting up what we have hidden. There is no such dredge in a cognitive/insight approach because the energy level is kept under control. The Freudian legacy dictated that the emotions should never be released in full because it would be disintegrating for the patient's mental health. That is why insight is given with an objective air devoid of feeling. The therapist delivers his truths in a calm, deliberate manner with a tone devoid of excess. He cannot imagine letting his patient roll around on the floor screaming and crying. This practice is all in the interest of being scientific and objective.

Thus psychological science and feeling have become antithetical propositions. The more scientific we become, the less we are interested in feeling; so much so that now in current psychoneurologic science, it is mostly a matter of what neuronal structures affect personality—a minute analysis of neurons instead of human beings. Neurology is the foreground, while the human being recedes into the background. We know more and more about less and less. That is why scientists can now know so much about brain function but cannot figure out how to insert that knowledge into therapy. What has been ignored is the whole human being and how his condition affects the neurons. We seem to be working backwards—how neurons affect personality, which they do, but we have left out history, humanity, and feeling. Neurons have become entities in themselves apart from the human experience. It is clear from the work of Alan Schore at UCLA and others that early experience affects the growth and even the existence of certain neurons. So we have two kinds of scientists working on two different ends of the human being: the neurologist working on the neurons, and the psychologist working on the thinking mind. In between there is a whole universe of feeling. Neurologists too often feel that their work is "pure science," not contaminated by therapeutic considerations. They must never forget that our science should be at the service of mankind. What other possible reason could there be to do research but to help humanity?

Why We Must Relive as a Total Experience

A reliving of pre-birth and birth imprints will evoke the exact same reactions as at the time of the original trauma. But in the absence of a reliving, the reactions or fragments of the memory will persist, such as a fast heart rate or high blood pressure. When we relive a complete early pre-birth memory of which high blood pressure was a part, then in the total reliving, that fragment of the memory will also be included, and the patient should consequently see relief from the intrusive symptoms. If aspects of the original reaction are missing, the reliving is not complete and therefore not curative. If we medicate blood pressure and keep the high level reaction under wraps, the complete reliving is not possible.

A person not in therapy needs tranquilizers for the same reason that our patients might need them as they approach feelings: repression is weak, and chemical help is needed to bolster it. The drugs help normalize our inner pain-killing pharmacy. We don't want patients with weak defenses to free-fall into remote and high-valence first-line pain. Medication allows for a slow, methodical descent; it keeps the patient in the Primal zone. For that reason I sometimes describe Primal Therapy as a "journey to the zone of the interior." When patients relive enough of their painful history, they no longer need alcohol, drugs, cigarettes, or painkillers. Less pain, less painkillers. This occurs without any discussion of the habit itself. Unfortunately, many therapies use tranquilizers as an adjunct to their therapy, which has the effect of blocking access to feelings and preventing a full reliving. In effect, it blocks the possibility of a cure. The habit, again, is a reaction to pain, and not the essential problem. Alcohol and drugs are like a good mother should have been: always there when needed, reliable, comforting, and relaxing. A person has to make no other effort than to reach for the bottle or the cigarette, and relief arrives. It is called "drug abuse," but drugs are not being abused; they serve a central purpose of trying to bridge the Janovian Gap, to bring harmony and relief to the system. Incidentally, over the years we have enough experience with medication to know that there are effective first-line blockers, while other medications are more effective on the second line. We sometimes want to quell the first line so that it does not continuously intrude into reliving on the second, specifically, childhood events. And we sometimes want to quell part of the second-line because the overall pain level is too much to integrate.

Recently I discussed drug addiction with a center specializing in rehab. They told me that they use various means to affect a cure, including hypnosis, acupuncture, EMDR, massage, and exercise, as an attempt to build toward reality. The result, in effect, is to pile on one ineffective technique after another, resulting in a massive unreality. In no other branch of medicine would we consider trying a plethora of old discarded techniques on a physical symptom, hoping that one might help. There is either a science or there isn't. If we did that in physical medicine, there would be chaos. Notice that each of the approaches mentioned is ahistoric; dealing not with generating causes, but involving external manipulation done by various means. The person is being "done to." The power is outside of her. Some patients prefer being "done to." They like hypnosis because it all happens while they are unconscious. We can't beat that. They don't have to participate and make an effort, and, above all, there is no need to feel any pain. Yet the pain is there; we can either deny it or feel it.

Now why should we make a fuss about history? We have only to look at research by neurobiologist Charles Nemeroff to understand. He studied rat pups who were separated from their mothers. He later found markers of hyper-secretion that one finds in acute stress. This early abuse left a lifetime vulnerability to stress. He also studied adult women—those with early abuse and traumatic, and those without. Again, later on they still showed all the secretions involved in acute stress response. This study showed that early trauma (history) results in "permanently hyperactive stress response."[3] The traumas, though 20 years old, still had an important effect. In brief, they were still victims of their history. History never goes away. In no other field could we imagine that history does not exist. In archeology, political science, astronomy—could we imagine a lack of historical perspective?

Recovering Hidden Memory

There is one important way we know that a reliving episode is accurate and that imprints exist. Once one is totally in a memory, body and soul, and one has to relive a lowering of oxygen supplies at birth, the system acts as though there is this enormous need for oxygen and accepts deep, heavy breathing for a long period of time as a normal reaction. (I call this locomotive breathing.) There is no hyperventilation syndrome—no dizziness, puckered lips, or the feeling of fainting. The brain system is crying out for oxygen. What brain system? The one that suffered anoxia at birth.

Here is the essence of my argument: If that early brain system is not engaged, there will be an immediate hyperventilation syndrome. We have tried this on many patients and it is unfailing. If the person descends to that early brain system, everything is still intact as it was originally. The memory is present and the patient is "back there." She is reliving the event with the brain system involved at the time, and therein lies resolution. Blood pressure can go from over 200/110 to 120/80 at the end of the session. The memory has left its storehouse and has finally connected to the frontal area. We react now as we should have back then. There is obviously plenty of oxygen in the therapy room.

Reactivity is paramount, because we have been reacting all along to our past with our high blood pressure and rapid heart beat. These are the physiologic fragments of the memory that cannot be hidden, that have escaped through the sieve of a leaky gating system. An example is low body temperature. We have treated a patient with vaginismus, a painful closing of the vaginal walls against penetration. She found, after months of therapy, that she suffered incest at a very early age. In sex, her body was reacting to that memory in terms of her anatomy. Feelings are everywhere in the system. In the trauma it began in the vagina and it remained there, coded and stored. That constricted, painful vagina was shouting out a crisis, a trauma that lay buried in the unconscious. She was told in a previous therapy, and she believed, that she was possibly a lesbian because she obviously didn't like men. Actually, she was unconsciously and physiologically protecting herself against a memory! And with the brain, that had little to do with the left prefrontal area; ideas were never going to affect that memory.

Fragments often become the presenting problem: blood pressure, heart rate, chronic fatigue, hypothyroidism, and so on. All of these are part of an ensemble of reactions congealed by a central feeling/sensation, just as is a constricted vagina. As I mentioned, the neurophysiologic change of a key fragmented sensation into a feeling is a Primal. We change a lower order imprint into a higher order neuronal event. Thus we change tachycardia and cardiac arrhythmia into a feeling/sensation in context, and then into a cortical acknowledgement.

Here we note that the expression of the pain moves up the evolutionary scale, the absolute necessity for resolution. Biologically, people always try to expel what hurts. It seems to be another biologic law. We forcefully exhale noxious fumes and we vomit out poisonous substances from the stomach. Painful feelings also obey that law. We try to expunge noxious feelings through frontal connection, but gating stops it. Gating has kept the sensation away from its context because that context means great pain. When gating weakens, pain rises. It is now not surprising when I say that my patients who have undergone electroshock therapy have to relive it to get it out of their systems. What comes in that is overwhelming and/or noxious, must go out.

Low body temperature or low blood pressure can be part of an overall memory of a terrible struggle at birth or a trauma before birth where abandoning the struggle was the end result. That end scenario is stamped in as a parasympathetic prototype and remains as a tendency thereafter. Each of the symptoms, low blood pressure, hypothyroidism, asthma, migraines, and finally depression, may be the silent reminders of this struggle and are permanent aspects of the imprint. When therapists or physicians isolate these symptoms in treatment, we remove the historical context. In that case all we can do is palliate. Migraines, we have found, often reflect severe anoxia at birth, which involves the blood vessels constricting and then dilating. Currently, one of the treatments for migraines is the use of oxygen. We cannot observe the birth trauma without the proper techniques, including a setting that is not time-bound, that is quiet, soundproof, and darkened. The patient must by lying down. It is only then that we can achieve deep access. A patient sitting up and talking to a therapist is not going to arrive at this kind of access. He is too much in the present, with too much external focus. He needs to focus inside; talking to or taking orders from a therapist prohibits that.

When a patient relives early terror, then ceases to compulsively check the locks on his doors 20 times a day, he has solved an important mystery. This, without any prolonged discussion of the obsession. He felt unsafe, profoundly unsafe early on; the obsessions controlled the terror that he didn't even know he had. The left frontal cortex was saying, "I'd better check the locks. It makes me feel more comfortable." Because the terror is there, he never can feel safe for long, and the obsessions continue. The feeling of being unsafe was seeping up in small increments from the right brain. It was immediately staved off by the obsession on the left. "I'll be safe if the house is locked" is the unconscious formula; in the same way that the woman discussed earlier felt unconsciously, "I'll be safe if no one can penetrate me." If we were to prevent the obsession, we would see terror, which is what we do in Primal Therapy. But it must be done in a safe, controlled atmosphere. To feel deeply unsafe, one has to feel totally safe in the present. That safety, dialectically, turns into its opposite.

One of my patients who had a cesarean birth complained, “I’ve got to get to the finish line.” She never felt finished, ever. There was always more to do, and she was always dissatisfied. She was driven constantly. We could have helped her develop more “healthy” ideas, taught her to relax and not drive herself, but her ideas were tied neuronally to birth. She finally felt the devastating effect of never having finished getting born. Her drive in great part came from that. I wouldn’t make such a psychological leap, connecting the current problem with birth; she did. How does psychiatry treat all this? Too often with medication to block the terror and the pain. It is psychiatry’s theory that becomes blinders that keeps psychiatrists from considering deep brain memories. Theories that evolve out of repression and intellectuality are bound to involve continued repression as part of the techniques. That is, theories that evolve out of left-side intellect are perforce neglecting right side feelings. Therefore, they tend to be superimposed on human behavior rather than evolving out of it. This is not a minor quibble; it is of the essence. Whenever the patient is being “done to,” there is little chance of feeling.

The same cesarean imprint can, depending on later experience, turn into something quite different. There is no universal application of one trauma that will fit everyone. One cesarean birth patient never seemed worried about anything. She had a false sense of security that “something was going to happen to solve the problem for her.” Some magical entity would appear and take care of everything. She was insouciant and engaged in magical thinking. Her credo: “Something is bound to happen to make things right.” And at birth it did. Someone did take her out of the womb and solve the problem. She had to make no further effort. This and the fact that she was totally indulged as a child. Yet another patient with the same birth thinks, “I am never ready for anything. I prepare meticulously for everything to keep any surprises from happening.” Obsessive preparations for a trip are an example of trying to be ready for a surprise yet still feeling unprepared because of the memory. Although every possible detail is attended to, the person still feels not ready. No cognitive idea in the present is going to change that because in a life-and-death situation the feeling was, “I am not ready.” We can try to change the idea, but unless we change the imprint it is useless.

This may be treated by the cognitivists by showing the patient that there is no reason to be so compulsive in having to finish everything so perfectly. “Ease up,” begs the therapist. “You’re too compulsive.”

"Yes I know," states the patient, and it stays in the knowing area of the brain. One of my patients always felt that she had to wash her hands at least 10 times so she could feel clean and finished with her task. It had so many implications: "I feel dirty. I feel bad."

The following are two patients with two different kinds of compulsions. The first, a woman who must hang all her shirts in the same direction. She gets very nervous if one shirt isn't hanging right. The insight in her feeling was, "I could never get it right. Nothing I could do would make my parents say, 'You've done a good job.'" As it is with her shirts, she had to check over and over again because she still felt she didn't get it right. She was acting out symbolically, "Everything I do is wrong. Nothing I can do will make them approve and love me." Another patient is addicted to video games. It is not something he just plays; he is addicted and must do it. Why? To feel like a winner. No matter how many times he won, however, he still felt like a loser, something his father called him constantly. He was trying to shake that feeling, but never could. In life he felt like a failure; he didn't know what else to do to get rid of that feeling. He chose, as in every neurosis, a symbolic channel. Until he felt in a session over and over again, "I'm not a failure, Daddy. Say I'm good—just once!" Feeling that stopped the act-out; he had to feel that many times.

In Primal Therapy we do not discuss compulsions, as such. The feeling has been put back into context. It no longer intrudes in one's current life. In the case of hand washing, we discovered incest by an uncle, a favorite uncle, that made the patient feel dirty. Washing her hands is about all she could do with an unknown and unreachable memory. It is a symbolic ritual where the person had no idea about origins. As soon as she discovers the origin, the ritual has no further purpose.

Self-Destructive Behavior

A woman who is insatiable in sex may, in the end, be trying to feel loved, a trauma that may have started in infancy. Should we convince her through cognitive therapy that her behavior is destructive? In the old days of insight therapy, I did just that. And the patient invariably agreed. I do not say that the cognitivists are making conscious errors. I am saying that until one has a proper theory and therapy, those errors have to be made, as I did for years. I am trying to point the way, and I hope that other therapists will take it that way. After all, we do not lack insights at age 1, yet we can sense a lack of love, and hurt because of it. Insights are not going to solve that lack. How do we express all that? We hurt. Ineffable wounds. There were no insights then or now that could change the problem. Words can never change the deviated structure of the corpus callosum in order for there to be a connected feeling.

> *In trying to kill the pain, we are sometimes forced into behaviors that ruin our lives.*

A sexually hyperactive woman may say, "Yes, I know it is self-destructive." But that insight won't change her behavior, because it is not just behavior. There is a person and a history behind it. Here again we are in the realm of theology. So let's see what self is destroying the other by insatiable sex, or by drink, for that matter. There is a need for love and warmth from one's parents. It is not given. The child needs desperately. She grows up with pain from that unfulfilled need and starts to drink and have promiscuous sex to ease her suffering/need. It ruins her life. She loses her job and husband. She seeks out help for her "self-destructive" behavior. All she was trying to do was quell the pain of the little needing self, not to destroy that self. She had sex with anyone who wanted her. In fact, having never felt wanted by her parents, she was an easy target for anyone who even looked as if he wanted her. Sometimes the pain was such that she tried suicide to kill the pain. The problem was that she also was killing her physical self—the ultimate in self-destruction—the self needing love and feeling hopeless about it. Her behavior was as insatiable as the need.

In trying to kill the pain, we are sometimes forced into behaviors that ruin our lives. We need holding so badly that we cheat on our spouses. Is it self-destructive? It is trying for fulfillment, but because it is symbolic, it may take a destructive turn, such as alcoholism. The aim is to discover the historical context, and only the patient can do that. Trying to dissuade a patient from her behavior is moralism parading as therapy. The patient's behavior is treated as though it were a choice she made. If we focus on the present, we are obliged to treat it as a conscious choice. How else can you explain it?

Compulsive behavior is not just a "choice" we make but the logical denouement of historical events. For example, a person may take painkillers every day even though there seems to be no rational reason in the present to make that necessary. It is just that the drugs make him or her feel normal.

In Alcoholics Anonymous the group member can give up his addiction because he is surrounded by "love, protection, and warmth." He is getting in the present, symbolically, what he needed in the past. He needs this shoring up all of the time. Perhaps it will help his addiction temporarily. "I've been off booze two years," he will say. He gets applause, hugs, and lots of approval. And it is true that he can get on with his life. He gave up trying to assuage his pain with alcohol and settled for a different painkiller—symbolic present-day fulfillment. Who can say that this is bad? At least he functions. But this means forgetting about the critical period when love was necessary *at that time*. He can get hugs every day from his group and still feel unloved deep down, and relapse into alcoholism again. Thus, he may have to go to AA forever. It is better than drinking. However, it is even better to get rid of the pain! Remember, "unloved" is now part of the neurophysiology, and remains so.

What Neurosis, and Reliving, Do to the Brain

As a result of four separate brainwave studies we discovered a brain system with better balanced right and left hemispheres after one year of Primal Therapy. Gaining access to the deepest levels of brain function allows us to see for the first time in history what resides on each level, and its purpose in the psychic economy. We can see exactly what kind of birth the person underwent and what the trauma was. We can see whether there was touch and holding immediately following birth or not. We don't have to guess or theorize. It is right before our eyes.

As the reliving takes place and a symptom disappears, we can see the connection between a symptom such as migraine and the birth trauma, specifically anoxic trauma. Let us not confuse the message with the label. One can say to a patient, "You are acting like your girlfriend is your mother. Demanding so much." He says, "Yes, that's right." It sounds brilliant, and no doubt is true, but it changes nothing. Words won't do it; they won't change the need to be cuddled and taken care by one's mother during the critical period. He must feel the original need, not deny it because he has been found to be "immature." His need is immature, but it was a matter of survival. He will act out that need on anyone he gets close to.

11

Toward a Therapy of Feeling: One Cure for Many Diseases

Therapy should not be a matter of anarchy, of each therapist doing his own thing, of each of us conducting psychotherapy without regard to the brain and its processes. There is a notion that we therapists, and patients, should do whatever we are comfortable with. The problem is that neurotics are comfortable with their own neuroses. Both patients and therapists may cleave to cognitive therapy. In that kind of therapy, where biology is neglected, the person is perceived not necessarily as sick, but rather as a client who is just behaving badly. Thus, in their view, the person simply has deviated ideas and not a deviated system.

Our view is that deviation is total and affects both our physiology and our ideas. They are a unity. If we think a patient is sick, then we have to look at the whole organism to see how the sickness affects her. But if the person is a "client," a kind of customer for our services, like a tailor, we only have to observe her, and adjust things here and there. The treatment therefore does not have to be so scientific and disciplined. And the theory doesn't have to be so rigorous; it doesn't have to cross neurologic lines. It can have the veneer of science. If I beat someone with a stick every time he takes a cigarette, sooner or later he stops smoking. Is that a cure? Or in the case of EMDR where distraction is the order of the day, there are hundreds of "scientific" studies *confirming* their position. Here again, if we only measure the superficial, the obvious and overt, then the criteria for proof lies in behavior and not in the total neurophysiologic state.

Suppose that as a result of their therapy, the person's behavior is more relaxed, yet her stress hormone (cortisol) level rises. What does that say? It means we have to look at the whole human being. We do know, for example, that the way we wave that wand in front of a person's eyes can shift the balance to the left repressive brain and away from the right side. Of course, the person, now more inhibited/repressed, does report feeling better, or less anxious or depressed. The key here is "reports." If we rely on verbal reports, then we can be easily deluded.

If criteria are narrowly defined, then the actual measures of progress will be also. Watch out for statistical truths; they are rarely biologic ones. They appeal to the lovers of numbers and are too easily manipulated in terms of the bias of the investigator. Research studies funded by pharmaceutical houses nearly always find in favor of the company. It is not easy to bite the hand that feeds us. Concepts beyond the statistical facts take a second seat in science today. It makes the job of those who deal in feeling very difficult because feelings are not always statistically verifiable.

If I say that we cure drug addicts and that the criterion is being off drugs for three months, I can offer "proof" of our cure by the patient's behavior. What price do the patients pay? We won't know until we look under the hood. If someone says that the Holocaust survivors have made a good adjustment, gotten married, hold good jobs, and are happy, who are we to doubt that? If we leave the criteria at that, then there is no argument. But when we address their inner life, their vulnerability to disease and premature death, we may find a different outcome. No one is arguing that someone who escaped the concentration camp cannot really be happy. No one will take that away. What we want to know is how they survive. Are they prone to depression, anxiety, and nightmares? We need to know the price of adjustment in therapy and in life. Criteria are a tricky matter.

We see that many diet regimes "work." The criterion may be that the client has lost 50 pounds. Is he cured? Not without generating sources. We can say that a combat veteran of the wars in Vietnam and Iraq is well adjusted because he has a good attitude, has a job, is married and doing well. That does not address unconscious imprints. When the pain or trauma is high enough in our adult life it, too, can be imprinted. It is simply that the trauma must be of high valence to be imprinted; several times the force necessary than if it occurred during the critical period.

In the analytic/insight world, neurosis is often a matter of the relationship between doctor and patient (the transference). The doctor is inculcating a theory into his patient. His school of thought—a series of beliefs, after all—becomes a rationale for his (the therapist's) unconscious, just as any of our thoughts are rationales for our feelings. Thus, some therapists raise their own unconscious problems to the level of a theoretical principal, such as the notion that neurosis is based on deep shame. We need to be careful to separate out our own feelings from those of the patient. If we are repressed and live "in our head," we are going to be attracted to a therapy that is more cognitive, dealing with changes in ideas as the goal of treatment. This is true for both therapist and patient. So here we have an unconscious pact in which both agree to confine therapy to the realm of ideas and attitudes. Nothing has to be said, as such. It is just understood. If neither have access to feelings, there is no question that feelings will be ignored, as will evolutionary science. Again, symptoms and neurotic behavior are not caused by a lack of insights, and insights will not cure them; anymore than headaches are caused by a lack of aspirin, even though aspirin sometimes can "cure" them.

Another variation on the cognitive approach is called Decision Therapy. The doctor helps the person make decisions in his life. It is unfortunate, but true, that many people need to be told what to do and how to live. It is part and parcel of fascism, deep fundamentalism, all religions, and Communism. The patient comes to lead a version of the doctor's life instead of his own. And what if he can't make the decision to make the decision? Then we need to delve deeper; unfortunately, that is where the cognitivists stop.

When we talk about a therapy for feelings, choice is immediately narrowed down. Feelings are few, and how to access them is in terms of precise yet confined techniques. Ideas and act-outs are myriad and lead to interminable therapies. It seems to me that what most of us want out of a therapy is what we want out of life: the ability to give and receive love, which is the basis for sustaining a rapport with someone else. If we open up the gating system within the brain, we help our patients to love. As a result, the person is no longer driven by unconscious forces that compel her to make irrational choices in partners.

For example, a woman who had a tyrannical father may seek out weak men who cannot be the threat her father was. She then may be deeply disappointed in his passivity and lack of ambition and drive. It is not a surprise, except to her. When we help her go back to her childhood and feel terrified of her father once again, she can then choose more aggressive, successful men because such men will no longer trigger her early terror. She doesn't have to act it out in the present. A cognitive therapist can try to convince her not to always choose weak men, but the unconscious fear drives her.

When one blocks a terrible feeling from childhood, the result is systemic. There is a general blockage of feeling, not just a specific repression of one feeling. This repression has the effect of not accepting love and not even being aware when it is offered. A study reported in the *Archives of General Psychiatry* (July 1997) found that pregnant mothers who smoked more than a half a pack of cigarettes a day while carrying were far more likely to have children with conduct disorders.[1] If we concentrate on conduct alone, we will not see the fetal months when that disorder was forming. There are literally hundreds of studies documenting the effects of fetal life on later behavior and symptoms. Thus, even if a therapist understood these effects, he might not know what to do about them; he would not realize the effects could be relived.

The great error in psychotherapy is often confusing speech with its underlying drive; believing that speech and language can solve the problem if the patient will just adopt another set of ideas. She can do that, but the drive does not change, it is just capped in a different way. So here is the dilemma: A high-level function, such as thought and concentration, is actually driven by a primitive, reptilian brain, something we generally have no access to and cannot even imagine is possible. So long as we neglect that history, we cannot understand the breakdown.

There has been no mechanism or brain structure found that can eradicate emotional memory or obliterate the need for connection; not even electroshock therapy. Electroshock, obviously, tends to enhance the disconnection. To destroy memory is tantamount to destroying part of the right side of the brain. All therapies that leave the imprint intact strengthen existing mechanisms of defense, diverting memory from consciousness. That means there can be no profound change. From that there is no escape.

Consciousness is our goal because unconsciousness defines neurosis. Consciousness is a unified event that no amount of words can produce. No therapy without strong feelings can give us back that alive feeling we achieve when consciousness arrives; no therapy that ignores feeling can return the ability to love, for love is all about feeling.

Tears are the avatar that leads to deeper brain imprints and higher level understanding.

According to Avram Goldstein, neurophysiologist at Stanford University, shedding tears lights up the right side of the adult brain, and not the left. What may be inferred here is that the evocation of tears leads to childhood memories. And those memories can explain so much about current behavior. And indeed, tears are the avatar that leads to deeper brain imprints and higher level understanding. What we find clinically is that as the patient begins to cry about something in the present, she will automatically be led to childhood-related events, assuming there is no interference. The ineluctable conclusion is that the right brain must be engaged in therapy if it is to succeed. Some years ago, we did research on tears with William Frey of the University of Minnesota. Tears do release some of the neuro-inhibitory transmitters and thus help with access by lowering repression. Therefore, crying must be an essential part of any therapy. And it eventually has to be powerful enough to dredge up heavy valence feelings from deep in the brain. Only then can we realize the forces that drive ideas, attitudes, and beliefs.

With each unblocking of feeling in Primal Therapy, there is an incremental increase in consciousness as connection from the right brain to the left prefrontal area takes place.

Suppose we were like the very early explorers who did not know there was a Down Under? Their explorations were random, without maps, a hit-or-miss proposition. We need to know that there is a proper destination, and we need to know how to get there; to be cartographers of all the elements of mind, not just the thinking mind. If physicians and therapists don't know about "down under," they will not solve panic and anxiety attacks, depression, suicidal tendencies, high blood pressure, sex problems, nightmares, and hormone deficiencies, to say nothing of heart attacks and other catastrophic diseases. To continue the metaphor, when we stay in the verbal neighborhood, we are never going to learn a foreign language—the language of sensations and feelings. *Even though these lower levels talk to us continuously, we have never learned to talk to them.* We haven't learned their language because their language is ancient, developing long before the newer verbal language we have today. We are trying to get one level of the brain to do the work of another level, and it simply cannot. We use words to control anxiety when it has nothing to do with words. With each unblocking of feeling in our therapy, there is an incremental increase in consciousness as connection from the right brain to the left prefrontal area takes place. Our goal is to widen and expand consciousness and narrow the Janovian Gap. There is no cure without acknowledging pain, and certainly no cure without descending to meet it.

The patient's ideas are not the problem in psychotherapy. They are an attempt at a solution. They are attempting to counterbalance the deeper forces. It is all about equilibrium. A bad feeling down below may force a counterbalancing idea up above. Hopelessness lying deep in the brain can lead to irrational beliefs that contain hope: a belief in a God who loves and protects us, for example. It is the counterbalance, unconsciously trying to control terrible despair with ideas.

> *When we operate on theories that are constructed out of the unconscious of psychologists rather than based on the internal reality of the patient, we become tinkering mechanics, altering our techniques more out of whimsy than science.*

We must take care in labeling ideas as neurotic or irrational. Take the feeling of hopelessness, someone who is despairing and feeling defeated. Before we go about talking her out of that feeling (because her current life is not so bleak as to provoke despair), we need to see how it works in the psychic economy. We as therapists may offer hope to the patient: "After all, things aren't as bad as you make them."

Here is how hope may work physiologically: A child feels hopeless about getting her mother's love. She is not aware of this feeling because it began its life before she had words. To block that painful feeling from connection, there is an increase in serotonin output. This serotonin may also control dopamine release, which can underlie ideas containing hope.

So serotonin kicks in to block perception of hopelessness. Then dopamine is released to help produce beliefs that involve hope. Hope arises out of hopelessness. Hopelessness gives life to hope. Any hope that we therapists proffer cannot produce any real change in the patient because she has to plunge into the depths of hopelessness, and put it in context; then there will be no reason for unreal beliefs. There will be no reason to create false hope (God or my therapist will save me!), because its wellspring—hopelessness—is no longer there.

What we need to do in psychotherapy is to rid ourselves of a class of elite cognoscenti who are the center of all psychologic knowledge. The patient is the only one who has knowledge of her unconscious. Therapists can only guess at it. When therapists operate on theories that are constructed out of the unconscious of psychologists rather than based on the internal reality of the patient, they become tinkering mechanics, altering their techniques more out of whimsy than science. Until now, there has been no theoretical web that encompasses both psychology and neurology, although there have been attempts to join psychoanalysis with neurology. It is, by and large, a shotgun wedding. It is the same as plastering an old, outdated notion onto new science and hoping it will stick. If psychoanalysis ignores key internal realities, it doesn't matter that we adhere certain neurologic facts to it. It cannot work. Why would we take a theory that is 100 years old and join with it research that may be six months old? The marriage can't last; the groom is far too old for the bride, who has new ideas and new information. The youngster is trying to lead the old man but the old man, is too feeble to keep up. Better a young theory that works within neurologic principles.

What the New Age, alternative therapies do tends to be haphazard without any guiding framework to give them profound direction—a kind of piling on of one technique after another, hoping to achieve improvement. It is true that certain vitamins and minerals help, but where is the overall theory that helps us make sense of it? We are trying to steady the ship without accounting for the waves. The cognitivists and insight therapists are plying a trade that skims along the surface while convinced of its depth. The so-called "depth" psychology is really a matter of ideas, which allude to certain deep feeling states without corroborating evidence. If they have never seen the depth, as we have, it is easy to make that mistake. A textured theory means to take into account the various nuances of the levels of consciousness. In any case, in the conventional therapies, patients come to get their neuroses validated. They want to change but without the pain, which is an understandable attitude. But without the pain there is no basic change.

If we say that someone is well who acts well, then that is the end of the discussion. But if we offer a different set of criteria that includes neurobiologic processes, the proof is different. Then we have to wonder if the cortisol level is lower or the serotonin level has been changed. What happens to the brainwave patterns? We know that in combat veterans, their norepinephrine levels are high (as measured in urine samples). Those with terrible childhoods are also combat veterans; the war is rather silent and subtle, but murderous of the soul, as well. Interestingly, when patients were given a medication to raise the norepinephrine level (galvanizing feelings), they had flashbacks to traumatic events during childhood. What we do in therapy is accomplish that *without medication.* We raise the emotional stakes, and history comes along for the ride.

We have the power to make an atavistic leap into our past and unlock the unconscious. We can peer down into millions of years of evolution by traveling back in our personal development. We can see how when feelings are too strong, ideas and beliefs jump into the fray. Each month of our personal fetal evolution and our infancy (ontogeny) seems to represent millions of years of human development (phylogeny). And, in this sense, in our therapeutic sessions, ontogeny recapitulates phylogeny. What we can do now is go back to our beginnings, and through reliving we can find what happened during birth. Further, we can discover how that event affected our lives. We can get to the beginning of our survival strategies, and each step means getting back more of ourselves. We fight assiduously against the liberation of the unconscious when that alone spells emotional freedom.

Let me summarize what I believe are the key phenomena in the development of emotional affliction (or neurosis), and the general principles of a proper therapy. As I mentioned at the beginning of this work, there are key phenomena in the development of emotional afflictions. They are:

1. The underlying cause of many emotional problems and symptoms is pain.
2. This pain stems from early in life, not the least of which is womb-life and birth.
3. The pain is imprinted into the central nervous system and throughout the body.
4. The pain is coded and stored in key brain systems, particularly the limbic system and brainstem, and spreads its tentacles to other parts of one's physiology.

5. The pain can be registered on three key levels of brain function or levels of consciousness.
6. The time or epoch in which the trauma occurred will determine where in the brain it is stored and the amount of damage it will produce.
7. This pain produces an overload of input into the brain system, which...
8. Produces a neurologic shutdown or gating to keep the pain from conscious-awareness.
9. As a result of the gating, the painful feelings on lower brain levels reverberate in a loop in lower brain structures.
10. There is then a dislocation of function in many key biologic systems as the energy of the pain spreads.
11. The pain produces a dissociation or disconnection among those levels, stopping a fluid access among them.
12. A proper therapeutic goal must be connection between lower-level imprinted traumas and conscious-awareness.

The principles of a proper therapy are as follows:

1. The therapist must help the patient access key imprints on the various levels of consciousness, and not offer his or her insights.
2. The suffering component of these traumatic imprints needs to be brought to cortical consciousness for connection. It is this component that lies in the unconscious and drives illogical and irrational ideas.
3. The connection is the sine qua non of an effective therapy and for the resolution of many symptoms and deviated behaviors and ideas.
4. Once connection occurs, the trauma is finally integrated, the overload of input is connected to cortical centers, and it is finally dispersed. Integration means that repression is lifted and there is no longer a constant need to hold down feelings. Nothing has to be said, as such. It is just understood. If neither have access to feelings, there is no question that feelings will be ignored, as will evolutionary science.
5. We need an experiential therapy that coalesces with current neurologic research, providing deep access to low-level neurologic processes.

6. This access is accomplished in titrated doses to permit measured connection and integration, which creates permanent changes in many biologic parameters, most importantly, in the central nervous system.
7. Once this is done, there will no longer be major dislocation of function and the whole system is normalized physiologically and in the realm of ideas and beliefs.
8. With resolution we can see changes throughout the biologic system from the immune system to the neurologic.

If one recognizes that early trauma causes pain, that the pain endures and is imprinted, that this pain is a measurable force, that it is possible to relive the pain and connect it to consciousness, that once that is done there is a cascade of changes in the system from brain function to immune system changes, then one knows there is only one cure for many, many diseases. The cascade I am discussing is the reverse of the cascade described by Martin Teicher, who discussed the changes in the brain associated with early trauma. He states that with early trauma there is a cascade of changes all the way down to the level of the molecular. In reliving, there are those same changes in reverse—a normalization that reestablishes the set-points where possible.

The new equilibrium can be achieved through reliving the trauma that has remained in pristine form in the system. Thus, there are two ways to have a normal system: the first is to be loved early on, and not be so damaged that many biologic systems are distorted or deviated (neurosis); and the second is to relive the damage to reestablish equilibrium. Nothing else can accomplish that. As I pointed out, if we brought the indifferent, cold mother into the therapy session and had her kiss and hug the patient for an hour, nothing would change. There might be a transient alteration here and there, but no permanent effects.

The reliving must embrace a total reexperience, and not just one brain system or biologic system, alone. Experience isn't just laid down as an idea, and ideas won't change it. Indeed, the key experiences that shape us are imprinted deep in the brain long before we have ideas. That is why, after a time in Primal Therapy, we see changes in so many different systems.

An article in a 2002 *London Times* headlines as follows: "We're stuck with our personality at age three."[2] It discusses research by the Institute of Psychiatry, London, on 1,000 children at age 3 and again at age 23. The article indicates that we change very little in character traits from the age of 3 on until adulthood, indicating that basic personality is formed by age 3. This makes sense because the right-brain limbic development gives way to frontal cortical development at the age of 3. To quote from the *Times* article: "This provides the strongest evidence yet that children's early emerging behavior can foretell their characteristic behavior as adults." We change little after age 3 in terms of confidence, reliability, outgoingness, decisiveness, anger, and self-control.

The right brain offers us a chance to recapitulate our history, relive it and change it. That is its miracle. It also allows us to observe ancient history and evolution of the brain. We see how each brain contributes to our humanity. We no longer have to rely on antiquated theories, which are superimposed on patients. Out of the mouths of those patients come all of the theory we need. Their feelings explain what we need to know.

One develops ideas out of the crush of feelings, which remain unconscious. To profoundly affect ideas, we need to affect the feelings that underlie them. We must remember that one evolutionary raison d'etre for the development of the left-frontal cortex was to produce a lie machine, a machine that could make us deceive ourselves and thus keep us out of pain. The result is an alienation of the hemispheres of the brain. It is here that disconnection takes place. It doesn't make sense to use that lie machine to get well, because we are using the defensive apparatus to get below defenses. Once we understand the role of feelings in the right brain, specifically the right prefrontal brain, we know that we must concentrate our efforts there. The difference between a feeling therapy and a cognitive one is the difference between cure and extinction of a symptom—between cure and palliation, cure and denial, between cure and self-deception, and between appearances and essences. It is the difference between emotions and ideas, of a holistic approach versus the treatment of fragments. It is the difference between a therapy of recall and a therapy of reliving. (We need to keep in mind that real remembering is something organic; we remember with all of us.) The danger in therapy is what the patient cannot recall. The body remembers in its gait and posture, in its facial set. Recall is a strictly cerebral event. One important factor: in the reliving we never try to change the outcome of memory. We do not try to rewrite history. We put the patient on the neurologic track and the rest is a matter of following history.

The history of neurosis is the history of misery; let us let the patient cry out that misery, and scream for all the times he was hurt and could not express it. Weep for a wasted life; for broken relationships and hurting one's family; for being forced to smoke, drink, and take drugs by forces unknown and unseen; for destroying one's life through behavior that did not seize opportunities for love. We need emotion in life and in therapy.

Jacques Chirac, president of France, in discussing the round-up of Jews in Paris for the concentration camps, noting something that we should never forget, said: "We must pursue the duty of memory to its conclusion." It is also true of each of us. Memory is a duty. And memory is medicine. No medicine can be effective when ripped out of its historical context because we are essentially treating history with memory. L.P. Hartley wrote: "The past is a foreign country." We must take that exhilarating trip there to make it our own so that we are no longer strangers to ourselves. We can go home again. We can undo history. Though feelings can twist and turn us in all directions, they are life itself. No therapy that relies on words can resurrect them and give us back our lives. The only person who can resurrect our feelings is us. We may need help, but we finally have the tools to feel what is driving us, take control, love, and live!

Appendix: What is Primal Therapy?

The essence of Primal Therapy is reliving, going back over early lack of love and traumas that remained in the system as imprints. Imprints are the linchpin of Primal Therapy work for they are engraved into all of our systems and the brain as indelible memories that direct our lives. They are most often unconscious forces laid down even before we had words to describe them. Our therapy is a systematic descent into history, into the patient's past, beginning with the most recent problems and then riding the vehicle of feeling into history; that history may be of traumas before birth and the birth trauma itself. It includes infancy and childhood, and as we move up the time scale, the pains are of lesser valence because needs tend to be less and less about survival. Lack of touch at age 10 can never equal the trauma of lack of touch at age 2 weeks. What we almost never get in conventional therapy is a return to preverbal events and lack of love, say, at 1 year of age. The events are then ignored as if they did not exist. But when a patient goes back on the vehicle of feeling to age 1 year and feels an anguish over parental indifference (for example, of a mother who is depressed and cannot pay attention to the baby) we know it exists. The adult can now beg for his mother's attention, something he could not do at the time. The pain comes spilling forth. One patient remembers being held by his mother at age 3 and recalls in the reliving the exact color and shape of her earrings. He asked his mother about them, and she confirmed that she had them, but threw them away decades ago.

We can ride feelings backward in time because feelings existed very early on; they are linked, usually by key frequencies, and thus a person is able to glide back to her origins. Once one is locked into those frequencies one is carried back automatically. We cannot *try* to go back in our lives because that is a self-defeating notion. The more we use the adult brain to make an effort, the less we have access to feeling. The notion of frequencies was espoused years ago by psychiatrist William Gray who joined systems theorist Paul LaViolette, Ph.D., in believing that all thought is embedded in feeling tones, which code and store memory as neuro-electric waveforms. It is the frequency of those waveforms—feelings—that connect one event to another and allow the resonance. The code responds to memory traces, and those allows us to lock into our history.

Another example: A patient had a fight with her husband because she wanted him to be strong for her and be concerned about her migraines. It brought her back to when she was little and her parents were not the least bit interested in her suffering; they wanted her to stop "whining" and be "up and cheerful." The feeling: they only care about my façade and not me. One patient was having trouble with a colleague who was harassing her. She was upset because she knew her boss would not support her. It took her back to when her siblings were teasing her and her father refused to stop them. He let her brothers bully her unmercifully. One of her feelings: "What about me and my feelings, Daddy? Don't I count?" Her later behavior was, "I really don't count for anyone." She continued to act as though what she wanted never counted, so she stopped expressing it. Incidentally, she came into the session feeling, "My boss really doesn't give a shit. He just lets my colleagues run rampant." Once in the feeling, it took her back and then she found the origin, not only of the specific event with her father but also why she gave up on expressing her needs. It clearly wasn't because of that one time, but an accumulation of many experiences that finally forced her into resignation.

The therapy is done in soundproof, darkened rooms with no distractions. The patient lies on a mattress with the therapist behind him or her. He/she discusses what is going on in their lives, what bothers them, and what is going on inside of them. At certain key junctures, they connect to a feeling which, once locked in, takes them back to childhood events that helped shaped them, to the pains that have resided in their system and have driven them. Although both patient and therapist talk at times during the session, the talk follows the thread of feeling, leading to reliving earlier experiences. This is not simply remembering earlier experiences but rather *reliving* them, as if they were happening again, activating brain circuitry that was operative at the time. Thus, a patient's cry may sound like a real baby during a session, but the same patient could never duplicate this sound afterward when he has come out of the Primal reliving. Let me put it succinctly: any therapy that focuses on the present, that uses gimmicks, methods, or special tools (for example, hypnosis) to go into the past cannot be effective. Only full reliving with the brain system operative at the time is resolving. If a therapy claims to deal with the patient's history but approaches it from an adult focus, it is bound to fail. If the delving into the past is at the behest or urging of a therapist, it will fail, because the focus is on the external instead of internal. If it is the result of any kind of encouragement or insistence it will fail. It must follow a natural evolutionary course of feeling.

We trust the patient to know when she should come for a session, once she has access to her feelings. The initial therapy is three weeks of individual sessions (once a day), which are open-ended, as only the feelings of the patient determine when the session ends. Usually it is between two and three hours. After the three-week period, which is designed to help the patient learn a "Primal style," and how to gain access to his or her deeper feelings and experience, there are two groups a week plus individual sessions, depending on the will and feelings of the patient. No patient is told when to come to therapy. The power is in their hands. They decide how much therapy they need, because they have access to their feelings that alerts them to the "danger" of rising pain. Generally, they come once or twice a week at first and then as the months go on, they taper off to less frequent visits. At the end of an individual or group session, there is an individual discussion period that can last from a half hour to an hour. Here the patient goes over her feelings and her insights. She discusses how the pain drove her to have certain symptoms or to behave in neurotic ways. How the need she felt, previously made her act out on her friends in needy, clinging ways.

In group, there is little confrontation. Each patient uses group to get to her or his own feelings. Someone's pain with his father may set off another patient with similar feelings. The problem may be between people, but the solution is within. These groups last three hours or more.

Every year we do a Halloween group where patients come dressed as their secret selves. This helps the patients get to their hidden feelings. One patient came dressed with pornographic magazines. This patient had no idea why he was addicted to porn. He found that the only feeling a woman ever showed was in these magazines; they were ecstatic compared to his mother, who was "dead." This then excited him sexually, but the real excitement would have been a mother who showed some ecstasy. It became transmuted. Another patient dressed as the Phantom of the Opera: her secret feelings were murderous against her father who molested her. Another was Quasimodo, the Hunchback of Notre Dame, shunned by everyone. That was this patient's feeling: no one liked him, and everyone avoided him. He felt ugly, unwanted, and that no one could ever love him. He discovered that he sought after women who really did not want him, and then he struggled to make them want him. But the feeling—unwanted—took over and he abandoned the struggle. Let me hasten to add here that although I speak of pain, there is no feeling so exhilerating as after a Primal. Suddently the weight of one's life just comes off; one feels light and really relaxed. One can face life again. Because we now know that it is the first-line imprint that gives so much power to impulsive-obsessive behavior, it is clear that when we are able to go deep and reduce the power of the imprint, we also reduce the tendency toward all sorts of impulsive behavior from sexual violence to uncontrolled rage.

Another patient came with religious placards attached to him and in a cage: he was prisoner of his beliefs and he never felt free from his upbringing, which was moralistic and controlled.

Those who come to us, by and large, have some access to their pain. They hurt and they know it. Those who make it in life, whose defenses operate efficiently, often by the addition of medication, are more drawn to the cognitive/insight approaches. We see those whose pain keeps them from managing life in a healthy way. There is no common type of patient nor is there any socioeconomic class. We see far more working-class individuals than upper class. There are those who lived in their cars, saving up for the therapy, although we do have a foundation that offers scholarships of the therapy to needy patients.

Our therapists are highly trained and still attend two training sessions a week, even those who have been on staff for 10 years. It is complicated, to say the least. We tape each and every session, as well as supervise them. We take vital sign measurements before and after every session to make sure there has been an integrated feeling. We used to do systematic brainwave tests of entering and leaving patients, but it became prohibitively expensive. Nevertheless, we take great care to prevent "abreaction," the random discharge of pain energy, because although it looks like a Primal, it is destructive to the therapeutic process. The patient may feel better after a session, but it is temporary and gives him a false sense of progress.

Does Primal Therapy have its failures? Yes, but not nearly as many as what I saw when I practiced Freudian analysis. We have a very hard time with those who took many LSD or Ecstasy trips, or those psychopaths who incorporated the therapy into their tendency to scam and fake. There are those who are very defensive and shut-off, who take a long time to open up, but if they stay with it, they are often successful. Because we are not an in-patient facility, we take very few psychotic patients. They need more care and supervision than we can offer. There are some patients who feel that they don't want any more pain and quit. We understand that. On the other hand, patients cannot wait to come to the clinic for therapy. They know that on the other end of the session there is often going to be relief. There are those who get into deep pain, who have had enough suffering and leave. Those are the ones with the most terrible childhoods—orphanages, incest, beatings, and so on.

A number of our patients return to their native countries and continue their treatments via phone or computer sessions. It can be done at times with telephone conversations, but it is always best to have a physical presence. Once they achieve access, patients can go on by themselves or call us for help. After a while it becomes a way of life. One feels pain and cries as one might laugh—part of the human condition. There is a buddy system at our clinic. Patients come with their buddies to the clinic, and each sits for the other. They are not doing therapy; they act as sounding boards for each other. Old patients often return to our retreats, which occur every few months. Patients at retreats stay at our clinic and have their meals there, as well. They see feature movies with Primal feelings, and they may have around-the-clock sessions and groups. It is a successful aspect of what we do.

Is there a common type of patient? Not really; although all of them sense a deep unhappiness, a lack of fulfillment, and feel they're not getting what they need out of life. We see many psychosomatic cases—asthma, colitis, migraines, high blood pressure, and epilepsy; as well as behavior disorders—those who are unable to sustain adult relationships, who divorce often, who cannot concentrate (ADD), and who are seriously depressed. We have seen about every kind of affliction extant. What patients get out of therapy is an end to their pain and a chance at a good life. They can be productive again, sleep well, perform sexually rather than suffer frigidity or impotence. They are not afraid of new experiences and seek challenges willingly. Above all, they are often no longer anxious or depressed. We have good luck with these patients because we know how deep the pain is and have the techniques to go there—gently, methodically, but inevitably.

There are few Primal therapists because there is a very long training period, and mental health professionals that have already spent years in graduate work generally have no desire to start over again. I understand that, but if a professional is convinced about what we do, he or she needs to do the right thing and train properly. I want to open our therapy to professionals; they have only to take time off and be trained by us. We are not guarding the therapy as a trade secret. We have found that those professionals who read my books sometimes set up Primal shop. The result is often disastrous. I got a letter this morning from someone in New York who has become a self-appointed lecturer and therapist in Primal Therapy. We can be sure that those who go to the untrained therapist will suffer. Therapists must get to need with their patients, and that is a difficult task. They need to learn when to do it and when not to, as well as *how* to do it. There are times when Primal Therapy gets a bad reputation from all of the charlatans practicing it and the damage they do. For years we had to undo the damage done by the rebirthers. Incidentally, in the fall of 2006 we shall open our training to professionals for a one year intensive course that includes experiencing the therapy, learning the current theory, and a practicum.

Primal Therapy is sometimes known as miraculous, but it is not a miracle. The miracle lies in feeling. It is based on sound, scientific principles and 35 years of research. Is it the only way? I wish I could appeal to democratic principles and say, "No. A person should try everything." But adding one method that is not efficient to another that is even less efficient does not add up to a proper, beneficial, efficient therapy. What I try to show here is how we have honed techniques over three decades, and have establish a rigorous methodology that has a confluence with the most recent research in neurology and biochemistry. Others may help a patient have a Primal from time to time, but I have never seen it done systematically and in proper sequence, and almost never with deep connections. The practice is only dangerous in untrained hands.

One last thought: As the therapy goes on, patients have to experience Primal level feelings less and less. They know how they feel, and they can lead much healthier lives, no longer being addicted to whisky, cigarettes, and drugs—and no longer addicted to therapy.

If we wonder how deeply ingrained the behavioral therapy approach is, look no further than the standard reference book all mental health professionals must use, the *Diagnostic and Statistical Manual*, which is a book as big as the Manhattan telephone book and contains every kind of behavior known to man. It is used mostly by insurance companies as shorthand codes for reimbursement. Almost every different type of behavior has its own diagnostic category. In short, diagnosis and payment are based on behavior, not feeling. Our diagnostic approach is internal, not external; it depends on what level of consciousness the patient operates on, the kind of access she has to lower levels of consciousness, and how much intrusion from subconscious imprints there is because there is a melange of lower levels of consciousness that puts the patient at risk of being overhwlmed by lower-level pain.

Notes

Chapter 1

1. "Thinking the Hurt Away,"*Science News* (Sept. 2005).
2. See full article in the September 6, 2005, issue of the *Proceedings of the National Academy of Sciences*.
3. Briley et al., "On Imipramine Binding," *European Journal Pharmacology* (1979): 347–348.

Chapter 2

1. John G. Vandenbergh, "Prenatal Hormone Exposure and Sexual Variation," *American Scientist* (June 2003): 225.
2. "Childhood Trauma Raises Risk of Heart Disease," *Science News* (Oct. 30, 2004).
3. "Prescription for Trouble," *Science News* 166 (Oct. 30, 2004): 278.
4. Associated Press (2002).
5. Robert M. Sapolsky, *Monkeyluv* (New York: Scribner, 2005): 52.
6. Ibid., 53.
7. See my forthcoming book *Sex and the Subconscious* for a full discussion of this point.

Chapter 3

1. N.I. Eisenberg, M.D. Lieberman, et al., "Rejection Really Hurts," *Science* (Oct. 10, 2003).
2. Joseph LeDoux, "Emotion, Memory and the Brain." *Scientific American* (August 31, 2002): 62–71).

Chapter 4

1. John R. Cirrito, Kelvin A. Yamada, Mary Beth Finn, Robert S. Sloviter, Kelly R. Bales, Patrick C. May, Darryle D. Schoepp, Steven M. Paul, Steven Mennerick, and David M. Holtzman, "Synaptic Activity Regulates Interstitial Fluid Amyloid-â Levels In Vivo," *Neuron* 48 (December 22, 2005): 913–922.
2. *Science News* 169 (Jan. 7, 2006): 4.

Chapter 5

1. Martin Teicher, "The Neurology of Child Abuse," *Scientific American* (March 2002).
2. W.J. Cromie, "Childhood Abuse Hurts the Brain," *www.news.harvard.edu*.
3. See the work of van der Kolk on the orbitofrontal cortex and post-traumatic stress disorder, as well as the many related research studies by Bruce Perry.
4. A recent study undertaken at Ghent University, Holland, confirms aspects of what I am discussing. Subjects were asked to focus on certain words or phrases and then on the meaning and feeling of them. First the left brain was activated, and then when dealing with feeling the right frontal brain was activated; but the left-brain activation did not diminish during this time. It took both sides to know the feeling *and* the meaning—the connection. It takes both brains to process the guts of feeling, to establish meaningful content and to label the feeling. We need to know not only the "what" of a message, but how it feels. It isn't only the right side that is responsible for feelings; it needs the left side cooperation, as well. If the focus were on words (as in cognitive therapy), the right brain is not fully engaged. It was the patterns of

rhythm, sound, and tone that activated the right brain. Citation: G.Vingerhoets, C. Berckmoes, and N. Stroobant, "Cerebral Hemodynamics During Discrimination of Prosodic and Semantic Emotion in Speech Studied by Transcranial Doppler Ultrasonography." *Neuropsychology* (Jan. 2003).

Chapter 6

1. D.F. O'Connell and Henry O. Patterson. In M.A. Reinecke, F.M. Dattilio, and A. Freeman (Eds), *Cognitive Therapy with Children and Adolescents: A Casebook for Clinical Practice* (New York: Guildford, 1996).
2. M. Szalavitz, "Love is the Drug," *New Scientist* (November 23, 2002): 38-40.
3. David Burns, *Feeling Good: The New Mood Therapy* (New York: Avon Books, 1999).
4. Steven Pinker, *The Blank Slate* (New York: Viking Press, 2002).
5. "Accentuate the Positive" (December 9, 2002): F5.

Chapter 7

1. *Journal of Environmental Science and Technology* (March 2006).
2. M.O. Huttunen and P. Niskanen, "Prenatal Loss of Father and Psychiatric Disorders," *Archives of General Psychiatry* 4 (1978): 429–431.
3. A.R. Hollenbeck, et al., "Early trimester anesthetic exposure: Incidence rates in an urban hospital population," *Child Psychiatry and Human Development* 16(2) (Dec. 1985): 126–134.
4. K. Nyberg, *Epidemiology* 11: 715.
5. "Neural Road to Repression," *Science News* 165 (Jan. 10, 2004): 21.

Chapter 8

1. N.I. Eisenberger and Matthew D. Liberman, "Hurt Feelings," *Los Angeles Times* (Oct. 11, 2002): A16.

2. *Science* (February 2004).
3. "Brain's Own Pain Relievers at Work in Placebo Effect," *Science News* (Aug. 24, 2005).
4. "Thinking Away the Hurt," *Science News* 168 (Sept. 10, 2005): 164. For more on this, see the Proceedings of the National Academy of Sciences (Sept 6., 2005).
5. March 9, 1991: 159.
6. July 2005.
7. David Darling, *Equations of Eternity* (New York: Hyperion Press, 1993): 24.
8. Ibid., 25.
9. Ibid., 26–27.
10. Ibid., 27.
11. Lynne McTaggart, *The Field* (New York: Harper Collins, 2002).
12. "How Life Shapes the Brainscape," *New Scientist* 26 (November 2005): 12.
13. "Depression May Play a Role in Stroke Risk," *Science News* (Aug. 12, 2000): 102.
14. Bruce Bower, "Early Stress in Rats Bites Memory Later On," *Science News* (Oct. 22, 2005).
15. "The Amygdala and Emotional Memory," *Scientific American* (May 2005).
16. *A Universe of Consciousness* (New York: Basic Books, 2000): 148.

Chapter 9

1. K. Demos, "Oxygen Shortage at Birth Linked to Schizophrenia," *Reuters Health Report* (June 12, 2001).
2. R.A. Ervin, C.L. Banker, and G.J. DuPaul, "Treatment of Attention Deficit/Hyperactivity Disorder." In M.A. Reinecke, F.M. Dattilio, and A. Freeman (Editors), Cognitive Therapy with Children and Adolescents: A Casebook for Clinical Practice (New York: Guilford Press, 1996): 44.

3. *Nature* 420(6911) (Nov. 7, 2002).
4. Research carried out by the Neuroscience Center, Drs. David Goodman and Harry Sobel.

Chapter 10

1. Lea Winerman, "Can You Force Yourself to Forget?" *Monitor* 36(8) (Sept. 2005): 52–53.
2. Ibid., 53.
3. From R. Restak's *The Secret Life of the Brain* (Washington, D.C.: Joseph Henry Press, 2004): 122.

Chapter 11

1. L.S. Wakschlag, B.B. Lahey, R. Loeber, S.M. Green, R.A. Gordon, and B.L. Leventhal, "Maternal Smoking During Pregnancy and the Risk of Conduct Disorder in Boys," *Archives of General Psychiatry* 54(7) (July 1997).
2. "We're Stuck with Our Personality at Age Three," *London Times* (Aug. 24, 2002): 11.

Select Bibliography

Aguilera, G., and C. Rabadan-Diehl, "Vasopressinergic Regulation of The Hypothalamic-Pituitary-Adrenal Axis: Implications For Stress Adaptation." *Regul Pept* 96 (1-2) (Dec. 22, 2000): 23-29.

Amaral, David G., and Ricardo Insausti, "Hippocampal Formation: A Review of Anatomical Data." In Amaral, D.G., and M.P. Witter, "The three-dimensional Organization of the Hippocampal Formation: A Review of Anatomical Data." *Neuroscience* 31(3) (1989): 571–591.

———. "Hippocampal Formation." In *The Human Nervous System*, edited by George Paxinos, 711–755. San Diego: Academic Press, 1990.

Barbas, H., "An Anatomic Basis of Cognitive Emotional Interactions in the Primate Prefrontal Cortex" [Review]. *Neuroscience: Biobehavioral Review* 19 (1998): 499–510.

Barbas, H., and D.N. Pandya, "Architecture of Intrinsic Connections of the Prefrontal Cortex in Rhesus Monkey." In *Neurobiology of Decision Making*. Berlin: Springer-Verlag, 1996.

Black, Harvey. "Amygdala's Inner Workings: Researchers Gain New Insights Into This Structure's Emotional Connections." *The Scientist* 15(19) (October 2001): 20.

Blum, K., and E.R. Braverman, et al. "Reward Deficiency Syndrome: A Biogenetic Model for the Diagnosis and Treatment of Impulsive, Addictive, and Compulsive Behaviors." *Journal of Psychoactive Drugs*, 32 Suppl: i-iv (Nov. 2000): 1-112.

Bohus, B., et al. "Forebrain Pathways and their Behavioral with Neuroendocrine and Cardiovascular Function in the Rat." *Clinical Experimental Pharmacology and Physiology* 23 (2) (1996): 177–182.

Bower, Bruce. "Left Brain Hammers Out Tool Use." *Science News* (April 19, 2003): 241–256.

———. "Smells Like Emotion: Brain Splits Duties To Sniff Out Feelings." *Science News* 163(4) (January 25, 2003): 49–64.

Canli, Turhan, Zuo Zhao, James Brewer, John D.E.Gabrieli, and Larry Cahill. "Event Related Activation in the Human Amygdala Associates with Later Memory for Individual Emotional Experience." *The Journal of Neuroscience* 20 RC99 (2000): 1–5.

Carey, Benedict. "New Surgery to Control Behavior." *The Los Angeles Times* (August 4, 2003): F1.

———. "Psychiatry and Preschoolers: More Young Children Are Being Diagnosed with Drugs Even As Doctors Grapple With a Lack of Research." *The Los Angeles Times* (June 30, 2003): F1.

Carroll, Linda. "Mounting Data on Epilepsy Point to Dangers of Repeated Seizures." *The New York Times* (Tuesday, February 18, 2003): D5.

Cloninger, C. "Genetic and environmental factors in the development of alcoholism." *Journal of Psychiatric Treatment Evaluation* 10 (1983).

Comings, D.E., and K. Blum. *Progress in Brain Resesearch* 126 (2000):325–341.

Cromie, William J. "Childhood Abuse Hurts the Brain, Raises Risks of Suicide, Mental Illness." *Harvard Daily Gazette* (March 5, 2001).

DeMoss, R. *Brainwaves Through Time*. New York: Plenum Press, 1999.

Dickey, Chandlee C., Robert W.McCarley, and Martha E.Shenton. "The Brain in Schizotypal Personality Disorder: A Review of Structural MRI and CT Findings." *Harvard Rev. Psychiatry* (January/February 2002).

Falk, F. *Brain Dance*. New York: Harry Holton Books, 1992.

Foreman, Judy, "Minds Fixed on Chemo Brain." *The Los Angeles Times* (July 14, 2003): F8.

Friedman, Richard A. "Self-Protection or Delusion? The Many Varieties of Paranoia." *The New York Times* (Tuesday, April 1, 2003): D5.

Gazzaniga, Michael S. "Cerebral Specialization and Interhemispheric Communication: Does the Corpus Callosum Enable the Human Condition?" *Brain* 123 (2000): 1293–1326.

Goldenberg, Myron M. "Pharmacology for the Psychotherapist." Accelerated Development Inc. (1990).

Goodman, David. "Biochemical Changes During a Dacrystic Regimen." Newport Neuroscience Center. Society of Neuroscience. Tenth Annual Convention. (Nov. 1984) Abstract 97.13., page 343 (approximate).

Hale, Malcolm. *Mechanisms of the Mind*. Pittsburgh, Penn: Hale-van-Ruth Press, 1999.

Heldt, Scott A., and William A. Falls. "Research Report: Destruction of the Auditory Thalamus Disrupts the Production of Fear but not The Inhibition of Fear Conditioned to an Auditory Stimulus." *Elsevier Science* (September 29, 1998).

Holden, Michael E. "The Neurophysiology of Feeling," and "The Profile of a Primal." *The Journal of Primal Therapy* 2(3) (Winter 1975): 181–205, 216–223.

Ingvar, David A., and Niels A. Lassen. "Brain Function and Blood Flow." *Scientific American* (October 1978): 50–59.

Janov, A. *The Biology of Love*. New York: Prometheus Books, 2000.

———. *The New Primal Scream*. Enterprise Publishing, 1991.

Jimerson, D.C., B.E. Wolte, E.D. Metzger, D.M. Finkelstein, T.B. Cooper, and J.M. Levine. "Decreased Serotonin Function in Bulimia Nervosa." *General Psychiatry* 54(6) (1997): 529–534.

Johnson, Steven. "The Brain + Emotions: Fear," *Discover* (March 2003): 33–39.

Joseph, R. "Fetal Brain & Cognitive Development." *Developmental Review* 20 (1999): 81–98.

Kalb, Claudia.. "Coping with Anxiety," *Newsweek* (February 24, 2003): 51–52.

Kovacs, G.L., Z. Sarnyai, and G. Szabo. "Oxytocin and Addiction: A Review." *Pyschoneuroendocrinology* 23(8) (1998): 945–62.

Lang, P.J., M. David, and A. Ohman. "Fear and Anxiety: Animal Models and Human Cognitive Psychophysiology." *Affect Disorders* 61(3) (December 2000): 137–159.

Ledoux, Joseph E. (Center for Neural Science, New York University). "Emotion Circuits in the Brain." *Annual Review of Neuroscience* 23 (2000): 155–184.

———. *The Emotional Brain: The Mysterious Underpinnings of Emotional Life*. New York: Touchstone Books, 1996.

Ledoux, Joseph E., A. Sakaguchi, and D.J. Reis. "Subcortical Efferent Projections of the Medial Geniculate Nucleus Mediate Emotional Responses Conditioned to Acoustic Stimuli." *Journal of Neuroscience* 4(3) (March 1984): 683–698.

Leshner, A.I., and G.F. Koob. National Institute on Drug Abuse, National Institutes of Health, Rockville, MD, Association of American Physicians (1999) Mar-Apr; 111(2): 99-108.

LeVay, Simon. *The Sexual Brain*. Cambridge, Mass.: MIT Press, 1993.

Levine, S. "Influence of Psychological Variables on the Activity of the Hypothalamic-Pituitary-Adrenal Axis." *European Journal of Pharmacology* 405 (1-3) (Sept. 29, 2000): 149–160.

MacLean, Paul. *The Triune Brain in Evolution: Role in Paleocerebral Functions*. Springer, 2003.

McGaugh, James L. "Memory Consolidation and the Amygdala: A Systems Perspective," *Trends in Neurosciences* 25(9) (September 2002).

Meratos, E.J., R.J. Dolan, et al. "Neural Activity Associated with Episodic Memory for Emotional Context," *Neurospsychologia* 39(9) (2001): 910–920.

Miller, B., L. Chou, and B.L. Finlay. "The Early Development of Thalamocortical and Corticothalamic Projections." *Journal of Comparative Neurology* 335 (1) (Sept. 1, 1993): 16–41.

Miller, Martin. "When Anxiety Runs Sky-High." *The Los Angeles Times* (July 7, 2003): F1.

Minugh-Purvis, Nancy, and McNamara. *Human Evolution Through Developmental Change*. Baltimore, Md: Johns Hopkins Univ. Press, 2002.

Neumann, I.D., et al. "Brain Oxytocin Inhibits Stress-induced Activity of the Hypothalamo-Pituitary-Adrenal Axis in Male and Female rats; A Partial Action within the Paraventricular Nucleus." *Journal of Neuroendocrinology* 12 (3) (2000): 235–243.

Papousek, I., and G. Schulder. "Covariances of EEG Assymetries and Emotional State Indicate that Activity at Frontopolar Locations is Potentially Affected by State Factors." *Psychophysiology* 39 (2002): 350–360.

Rauch, Scott. "The Amygdala in Brain Function: Basic and Clinical Approaches," The New York Academy of Sciences, Neuroscience Conference. (March 24–27, 2002): 47.

Samson, W.K. "Evidence for a Psychological Role for Oxytocin in the Control of Prolactin Secretion." *Endocrinology* 119(2) (1986): 554–560.

———. "Oxytocin and the anterior pituitary gland." *Advanced Experimental Medical Biology* (1995): 395; 355–364.

Santouse, A.M., D.H. Ffytche, R.J. Howard, et al. "The Functional Significance of Perinatal Corpus Callosum Damage: An FMRI Study in Young Adults." *Guarantors of Brain* 125 (2002): 1782–1792.

Schacter, D., and Elaine Scarry. *Memory, Brain and Belief*. Cambridge, Mass.: Harvard U. Press, 2000.

Schore, Allan N. "The Effects of Early Relational Trauma on Right Brain Development, Affect Regulation, and Infant Mental Health." *Infant Mental Health Journal* 22 (2001): 201–269.

———. "The Effects of a Secure Attachment Relationship on Right Brain Development, Affect Regulation and Infant Mental Health," *Infant Mental Health Journal* 22 (2001): 7–66.

———. *Affect Regulation and the Origin of the Self*. Mahwah, N.J.: Lawrence Erlbaum, 1994.

Stuss, D.T., T.W. Picton, and N.P. Alesander. "Consciousness, Self-Awareness and Frontal Lobes." In *The Frontal Lobes and Neuropsychiatric Illness*, ed. S. Salloway, P Malloy, and J. Duffy. Washington: Psychiatric Press, 1999.

Szalavitz, Maia. "Love Is the Drug." *New Scientist* (November 23, 2002): 38–40.

Teicher, Martin. "The Neurology of Child Abuse." *Scientific American*. (March 2002): 41–42, 75, and Mara M. Sanchez, cited, page 74.

Vedantam, Shankar. "A Mother's Touch, a Lover's Caress." *The Washington Post* (July 30, 2002): 7.

Wallace, J. "The New Disease Model of Alcoholism." *Western Journal of Medicine* 152 (1990).

Wang, Zuoxin, Larry J. Young, Yue Liu, and Thomas R. Insel. "Species Differences in Vasopressin Receptor Binding Are Evident Early in Development: Comparative Anatomic Studies in Prairie and Montane Voles." *The Journal of Comparative Neurology* 378 (1997): 535–546.

INDEX